AUGMENTED HEALTH (CARE)™

THE END OF THE BEGINNING

LUCIEN ENGELEN

ISBN: 9789082874013

Table of Contents

Introduction to Augmented Health(care)™, "the end of the beginning"

Be my guest: You can read this book in 5 major themes, that can be read separately as well.

Theme 1. What's been going on?

In 2007 the first iPhone was introduced, changing the way we interact with technology forever. Who would have figured, back then, that these powerful supercomputers in our pocket would become an important part of data collection for medical purposes and clinical trials? The world has changed fundamentally since the turn of the century: technology grows with exponential speed. "Omnia mutantur nos et mutamur in illis": Everything changes, and we change with it.

That notion seems even more true in 2018, and beyond. The way we interact with new technologies has changed our social, cultural and economic systems, health(care) included. We are entering a world of Augmented Health(care)™, as I coined it.

What are the main changes I have witnessed in healthcare and technology in the past eight years I've been in health(care) innovation and part of 'the system'?

Theme 1, will touch upon some major developments, from an international perspective. With a number of noted guest contributors, I will dive into the emergence of #patientsincluded™ and #nurseincluded™ as an unstoppable force, the digitization of the healthcare sector and the need for alternative business models, coming from international tech companies such as Apple, Amazon, Google, with a strategic focus on healthcare. We will start with the earliest uses of the Internet in healthcare – mostly as a source to search for medical information – and fast forward to crowdsourcing medical data and novel ways of doing clinical research.

We will share about the future of real estate. At Radboudumc, we are about to begin the biggest real estate transformation in years, building a hospital that is fit for the future. But how do you build a future-proof building in an era of exponential technology? It's like building a plane in mid-air.

As Rene Bleeker points out: a strategy must be built on bricks, bytes and human behavior.

These are not abstract visions, these are the things that are happening right now, this very moment. Want to know what's been going on in healthcare? Start here.

Theme 2. Cracks in the system

As we continue to live longer, we are not necessarily living healthier: more and more people develop one or multiple chronic diseases, which will cost money and demand services in terms of healthcare. We will have a huge number of people that are moving into retirement age: a "silver tsunami", as HIMSS CEO Hal Wolff calls them in his contribution. These are the economics that will drive the next ten years in our healthcare systems.

What are these "cracks" in the system? How do they manifest? This theme will not only focus on the increasing pressure that (inter)national healthcare systems are facing. As I will argue in this book, our medical systems mostly consist of logistic processes I reckon 80%: only 20% of our time and energy goes to medicine. Solving the current inefficiencies in this system could be a possible solution. Therefore, we need a new perspective on supply chain management, providing service and customer excellence, as experts from outside healthcare are eager to point out (see, for example, Michiel Muller's vignette: "We need to optimize the chain with the use of data").

At the same time, digital healthcare seems like a different planetary system. We come up with separate names, separate reimbursement models and separate workflows when it comes to digital health(care). And as long as a separate digital portal or an app per institution to access your medical records is needed, a challenge (at least, in the Netherlands) remains, we will continue to experience inefficacy and information asymmetry in healthcare. The only solution to stud these cracks in our system is to fully embrace the digital transformation.

Theme 3. Taking part is the only way

"Stop talking, start doing." It seems so simple, yet most people find it so hard to make the first step and just begin. It's is one of my mantras that I must have shared almost a thousand times on stage: taking part is the only way. We've seen over and over again the hurdles we've discussed in all of those sessions prior to the start, in the end, appeared to be different ones. You have to get your feet wet, get into the mud and take the messy, slippery road of innovating in healthcare. It is the only way to excellence in the end. You neither can't learn how to bike from a book, can you?

In this theme, the learnings and experiences from the REshape Center, the innovation department at the Radboud University Medical Center that I was granted to found in 2011, take a central place. How do you "manage" innovation? How do you prepare an organization – in our case, a university medical center with 13.000 students and professionals – for the future? What can you learn from our mistakes?

Theme 3 takes you on a – by no means all-encompassing - guide for innovation. What is a "moonshot project"? Why is focusing on the "day after tomorrow" so important, yet so hard for most teams or organizations? How do you tackle resistance in your team, amongst your colleagues or in your board? What is the role of leadership and management in organizations when it comes to innovating?

For those interested in our journey of innovation at REshape: I have included some of my memories and recollections in this theme as well, by including some of my Linkedin blogs (still stunned it has over 750.000 followers already) from earlier days to give some perspective. I have not only been using Gartner's Hype Cycle to handle the predicted breakthrough moment of technology, but we used it internally as well, as I noticed that every innovation project was roughly going through the same phase of the Hype Cycle. I started to try to influence a specific portion of it, more as a guidance of how projects evolve. Speeding up the Hype Cycle, in my opinion, could increase the actual access to and use of innovation and adoption of the #patientsincluded™ model.

Theme 4. Digital Strategy

The digital evolution is impacting the way we work, the resources we use, and the nature of technology itself. If organizations hope to respond swiftly to change, reap the business benefits of new digital innovation, and attract top-tier talent in the future, their operating model must evolve accordingly into a digital TOM (Technological Operating Model).

For a lot of organizations, however, the digital strategy that they have identified does not fit their current (traditional) OM: it's like trying to fit a UK plug into a US Power socket or to fit a square peg into a round hole as they say. I have joined forces with Deloitte, to translate into health(care) the nine significant shifts they've identified that will influence the model of the future and that need to be discussed in conjunction with each other since they are highly interdependent.

This theme is the strategic core of this book. It is not a handbook, nor a blueprint or a generic approach. Consider this 'Digital strategy' merely as the start of a framework for the different steps one could set to see whether or not they're ready for the things that lie ahead and to offer some assistance.

Theme 5. This revolution will not stop

A book on healthcare innovation would not be complete without a brief look into the future. I am grateful for an international team of guest contributors to share their vision of healthcare in 2030, whether it is the future of pharmaceutical care (Claudia Rijcken), the digital skillset that is needed in an exponential age (Daniel Kraft) or how an average day of a general practitioner looks like (Bart Timmers). These vignettes will transpose readers to the future of healthcare.

In this final theme, I share my own vision on the future of healthcare as well. We will be entering an era of Augmented Health(care)™, a layer of smart technology and data that comes *help a person make (a Action) a better deal!*

here

Lucien Engelen

around us and that helps us make better decisions. With us, I mean everyone who is involved in the healthcare: care providers, patients, family, government, industry and informal caregivers. Whether that layer is projected via glasses or in another way such as on your phone, refrigerator or smartwatch, is not that important.

What matters most is that in the future, everyone will have exactly the information they need to be able to do their profession or work well, follow a therapy well, or receive the right information at the right time. With Augmented Health(care)™ healthcare professionals and patients are given digital tools to process and analyze the ever-expanding oceans of data in a meaningful way.

Note: as some of the images in this book are hard to read in this small format, so I have put them online on my website http://www.lucienengelen.com/book/images

Prologue

"Omnia mutantur nos et mutamur in illis": Everything changes, and we change with it.

The world is changing, society is changing, technology is changing, and so health(care) is. And it does so at ever increasing speeds. Platforms like Facebook, Youtube, Spotify, and Amazon have entered our life and are here to stay. Many of these platforms did not exist 15 years ago, and some of them will no longer exist 10 years from now. Healthcare apps for smartphones, portals and big corporate electronic health record (EHR) systems struggle to adapt to a new reality where algorithms and platform thinking emerges. Where patients are in control of their own personal data. And where everything is INTERconnected and traditional healthcare systems (still) are just INTRAconnected. They will enter the 'End of Life' phase of their current product cycle.

While many digital health critics at present address privacy and security issues - next to the looming market domination by modern tech-titans - I expect these new global corporates will be compliant to the European GDPR sooner than many of our healthcare institutions. And although I share the worries on the risk of monopolization by tech corporations, I trust the current and future governance systems to handle this. Even though we will see hiccups on the way like recently with the 'Cambridge Analytica files' - officially not a 'data breach' but a flagrant crossing of ethical borders - I believe that law will follow the practice.

New players like Apple, Amazon, and Google (Verily) first explored the healthcare scene and now aggressively fight for (the data of) patients, offering a consumer-friendly user interface and removing the friction that the traditional silo-structured health-care industry has been reluctant to address. Meanwhile, these tech-titans create interconnectivity 'by design' and on a global scale. Together with their ambition to enter the health(care) domain at an increasingly speed as you can see in this graph below. In it I have pictured the announcements of these non traditional players into the healthcare arena over the past year, starting May 7th 2017. I think this picture needs no further explanation.

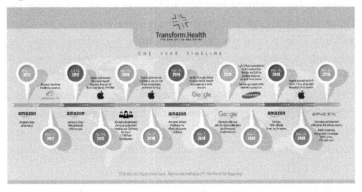

We have entered the fourth industrial revolution where everything will connect with everything. In this book, I elaborate on the four pillars of change that I sense healthcare is facing: Delocalisation, Democratisation, Digital, and Dollars, hence my 4D's.

Why are we at the "End of the beginning"?

I think this current digital transformation is at the "End of the beginning". In an era where data will be continuously and easily gathered, analyzed for new patterns and used for machine learning at meticulous speed, technology will 'augment' the way we deliver health(care). Not only in industrialized countries: due to the increase of network coverage, Augmented Health(care)™ will become accessible for all people all over the world, supporting citizens to stay healthy and professionals to help people with a condition even better than today.

Some people try to change healthcare by focusing on the quality of care and service. Others focus on safety or healthcare economics. I choose to focus my research on the impact and opportunities digital technology can bring, transforming health(care).

Healthcare has been subject to waves of change in the past centuries when developments came together. We are on the brink of a new wave right now. Although we all want to progress and we need more sustainable health(care) to cope with societal challenges such as aging populations, we also face a daily struggle with implementation of new tools. In this daily struggle important issues like workload, reimbursement, policies, culture, knowledge, and information are all roadblocks in the way to a gentle transition. We need to remove these roadblocks and change the way we educate and train health(care) professionals, change the way we pay for health services, and change how we measure and research digital health(care).

It requires continuous awareness of the ever-changing technological horizons. It requires a thorough implementation of those innovations and the incorporation of digital tools and a digital mindset in daily workflow, becoming "the new normal". It is almost like building a plane while it is already in mid-air. Maybe we should call this an 'adaptive digital transformation'.

This book is not a guide, nor a plan. Health(care) organizations, their contexts, and their cultures are different. These external and internal influences vary in each and every organization, so there is no blueprint for innovation. Hopefully, this book will offer some guidance on the next steps, to take on the challenges that lay ahead of us.

I have stepped into this arena almost seven years ago, starting with a shared ambition and the notion to address change. But there was no detailed, worked out plan at REshape, the Center for Innovation in the Radboud University Medical Center, back then. In these early days, we've experienced that a shared vision and awareness are powerful motivations for change.

Adjusting over time to the level of awareness, we now face a bigger overhaul, because our organization is ready for the next steps. Creating awareness, inspiring people, creating concepts and a compelling vision alone are not enough anymore. We now need to address the "how-to"-question. How to create meaningful digital tools for professionals and patient, how to organize and align stakeholders, how to scale digital health solutions?

This "how-to" has not been done yet. To me, it appears that a whole network of healthcare innovators across the globe is struggling with the same issues. Some organizations and individuals have a plan, some have partial success, some fail. It looks like we are all 'writing the book' as we speak, and yet we need to create tempo and build capacity.

Back then when we started REshape, I would have loved to have a book to learn about that first phase. A tour d'horizon of what is next when you start working on health(care) innovation. While some people think their organization can surpass that first discovery phase, or simply hire someone to come do this or even stop exploring and testing at one point in time, I would urge you that this exploration is vital. You really have to 'live' through this phase with your own people. You have to "feel the joy and the pain" as my friend Chris McCarthy - who ran the innovation center at Kaiser Permanente for twenty years - likes to say. What I am saying is: you can't learn how to bike from a book. To innovate in healthcare, you have to experience it.

Although the current increase of demand for scaling is valid, there also is the risk of losing sight on the constant change that will be permanent if we only focus on scaling. The world will not pause to change. There should be a fair balance in creativity and room for exploration, and meanwhile implementation and scaling.

In the journey towards this publication, I interviewed some great friends that we have partnered with over the past years. Some of them have written a brief perspective on the changing healthcare landscape. They enrich the broader picture with their 'vignettes' throughout this book.

This book is merely a reflection on the seven-year innovation-journey at Radboud University Medical Center (Nijmegen, The Netherlands), my work as faculty member at Exponential Medicine (Singularity University, Silicon Valley) and as CEO of my small company Transform.Health. At all of these positions, I have always been aiming to create sustainable health(care) change together with great professionals, with patients, and with the latest useable technology.

All my personal and professional learnings, the joy and pain, the lessons from others and my observations: they come together in this book, Augmented Health(care)™. I wish it was available as a direct 'download' from my brain, but since we're not in that exponential era yet and since there still is no USB plug in my brain, we had to write it down ourselves ;-)

The way this book came about is a journey in itself, with the use of modern and classical tools and means. You can learn more about in the chapter "how this book was made".

The combined mission of my work at REshape and my other endeavors was and still is to help prepare healthcare for a soft landing into the future. I do hope sharing these reflections and assumptions with you can inspire, assist, and help you to (re)think and encourage you to see the opportunities in this current era, to change health(care) for the better.

I'm grateful for the past and current executive board to have the courage, the boldness, the vision and trust in sending me out there to be their scout, ambassador, and rebel for change. Everybody thinks they're innovative, but it takes more than throwing some money against the wall and put up a shield "innovation center". The majority of the things they allowed me to have a long lead-time, before having any impact. There is a lot of tokenism in health(care) innovation, and some think you can change or even fix health(care) overnight. It is not about technology, nor about the process, it is about changing the culture of an organization. As we know culture eats strategy for breakfast. So sticking in there with me for over seven years, so past the 'seven years itch,' is to their credit. And last but not least my stellar team, what can i say: you are my fuel, my northstar and my passion. Being able to guide you is an honor in itself.

All of this takes time, dialogue, and understanding from those surrounding us. There is no quick fix, no silver bullet, and our world will never stop changing. So get on with it!

@lucienengelen, 2018

Introduction

And then there was a painting...

We can hardly speak of "empowerment" in the painting "The Doctor" (1891) by Sir Luke Fildes, a nineteenth century snapshot resembling how healthcare was delivered back then. A Victorian doctor would visit the house and sit down next to the patient to examine and observe the stage in the patient's illness. A little child lays in bed, father and mother gaze on helplessly from the background, anxiously awaiting the decision of the doctor.

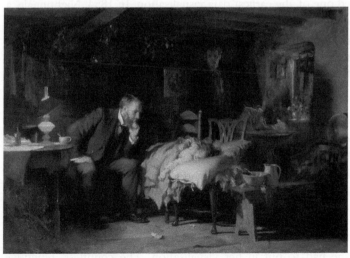

A lot has changed since 1891. Most doctor's house visits have become a thing of the past. People have become more empowered within society as a whole, as well as in healthcare. Technology has often played an important role in making it possible to do things differently, bringing new technologies in the hands of more people. But most importantly, patients and their family members have moved out of the shadows of Sir Luke Fildes' painting, from helplessly awaiting the verdict of the physician to empowered, informed individuals, with a wide range of technological tools within reach.

Apart from technological advancements, there are scientific breakthroughs. In the course of history, the combination of science and technology has been profound. In the future, we will see an even more intimate marriage of the two, a future where science and technology intertwine.

Think for a moment about how Florence Nightingale created one of the earliest data visualisation. In 1854. Nightingale, a nurse working the British Army 'in the East', created a diagram of the causes of mortality amongst the British Army, to illustrate seasonal sources of patient mortality in the military field hospital she managed.

Nightingale's visualisation demonstrated that sanitary conditions such as bad drainage, contaminated water, overcrowding and poor ventilation were causing the high death rate in India. Her breakthrough work and research drastically brought the mortality rate in the army down, and improved the sanitary conditions in India as a whole.

We can hardly envision of the circumstances that Nightingale had to work in. Try to imagine all the hours of work she had to put in her visualisation. The countless, repetitive administrative tasks, the endless lists of names of sick and fallen soldiers. Imagine for a minute she would have the technology to automatically collect, process and analyze that data to make models, visualisations and eventually see the impact of improved sanitation for the army in India.

Even though Nightingale was born into an upper-class, well-connected British family, it was her gift for mathematics and her crisp mind, her knowledge and her experience that brought her to the notion that sanitation could be the problem for high mortality rates. Her prior experiences and human ingenuity were essential. Technology might have sped up the process, and even raise the impact of her clarity. For me, it would be a nineteenth century example of what I call Augmented Health(care)™, or healthcare extremely supported by technology. Where technology can augment and support our human capabilities, one could only imagine what this could mean for humanity in the future.

The profound effect that technology has on our lives can best be witnessed in remote places, where access to medical facilities and basic primary care is limited, and medical knowledge is scarce. In these areas, technology can help to deliver often critical healthcare, via mobile phones, smartphones, or even SMS. To speak with a doctor with a video consultation, get a prescription online or monitor pregnant women via SMS-service. It is a testimony to the fact that healthcare is, in my opinion, for almost 80 percent a purely logistical operation.

Having access to a physician or nurse often is merely a logistical challenge: enter digital tools and these logistical barriers can be removed. The patient is going to the professional, or a professional is coming to the patient. Translate that thought to the current state in healthcare and a logistical issue remains: data has to go to the professional or the professional has to go

3

to the data. Again, a purely logistical challenge, in my opinion.

In this perspective, it's very interesting to see and dream about the impact of the orbital internet, that is now being launched by companies like SpaceX and others. This satellite internet network can reach the entire globe, competing with more traditional forms like cable internet.

More than 4000 small satellites of SpaceX will provide access to the internet literally on a global level. As we have seen countless times before, technology's exponential growth curve will decrease the now fairly high costs of global internet within years. Eventually, orbital internet will cost a lot less than digging cables and bringing them to sub-Saharan Africa or in the midst of the Amazonian rainforests.

The next orbital stop you could think of is how to deliver healthcare in space. How can digital health be of help for astronauts traveling to Mars? They don't have the ability to just quickly turn around and come back for whatever medical intervention that is needed. So keeping astronauts healthy not only brings the challenge of remote prevention of diseases but also of remote treatment and healthcare. As John F. Kennedy's famous Moonshot speech at Rice University in 1962 spurred technological advances in space aviation, the ambition to explore different planets could also spur the use of technology for health and healthcare.

Over the centuries, healthcare has changed with waves. It is my belief that we are facing such a wave at present again, and we are only at the beginning of it, hence "the end of the beginning".

THEME 1:

What's been going on?

CHAPTER 1

The End of the beginning

I welcome this European framework of legislation to improve privacy and security as it centers around protecting and empowering European (healthcare) consumers. With this new framework, corporates and organizations are legally required to make sure that every citizen is aware and is as safe as possible from being exploited. The big debate, of course, is how to implement this set of rules and regulations and how to adapt organizations to this new setting, shifting from the old setting where every country created some form of the legislation itself.

Empowerment

To me, the GDPR stands for a significant shift of influence - or power/empowerment for that matter - that I dearly wanted to happen in the past seven years I have been in health(-care) innovation. Healthcare still is the only branch where the consumer does not own his or her data. Even trying to get a view on or access to your data has been made as difficult as possible.

Sure, there are laws that give you, as a patient, the right to see some of the data regarding your laboratory results, letters that were sent to other healthcare professionals, your medical treatments and so on. But these laws are based on a right to view a medical record, which is entirely different than owning your record or having it accessible at all times. So, whereas the healthcare IT industry has been reluctant to pro-actively make this data available to the patient - sometimes with the argument that patients cannot handle that amount of sensitive data - with the GDPR, change has come.

The shift of power that derives from this is that patients can collect all their personal data. They will eventually be the only ones who have a complete overview of data coming from the GP's office, hospital, fitness club, dentist, pharmacy, etc. thereby creating a holistic perspective on everything that matters to them. This will make healthcare professional will be the one to take a subscription to the patients' data.

Tech Titans

Of course, this raises the question: how would consumers handle that amount of medical data responsibly? Keep in mind that it's not only healthcare professionals or the healthcare IT industry in this equation: tech titans like Apple, Google and Amazon are setting the international stage as well.

Take Apple, for instance. In 2014, Apple introduced Health-Kit, a software framework to collect health data via the built-in sensors of our smartphones or connected devices. Apart from storing personal health data (with the app Health, a standard feature of every iPhone), HealthKit is Apple's data platform to develop healthcare apps as well. In fact, Apple introduced a feature for American customers to see their medical records directly on their iPhone (spring 2018). Apple worked with the healthcare community to take a consumer-friendly approach, creating Health Records based on FHIR (Fast Healthcare Interoperability Resources), a standard for transferring electronic medical records. Making it easy for the patient to request data at the hospital, in a standard format, and store it on their own device.

To me, Apple's digital framework is a clear sign of the digital transformation that we are witnessing right now. Apple started with creating standalone (wellness) apps, then created a framework (HealthKit), adding CareKit and ResearchKit along the way, and is now offering a kind of personal health record (PHR) within Apple's operating system. On top of their knowledge of consumer-friendly apps and experience with innovative design, Apple is now even creating medical clinics for its employees and their families.

And we are just at the beginning of it. Take the Apple Watch, the smartwatch that is currently in its third edition (Series 3). Whereas most people would consider a smartwatch as a gimmick or a gadget a few years back, the Apple Watch is now increasingly being used as a fitness and wellness device, and even a medical device in the foreseeable future. Of course, medical grade apps and functionalities have to be approved by the FDA or European regulators before they come to the market. Apple is gearing up with the largest medical institutions in the United States to explore innovative, new ways of medical research. The biggest heart study is now being conducted by Stanford together with Apple, with the help of thousands of Apple Watch users that have given their consent to participate.

As data collection becomes easier with the growth of smartwatches, wearables and fitness trackers, more and more research studies are carried out with data such as heart rate variability (HVR), our daily number of steps, our sleep, activity and - combined with contextual information - the relationship between all these parameters. They can run some data points helping to keep track and subsequently advising you about better health.

We are not only entering a new era of medical research. We are entering a new era of personal health as well. At the REshape Center for Innovation (Radboud University Medical Center), we are conducting an interesting study on that. We combined a wearable patch - loaded with sensors - that a patient wears on his chest. This wireless patch measures vital signs such as heart rate variability, and wirelessly transmits that information to a dashboard. From there, our REshape team combines the data from the patch with another dataset, concerning glucose levels of a patient with diabetes, collected by a finger prick.

Next, we build an algorithm combining the data from the wireless patch and the patient's glucose levels. The algorithm gives us the ability to warn the patient 30 minutes before they have the risk of running into a hypo (short for hypoglycemia, when your blood glucose level is too low). We learned that heart rate variability (HRV) and blood glucose levels correlate and that a drop in HRV indicates an upcoming hypo. Imagine a wearable device that indicates that these changes are happening inside your body, while you might have no clue about what's happening with your blood glucose levels. If this wearable (embedded in a watch with GPS) could sense that a person is driving, it might even advise them to pull over, pause for a moment and take a snack, to prevent a hypo happening while they're driving at 120 km per hour. So now imagine that a technology giant like Apple would be able to do the same thing, based on just the Apple Watch on your wrist.

You get my point here: this new generation of applications, wearables, and smartwatches are consumer-friendly and most importantly: convenient and more and more ambient. Tech companies make products that you could wear the whole day.

As new medical research and algorithms enter the domain of consumer products, we will see more tools that help you run your life, with a subtle nudge or a shallow intrusion, instead of the invasive pricking of needles a couple of times a day that people with diabetes are used to right now.

The word 'comfortable' is of the utmost importance here: in our daily lives, we use digital products that make stuff easier and more efficient. Nowadays, a patient has multiple portals with multiple passwords and fragmented information stored away in all kinds of different systems. With their experience of the user interface, companies like Apple and Google could transform this data into an attractive overview, a rich digital environment with all available information and context. Again, my point is the convenience that these new players in the healthcare domain offer, removing friction from the current system. With seamless, frictionless products and services that citizens (using citizens on purpose here) are used to in their daily lives, but which are still not standard practice in healthcare.

Verily, sister of Google as an Alphabet company, has done its fair amount of data crunching as well. Verily used X-ray images and other healthcare data as datasets to train their machine learning algorithms, for instance, in recognizing notorious spots in X-ray images. Besides creating these care-oriented applications, Verily has created an algorithm that they are discussing with healthcare insurance organizations in the United States. This algorithm supposedly would drill down costs to an amount that could hardly be reached with traditional models of process improvement.

Although this algorithm is in the works, it already looks like their business model is taking a portion of the cost savings from the healthcare insurance organizations, enough to offer their API for free. So, one could expect that Google will also offer an easy framework for that data - that is increasingly getting unleashed - to be stored and processed in a very convenient way for patients.

The platform economy is coming. It is without question that the ease-of-use and the fact that the majority of the platforms are free to use, have a profound impact on society. There's almost no aspect of our social life or work life that has not been impacted by platforms. YouTube, Facebook, Google search, Twitter etc. but also the sulfur of Microsoft running our email systems, our computer systems our Outlook and all kinds of embedded systems in devices and other infrastructure control the majority of our life. We all know "there is no such thing as a free lunch" or "if you're not paying for the service, then you're the product." This is so true!

Amazon also fiercely seems to be entering the healthcare arena. In May 2017 Jeff Bezos, the CEO of Amazon, announced he wanted to step into the American pharmacy market with a multibillion investment. In July 2017, Amazon announced the acquisition of Whole Foods for $13 billion dollar, acquiring 550 brick and mortar stores throughout the United States. Of course, investors and international press speculated about the intent and underlying strategy of the Whole Foods acquisition. Was it a deceivingly simple step to sell more groceries? A strategic move to combine brick and mortar stores to drop off and collect online parcels, to create a convenient way of shopping for Amazon customers with the ability to run some errands?

In January 2018, things became more evident when Amazon teamed up with insurance company Berkshire Hathaway and JP

Morgan bank, announcing they will start delivering healthcare services to their combined 1.1 million employees.

So just imagine you would have a fully trained nurse on site in those 550 Whole Foods/Amazon stores. Grocery stores turned into local mini-clinics, stuffed with all kinds of easy to use technology, to do blood tests, take urine samples, blood pressure measurements, provide coaching sessions and offering pharmacy services. Just as online shopping has become 'the new normal' for American and European consumers, why wouldn't Amazon's pharmacy services become the user standard, as opposed to going to the pharmacist?

Picture this: your smart voice assistant, for instance an Alexa Echo system in the living room, would remind you during the day to check whether you have taken your medication. If you reply with a confirmation, Alexa could also count the number of pills you say you have been taking. Next, Alexa could know exactly when it's time for a refill of your prescription. The system adds a line to your shopping list, reminding you to take care of your prescription. Alexa might even order your approved prescription independently in the future.

Voice assistants

Roy Amara, an engineer and futurist way before "futurist" was even a title, coined what eventually become known as Amara's law: "We tend to overestimate the effect of a technology in the short run and underestimate the effect in the long run".

One of the clear recent examples of Amara's law is the recent introduction of Google Duplex; a conversational tool that lets Google Assistant make appointments with your barber or restaurants, for instance. This conversational agent not only amazes me due to its human-like style of conversation, including the "hmms' and "ahhs", but also because of the natural sounding language and the intonation of the computer system.

Google Duplex combines years of developments in machine learning, ARI and all the technologies that Google has invested in over the last decade. As Roy Amara's Law states, we overestimate the speed of developments but underestimate the impact. For years people have been debating the use, the accuracy and the efficiency of voice-activated systems. But with the introduction of Google Duplex) Google takes a strong advantage over Amazon Alexa and Apple's Siri, I think.

However, just one day after this introduction by Google, Deloitte and Amazon jointly launched Deloitte Assistant: d.assistant. A dot version for healthcare, implemented in a hospital in Australia, that acts as a 'next generation nurse-call'. Patients can talk to d.assistent asking for a pillow, a glass of water or stating that they are in pain. An algoritme triages the dialogue and alerts the nursing staff accordingly. Think about all the applications of these tools for healthcare. One can easily see now how development starts to accumulate and how one innovation stands on the shoulders of another one.

Legislators are noticing this breakthrough in technology as well. Early May 2018, the White House cleared the pathway for strong developments of artificial intelligence (AI), by taking away boundaries that were still in place. The US government has created a separate committee to support, control and steer the development of artificial intelligence in the United States, and we see similar developments in the EU.

Although it will take a couple of years before this technology is fully immersed in society - as well as in healthcare - the

15

impact will be enormous. More and more, we will become accustomed to talking to a voice-assistant. Whether it's an Alexa device, an Apple HomePod or Google Assistant embedded in your smartphone, this decade will see us humans interact differently with machines. The announcements of Google, and Deloitte and Amazon clearly show what's ahead of us.

Back to Amazon: starting as a small online marketplace for books in 1994, Amazon has become the largest Internet retailer in the world in 2018 (regarding revenue) and an extremely profitable cloud computing company. Amazon's supply chain management and inventory management - whether it is books, music and consumer goods - could revolutionize the healthcare sector as well. Amazon is also offering a whole framework for hospitals and other institutions to organize their entire medical supply chain in an easy way (the tech company might even start its own hospitals at one point in time!).

Amazon's supply chain management could not exist without a layer of data. The gathering of all kinds of data points helps hospitals to eliminate waste and organize effectively, removing friction from the system. The king of e-commerce not only strives for a convenient shopping experience for consumers (or citizens, patients, and their family in the future): it also provides convenience and practicality for healthcare organizations running their operation.

And there you have it. Verily, Apple and Amazon. Three of the most current examples of technology corporates stepping into the healthcare scene. Often starting in the domain of fitness and wellness, but gradually and steadily moving to traditional healthcare and medical interventions. These tech companies even hired hundreds of doctors, nurses, pharmacists, nutritionists and so forth. If you consider the developments above, there are a couple of notions that I would like to share with you.

First of all, the locked-in data inside healthcare IT systems, like the electronic health records of hospitals, are going to be unleashed, collected, processed and enriched in very user-friendly user interfaces and in the hands of the patients. The original health record systems were never built to have an interface for the patient, as they were built for billing, ordering and supporting data for the healthcare systems themselves.

So the current transition - or maybe I should say 'struggle' - of those enterprise systems is completely understandable. They simply were never intended to act as a patient-friendly system. So, to migrate from an Electronic Healthcare Records (EHR) system into what they now like to call Comprehensive Health Record (CHR) is a necessary but extremely challenging path. What we need is a Connected Healthcare Records system, and I think those will be provided by tech companies. As I started this chapter referring to the GDPR laws in Europe, personal medical data has to and will be unleashed. We will experience a shift of power that will remove constraints that healthcare institutions now have with their EHR vendors.

This new era of empowerment and personal data will also open up the possibility for new organizations and companies to make good use of data - with the explicit consent of the patient. Personal data that patients own and share with professionals. We will move from having the right to view a medical file to have the right to own and share our medical data and files. That could even mean a subscription to the data of the patient.

Secondly, I also expect that the current Electronical Health Record systems will transition back to their original function of a billing system and interoperability layer between different departments for their patients and order processing. Something they have been good at for the past years and functionality that is necessary to make modern healthcare institutions function. That also implies that current Electrical Health Record vendors could stop struggling to include the patient's perspective into their systems, other than offering a data sharing service.

These two notions bring me back to something that I often state in my keynotes. We are witnessing "...the End of Life phase of the product cycle of EHRs, portals and apps...". Some people think that it's the end of those systems, I don't think that will be the case.

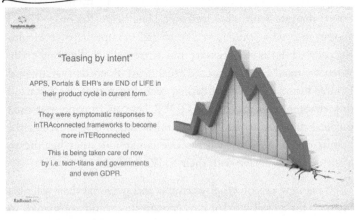

"Teasing by intent"

APPS, Portals & EHR's are END of LIFE in their product cycle in current form.

They were symptomatic responses to inTRAconnected frameworks to become more inTERconnected

This is being taken care of now by i.e. tech-titans and governments and even GDPR.

Traditional healthcare IT vendors have systems with indispensable functions. What I am referring to here is their role in the total eCo-system and also to the upcoming standard practice of interoperability that is going to get a boost by these international developments.

This fourth industrial revolution, this era of technology, this new European landscape of privacy and data protection.

Whatever you want to call it, one thing is for sure: this era we live in will be recognized as a pivotal moment in history.

As Winston Churchill said so eloquently halfway through the Second World War: "Now is not the end. It's not even the beginning of the end. But it is, perhaps, the end of the beginning." Of course, the context was a very different one, but anyone living in the present time might very well think that he was talking about the path that new technology goes through currently.

CHAPTER 2

Internet emancipates patients

Journalist Harriët Messing interviewed in Lucien Engelen 2011, it gives -looking back- a great vignette of the then current thinking.

Do you know what e-health or Health 2.0 is? Lucien Engelen is Health 2.0 Ambassador at Radboud University Nijmegen Medical Centre. He explains why this development in healthcare is important for patients. Because they will encounter the products of this development in the near future, if they have not already. Engelen: "Health 2.0 will create a level playing field in the relationship between patients and healthcare professionals."

"Internet technology gives patients the opportunity to make better health decisions", says Engelen. "They can research how to prevent illness and which doctors and treatments best suits their needs. Internet offers knowledge and knowledge is power. It emancipates patients. They can speak with their doctors about their illness and cure at a more equal level. And it offers more. Web 1.0 is the term used for websites that are often just a digital flyer. TYou still see a lot of those websites in healthcare. Web 2.0 means interaction, sharing information, knowledge and experiences. Examples are forums where patients meet to talk about their illness, experiences with hospitals and doctors and give each other advice. But patients also talk and exchange information on social media platforms like Twitter, Hyves and Face-

20

book. Health 2.0 is Web 2.0 in healthcare. Health 2.0 is not only about online contacts between patients. It is certainly also about interaction between patients and healthcare professionals."

Doctor Google

"More and more people first turn to the Internet in search for information about their illness", says Engelen. "In 2003 only one in ten people according to Dutch researcher TNS Nipo, in 2008 already seven in ten. The amount of information available online is enormous. The sources of the information are quite diverse. You can land on a page of a website belonging to a patient association, to an 'independent' health organisation, to a hospital or land on a patient's blog and so on. In 2010 the Dutch Patients and Consumers Federation (NPCF) stated that 24 percent of people already use websites like ZorgKaartNederland.nl to compare and choose doctors and hospitals. Three in five patients exchange information online about illness and health. One in seven patients publishes a blog about their own illness and medication. By doing so, they help others to go to their doctor better prepared."

Patients emancipate

Many health care professionals do not like their patients to turn to Doctor Google. Let alone patients giving other patients advice. Is a patient with vague complaints able to find the right path in the online information jungle? And how reliable is the information found? What if someone did not choose the right diagnosis or treatment? Furthermore, many websites belonging to healthcare institutions and patients associations still have a long way to go before they can provide that kind of information. The opinion of most healthcare professionals is that the patient should not be in charge. Ostrich politics according to

Engelen: "In many public domains Internet and social media are causing citizens to emancipate, demanding open, correct and reliable information. WikiLeaks is a good example. Healthcare professionals and organisations better prepare for this change and embrace it. Offering digital flyers is not enough anymore. Furthermore, what these digital flyers offer often is a far cry from the real information needs of patients."

Participatory healthcare

The Radboud University Nijmegen Medical Centre is the first Dutch hospital to notice at an early point in time that internet was changing the relationship between patients and healthcare professionals. "When I have to give a talk about Health 2.0, I often first give my audience a little startle", Engelen says laughingly. "I tell them Radboud stopped centring on the patient. You can see the audience looking at each other in bewilderment. Because they have only recently learned they have to work patient centred. I then explain that this model still presupposes that the caregiver knows best what the patient needs. Then I tell them that we take this a step further at our hospital. We ask the patient to be a member of the team that treats him.

The patient is the 'owner' of his disease and health and as such he has a role in making treatment choices. That is what participatory medicine is about. The doctor is not an all-knowing expert anymore; he is a competent advisor and coach."

Digital clinics and healthcare communities

The new patient wants to be regarded as an individual; and not as a diabetes or lung cancer patient. He wants a dialogue. "Talk to me, face to face and online". By telling his own story online, he comes into contact with others that can help him and his doctor. For instance, he could get the name of a specialist who will have a look at his file and give an advice. Or another patient can give advice about complementary treatments that support his therapy. In this way a healthcare network is created that can change per patient en per treatment stage. The patient also needs to be able to have a look at his own medical files. Engelen: "We offer our patients ten digital clinics. In 2011 we will start some more. These are websites where patients can check their own medical records, including test results, and find relevant information about their illness.

Soon patients will be able to make and check their appointments online too. The websites also enable online contact with their doctor and with other patients. Of course we are planning to add other services. For instance Skype consults. Furthermore, we have an online hangout for young adults with cancer. On this website called AYA4 they can meet and exchange experiences: from illness and treatment to finding insurance and mortgages. MijnZorgNet.nl is an example of a healthcare community where healthcare professionals, patients and their caregivers at home can find each other. It currently services IVF patients and people with Parkinson's disease."

Prevention has the future

"To keep the rising costs of healthcare in check, we also have to start using the internet for the prevention of illness", says Engelen. "In Holland we already have online courses to treat depression in an early stage or to prevent people from developing a depression. But we have to go further than that. We will have to improve research on how to help people make better health choices and stay healthy longer. An interesting

23

book about that is 'The Decision Tree' by Thomas Goetz. Our government already says they want to go into that direction. Read for instance the report by a government advisory board on healthcare (RVZ) 'From illness and care to health and behaviour' (Dutch) and their Perspective of health 20/20 (English). Yet we spend not even one percent of our national healthcare budget on prevention. That will have to change. We have to move to Prevention 2.0 very soon!'

E-health explained

E-health does not only encompass the use of internet and communication technologies in healthcare in order to make processes between caregivers and care receivers easier, faster and cheaper. It is also a way of thinking about healthcare that puts emphasis on convenience, service and promotion of health. It can support patient in self-managing their (chronic) illness. E-health models:

- Telemedicine is remote care. The patient is at home and communicates health data to his healthcare provider over the internet. For instance send him blood coagulation values or daily diabetes test results. The healthcare professional can monitor these from his computer and act when necessary. But telemedicine is also used between doctors. For instance with teledermatology: a GP sends a picture of the patient's skin condition to a dermatologist and receives a diagnosis and treatment plan, completely online.

- Tele-health is mostly about health education of patients and training of healthcare providers. Examples are online courses supporting the treatment of depression and supporting weight loss programs.

- M-health is the word used for the recent development in mobile internet that uses mobile software or apps on smart phones for monitoring, coaching or promotion of health. An example is an app that coaches autistic children to manage their daily schedule. Or an app that warns the patient at a preset time to take his medicine.

- Electronic Patient Dossier (EPD) versus Personal Health Record (PHR): the Dutch EPD is foremost a central online data exchange centre of medical files stored on decentralised computer systems of individual healthcare providers and organisations. At the moment it is only accessible for healthcare providers. The government wants to give patients future access, but it is still unclear what this will encompass. A PHR has the patient as a starting point. The patient collects and manages his own medical files en determines who he gives access to the data.

©Harriet Messing, 2011

CHAPTER 3

Pre paradigm shift

Signals that point in a certain direction

As developments proceed, small, almost non-noticeable signs occur, that often are only picked up when they cummulate or happen together, and all of a sudden a pattern becomes visible and together pointing to a <u>paradigm shifting</u>. Given the change in healthcare, I tend to refer to them as "pre-paradigm-shift signals".

- The request for "measurements, EVB and KPI's". Whenever it's no longer possible to neglect developments in a certain area, people start asking for evidence based proof and want to have Key Performance Indicators (KPI's), as they also try to get a hold on structuring things that typically cannot be structured like 'front-end innovation' in its early phase.

- Thesis proposals by the day. On a daily basis, we get requests from students wanting to do their Master thesis or internships at our REshape Center about innovation and the change in healthcare. Apart from these daily request for proposals and internships, a broad spectrum of educational programs has emerged that have a focus on innovation and healthcare.

26

- Critics starting to shout to keep "the virus" out. In a recent article <u>Drew Weilage</u> coined a new 'disease' : "<u>innovation autoimmune disorder</u>" referring to the discussions of the activity of the noncompliance actions that are being taken to block, prevent or at least not to encourage the change of innovation that's coming in. I think there's a strong resemblance with the biological process that happens within the body whenever a virus from outside enters the body.

- Nurses are getting engaged via #nurseincluded™. Including nurses as part of the innovation team is badly needed. Luckily nurses are increasingly needed to be included in innovation projects. Nurses are the biggest workforce in healthcare. Imagine the shift that will occur when they fully embrace digital health and technology.

- Patient involvement loses its ‹tokenism›. Since the introduction of the patient-included charter in 2011, we now clearly see that patients are getting more and more involved in processes in healthcare as a more genuine process. In science, in conferences, but also in workshops, design sessions and structural meetings and programs in healthcare institutions and even ministries. We have moved from including patients, as some sort of token, to making working with and for patients a logical and hopefully the standard procedure for healthcare institutions, hospitals, and (local) governments.

- Consultancy firms jump on board. I've always learned that whenever consultancy firms jump on certain developments, you know it's going to get mainstream, as there is business to gain.

- Masterclasses and workshops are being offered. The number of workshops, masterclasses, conferences and consortia that are being formed around a particular topic - like healthcare innovation, the digital transformation or patient empowerment - are clearly signals that a topics starts to move into the mainstream. Or, in others words: digital transformation and healthcare innovation are hot topics.

- Patients get vocal, demanding IT-services and digital products. You know that things are getting real when patients are starting to call their healthcare insurance organizations, demanding digital healthcare for themselves or their family. They no longer accept the current situation, having to take a day off to for an 8-minutes visit to a healthcare professional or in the hospital.

CHAPTER 4

From the valley of disillusionment

"It is the end of the beginning". At the moment many new digital healthcare concepts are at the top of the Gartner Hype Cycle. Some innovations are already over the top and on their way down to 'the valley of disillusionment'. All those wonderful digital healthcare concepts, that seemed so great as a Proof of Concept or so promising as a prototype, haven't been widely implemented, yet. But anyone who knows the Hype Cycle, also knows that there will be a new ascending line.

The Hype Cycle starts with a technology trigger: a new technology or concept gathers more and more media attention, which leads to a broad discussion within the market about the opportunities of this new technology. Expectations grow. A prototype is developed. More prototypes and Proof of Concepts (PoC) follow that show the potential of the new technology. Enthusiasm is growing bigger and bigger, as we are heading to the peak of inflated expectations, as Gartner calls it.

As our expectations get out of sync with reality, a collapse is on the way. We have seen this many times like with the internet bubble that bursted at the beginning of this millennium, after the enthusiasm and expectations of the Internet were at an all time high in the late 90s. In practice, it turned out to be difficult to find proper business models for Internet technologies. And the growth and expansion of innovative concepts was often difficult. In the path downwards we enter the Trough of Disillusionment, as Gartner calls it. After this valley of disillusionment, some companies remain testing and using the new technology, often in stealth mode and in relative silence. This will, in turn, lead to a new period of growth. Eventually, the companies and technology concepts that do find traction, will get on the path upwards to the Plateau of Productivity. Today, no one can say that the promises of the internet have not been met.

New healthcare concepts will also follow this path. Many healthcare innovations are currently at the top of the Hype Cycle or are in the downward phase and entering the valley of disillusionment. Some even appear to go completely up in smoke. Although the exact numbers vary, it is estimated that of all innovations, only 10 percent will eventually reach the market. Not every bright idea will become a success.

Take Theranos, the company that claimed to be able to do numerous blood tests with just a few drops of blood, for a few dollars. Theranos was considered a "breakthrough", "revolutionary" and "disruptive", according to the international newspaper headlines. Holmes - a Stanford University dropout who founded Theranos at the age of 19 - graced the cover of Time Magazine. Dressed in her typical black turtleneck sweater and black pants, the Theranos founder won prize after prize. I was also very excited about this newcomer, more specific about the promise of change that came out of it.

Even though the Food and Drug Administration (FDA) had still not approved Theranos' technology, Holmes was on her way to disrupt the diagnostic and lab market in the United States, unleashing a true revolution in on of the biggest sectors in healthcare.

I mentioned Theranos in just about every presentation as one of the leading examples of a company that did succeed to find the way to the market. In my LinkedIn blog, I periodically updated the unfolding Theranos story, covering news like the deal that pharmacy chain Walgreens and Theranos announced. Walgreens choose Theranos as technology partner to offer their services in their national chain of pharmacies.

Theranos story ended abruptly. In October 2015, the Wall Street Journal published an article that punctured the bubble. As the Wall Street Journal found out, Theranos had not only omitted and falsified information on its own research, the company had also concealed these facts from investors and partners. Former employees opened the book about the company and the founders, who had lied about the core capabilities of their supposedly disruptive lab technology.

The Theranos situation went from bad to worse. FDA officials carried out several inspections at Theranos facilities, closing them down. The company faced a string of legal challenges from medical authorities, investors and the U.S. Securities and Exchange Commission. And as we now know, Elizabeth Holmes has proved to be a liar and a fraud. Sad, but true. If Theranos could live up to its claim, we would have seen better, cheaper diagnostic tests on the market, that could have been a blessing for many people. Apart from this unfulfilled promise, the Theranos case was also a setback for a sector that desperately needs innovation.

On a daily basis, I send messages to people in my network when I see something happening in the field of innovation that I think can be relevant to them. I rarely get any feedback or anything from others. That week in October 2015, however, I received the same message more than 50 times, about how Theranos had been in a race to the bottom. These messages were often accompanied with texts such as "it doesn't seem to go so well with 'your' innovation..." or "as we had already promised you, this could not be true."

Of course, I understand the criticism and the skepticism. But I also want to point out: every epoch has its bad guys. There were crooks and villains in the Middle Ages, and there will be villains in the future. We cannot ban these bad guys completely. In the meantime, several organizations are busy developing similar services. Fortunately, Theranos has inspired them. Just as the hypes surrounding the Internet lead to a punctured bubble almost twenty years ago, we will witness hypes and inflated expectations in healthcare as well. But eventually, some technologies and companies will survive the valley of disillusionment. It is only a matter of time.

Back to the Hype Cycle. We are still in the middle of the descent. A completely logical development is that it takes a while before Proof of Concepts that have proven to be successful, will evolve into working products and services. This is perhaps the most difficult phase of innovation. In this phase, as i call it 'groundswork', must take place I will elaborate on these phases of innovation in another part of this book.

This groundswork requires different skills, different people and other forms of financing and governance than the ideation phase, the search for an idea, a new product or new service. In the groundswork phase, you need to arrange a governance structure, align stakeholders and provide more structure for working on innovation. Soon, you will experience resistance. Questions start to arise: how are we going to implement this concept? Where is the evidence? What is the revenue model? What about the security?

In many cases, a healthcare innovation is put up next to an existing service, as a digital layer on top of existing work procedures. That means that healthcare providers primarily experience more work. For example, most remote monitoring services are initially offered as an extra digital service, in addition to the regular visitations. As the workload increases with a new digital service outlet, it is not surprising that resistance arises. We are still descending further towards the valley of disillusionment.

For the innovation team that has been there from the start of the journey, this is a difficult time. Typically, an innovation team excels at creating new ideas, visualising these into designs, and translating the needs of patients, clients, residents and informal carers into a vision and a concept. An innovation team can work with anything they have at hand: some prototypes are made up with adhesive tape and paper clips, others starts as a digital mock-up of an app or website. Anything works, as long as the idea or concept is clear.

But often, the management or the organization also expects this innovation team to guide the implementation of their innovation. They are much less, or even not at all, equipped to do that task. Suddenly, there is more structure and much less room for flexibility and creativity. I elaborate on the difference between this "left brain and right brain" approach later in this book.

The need for structure and the desire for 'certainty' (see theme 2) often lead to a situation where the most complex parts of the innovation are put on hold.

The scheme below of Victor H. Wang puts them alongside.

Values of Innovation	Values of Production
1. Openness	1. Excellence
2. Diversity	2. Loyalty
3. Serendipity	3. Dependability
4. Fairness	4. Success
5. Experimentation	5. Quality
6. Play	6. Precision
7. Giving	7. Reciprocity

B.

In other words: everything that is truly innovative is taken out and the project that once started an ambitious, audacious goal, now only achieves incremental improvements. All enthusiasm and spirit evaporates from the team: in the end, you run the risk that nobody will be enthusiastic about this - once highly anticipated - project.

Organizations that stick to the maxim that the inventors of an innovative idea must also implement it, have a problem. Chances are that team members, their innovation - or both the team and the innovation - never come out of the valley of disillusionment. The innovators and creative minds become either sick of misery or leave to other organizations that do acknowledge their talents.

If you judge a fish by its ability to climb a tree, it will live its whole life believing that it is stupid. Organizations that realize this on time, often end up in a new phase of growth. They realize that people other than the innovation team have to do the groundswork. They stimulate the creative phase by actually putting part of the radical solutions into practice, with courage and bold leadership. The 3M case described in this book (*Eleven small learnings that will boost your innovation*) shows you how to do just that.

As I already pointed out with the subtitle of this book, we are witnessing 'the end of the beginning'. It seems like the big promises are not being fulfilled, but nothing could be farther from the truth. In fact, the world is accelerating: just look at the steps that tech giants such as Apple and Amazon have taken in the healthcare market. In the meantime, in Europe we continue to discuss: a lot of talking, much less doing.

The outside world really does not take a break because we need more time to discuss regulations, privacy matters or healthcare policies. All parties in the health(care) market, from hospitals and GPs to pharmaceutical companies and insurers, will have to take action, now, if they do not want to lose their relevance for the patient. Bringing care closer to the patient, making it easier for patients to receive the right care at the right time and place in a friendly userinterface. That must be the starting point for organisations. Try to remove yourself out of that process, if often urge our teams to try to become obsolete. Because if you will not try to become obsolete yourself, some-one from outside of the healthcare sector will probably make you and your business model obsolete in the future.

As I point out in the chapter *The day after tomorrow*, we are still too focused on today and tomorrow. But it is the day after tomorrow that matters. Only with an eye on the future, you can make the difference. An organization that does not have a vision of where they will be in ten years' time, with due regard for all developments around them, will hardly have a right to exist by

2028. If you do not have the courage to include radical innovation as part of your DNA as well as process improvement and incremental innovation, you are insufficiently able to cope with the changing world around you.

In healthcare, the time it takes for innovation to take shape is substantially different than what we have seen in, for example, the music industry, travel industry or taxi business. But even though healthcare has its own dynamics, change is knocking on the door. The (inter)national developments that we are witnessing at this time, cannot and will not be reversed. In my view, healthcare will not be changed from the inside, but rather by forces from the outside, driving innovation and driving change at speed.

Organisations really have to think about their future. Not about today, not tomorrow or next week, but five or ten years from now. In this context, I always like to quote famous football player Johan Cruyff - also an amateur philosopher - who put it this way: "Football is simple. You don't have to be where the ball is, but you have to be where the ball is GOING to be." Healthcare must become more aware of this.

Experiences at REshape Center

At our Radboudumc REshape Center, we also experiencing the Gartner Hype Cycle in our own evolution. In 2010, we formulated nine projects, that we took from idea to a first prototype in nine months. These individual projects needed to be completed in about thirty days. Starting with almost no clue, we quickly came up with first learnings. As a team, we went through a very steep learning curve (read: Hype Cycle's). Enthusiasm grew, both in our REshape Center and at the Radboud University Medical Center Nijmegen, as well as outside the hospital.

However these prototypes and Proof of Concepts did not change the existing healthcare processes. These innovations were all ideas that came alongside the regular care, added a digital layer on top off existing workflows, such as our Adolescents and Young Adults (AYA) community for young people with cancer.

In the years that followed, an increasing number of these prototypes and Proof of Concepts were gradually implemented, it sometimes even took 6-7 years. Digital innovations such as video consultations (FaceTalk) to facilitate contact between physicians and patients, wireless patient monitoring both at the wards and at home, and incorporating and researching the use of social media in healthcare. Adjustments to our real estate and building concepts, structurally involving patients in all changes, and making adjustments in the curriculum of the Medicine and Biomedical Sciences study program and our Health Innovation School to train our future leaders.

We could not simply put these innovations alongside the existing care process. Rather than being put on top of existing processes, innovation changes how we work or learn. Innovation or new processes must lead to 'profit'. Profit in quality, profit in effectiveness, profit in costs or profit in the experiences that the patient or the professional has. Innovations must enable healthcare providers to do their work better, preferably in less time. So there must be a clear business model. And it must be embedded in processes.

Our board at Radboud University Medical Center Nijmegen expects us to play a role in this, as REshape Center. At the same time, we urge them to find other people for this implementation and process optimization phase. Find the right people who do understand structure and governance, who know how to approach an implementation project and who do like such a task or role. People with very different knowledge and experience, and also with very different skills.

We're having are having a fierce but fruitful discussion about this. You can read more about this in the chapter "*To REshape or not*

"And yes, it often leads to a valley of disillusionment. But we also see that at the department or groups where an implementation team is appointed with proper implementation skills, things move fast. The initial enthusiasm comes back. The enthusiasm that is so badly needed to enter the next phase of growth.

CHAPTER 5

Uberization of healthcare

A LinkedIn blog from me - 24 okt. 2014

So, I woke up last night from a nightmare. I dreamt that our healthcare system was taken over, just 'overnight'. Healthcare being Uberized.

What I'm witnessing is that both large and small companies, most of them without any track record in health(care), have been able to 'seduce' people within the last 12 months - to join them, and put their data from smartwatches, fitness trackers and weighing scales into their platforms and apps.

The problem is, the scatteredness of all that data is increasing instead of declining. There is no way you will be able to handle all the information from the hospital community, from the GP's office, from the pharmacist and/or physiotherapist all together: it is difficult - sometimes even impossible - to gather all data in one place. Let alone adding your own data from your favorite cycling or running app, or from your dentist, who still works on paper.

Awareness is great, it is one of the things I have been working on fiercely over the past 5 years. Awareness hopefully leads to a higher level of taking self-control of your own health(care).

And how does this relate to all those different vendors of electronic medical records (EMR's) and operating systems? Are you at risk of being "out" of a certain health system if you have either an Apple or Google smartphone? Android or iOS only?

So YES, it is a good thing that there is something going on. The problem however is that healthcare professionals and institutions are just starting to think of these kind of solutions, whilst the (consumer) driven market is ready to roll. There is a reason why Apple, Google and most recently also Facebook are working towards health(care): for them, it is a huge market and we're all are going to be in need of it, at one point in our lives.

More and more tangible steps are being made by non-medical companies like Walmart, wanting to be the #1 health provider. So what will your future hospital look like? Will it resemble a hospital or look more like a supermarket?

Why bother? Well, I am not the kind of guy that states that 'we' are the only ones to understand health(care). As a matter of fact, I can't wait until we are on the intersection of clinical excellence and consumer/patient engagement like Apple, having a great track record in design and customer user experience. At REshape, we started out working for patients, now we are working and innovating with them, but I really think we should enable patients, family and informal care to innovate themselves. And just that is something companies like Apple figured out a while ago So, a close collaboration would be great, like the one we have with Apple and Epic.

And apart from the impact from companies from outside the healthcare domain, let's not forget smart patients who come up with innovations themselves and start a business out of their own creative ideas and needs. With ready-made building blocks available, for instance for payment, app design and security, anyone with a bright idea can start a business - you don't need to hire an expert any more. I really think the best is yet to come from them.

But what's keeping me 'awake at night' is the fact that change will be ignited from outside healthcare. Change will be driven by other corporates and patients (or consumers) themselves. We've seen that before in the travel, music and media industry, right? At first sight, I would have no problem with that. But there is also a reason why doctors had to study that long, why medical professionals take years and years of training and practice. It takes time to understand how our bodies work: a computer just can't replace a doctor.

As with any industry that is disrupted, there will be some 'clutter' and 'harm done' along the way. I really think that health(care) will become a software business within 20 years from now, run by algorithms i.e. on Dr. Watson based on big data and remote measurements. However, we are talking about people here: healthcare is about persons, not taxis or rental apartments. So there is no time to 'talk'' about change anymore, we have to execute it.

What I'm witnessing these days, on the axis of exponential technology and newcomers in the health(care) market, is that it's no longer about 'ambitions', 'planning' or 'intentions'. It is about real and actual steps being made at lighting speed. Apple wants to become a health data-broker, and Google and Novartis are creating a way to measure glucose with contact-lenses for diabetics.

At Radboud University Medical Center, we have been working on transforming health(care) over the past 5 years.

Sometimes, we moved way ahead of the curve, for instance with the Hereismydata platform with Philips. Hereismydata

(HIMD) started out as a vision: that patients should be in control of their own healthcare data. HIMD eventually turned from a vision into a Proof of Concept and spurred the movement of personal health records (PHR) and platforms for patients.

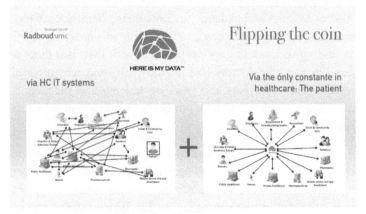

Looking at what is happening around us right now, the question is: will we be in time to keep the great knowledge and passion that's a characteristic of this sector alive, or have we already been 'Uber-ized', an industry taken over by new entrants? New innovations in healthcare tend to take 7 to 10 years to reach the market. I'm starting to think things will happen sooner from the outside, moving towards the inside.

I woke up in the middle of the night. Sweating, heavily breathing and with a pulse-rate that meets a good workout. Luckily it was just a nightmare! Or was it?

CHAPTER 6

A real estate perspective

As more and more tasks within healthcare can be performed at a different location, this will have an effect on the way we handle our real estate in this branch as well.

If let's say 5% of all the outpatient visits in our university medical center would have been done by video consultation, that would save us as much as 200 parking lots at day. That's an entire parking garage a year.

One could easily imagine a whole department specifically tailored for running virtual visits, including a medical control center where you could be it eight or have extra technology to monitor or measure the patient. These departments or rooms for virtual video visits and outpatient monitoring could be shared with other professionals.

In the United States, Mercy Virtual offers a complete hospital without a single bed, as they claim, and in China tele-care has almost become standard procedure in certain regions. Healthcare professionals in China and the United States provide low complex healthcare virtually and thereby help in treating people earlier, to prevent worse. Aided by algorithms, artificial intelligence and machine learning, healthcare professionals can keep an eye on their patient, even when a patient himself is not paying attention, and give them a call to run some tests.

So maybe the spaces needed for physical outpatient visits need to have a different structure. Eventually, real life visits and virtual care have to blend, based on the preferences of patients and based on the type of condition. With the right technology, trained professionals and a proper follow up procedure, the amount of people in the waiting room could and should decrease.

Think about other possibilities as well, from a real estate perspective. We could do much more to provide service and assurance to patients that do visit a hospital. Image that you - as a patient - would receive a message that the physician's schedule is running late. The message indicates that you can leave your home a bit later as well, preventing waiting in the waiting room but rather at home. Even when you've already entered the hospital, we could send you a message about the 10 or 20-minute delay, and give a QR code to get a cup of coffee in our visitor restaurant. By that, we could turn an unpleasant experience, waiting for an appointment, into something -a bit more- positive direction, providing information and services.

We often invite patients at the hospital for their preoperative procedure: an appointment where typically a nurse would run you through your list of medications, preparations and questionnaires for the operator's intervention, special needs and so forth. This control takes time and a visit to the hospital is required. But once this information - medications, questionnaires, personal information - would be residing in a personal health record, nurses don't have to ask the same questions over and over again. As a result, we would need less professionals sitting at a desk, filling in paperwork all day for all types of preoperative procedures. The hospital pharmacists would benefit greatly from having access to a personal medication file, including the over the counter pharmaceuticals, as well.

Why do we need to bring patients to a hospital, only to take some blood, measure their weight, blood pressure or oxygenation level? Why do patients - and their family members, spouses or caregivers - need to take a day off, arrange transportation, and free up their valuable time, only to run these quick typical tests, that can also be done remotely in the comfort of their homes? For those who are not able do to these tests or measurements at home, the 'mini clinics' that soon will be created within supermarkets near their own homes will offer an alternative. These local clinics will be staffed with nurses and even doctors, will be equipped with easy-to-use technology and will have a low threshold for patients to come in at a moment and time that suits them.

If you take all of these developments in consideration, it means that for us - as a university medical center - the patients we will see and admit will probably become more and more complex cases, as the more frequent and simple consultations and procedures will move to top clinical hospitals, mini-clinics at the supermarket, or even in your own home or in your car.

Emotional burden

Patients who will start their chemotherapy need to come to the hospital first, since we need to draw some blood on the same day their chemotherapy is bound to begin to see if the values a good enough to start the round of chemo. Patients need to come to the hospital early morning, we'll will take some blood and then they wait, often for a couple of hours.

If the values are OK, they would start chemotherapy within an hour from that moment, but if the values are not OK, patients will be sent back to their home, with the request to return the next morning. The next day, the same procedure follows.

Can you imagine what it would mean for people with cancer to be able to run these tests from the comfort of their own homes, with a small dianostic test kit? The results from the test kit will be sent to the physician, who measures the values and then decides whether or not the patient has to come to the hospital to start, or whether the patient can stay at home for another day or two.

Just imagine the emotional burden of being sent back home, over and over again, with such an impactful treatment as chemotherapy. With new diagnostic tests, it will become possible to measure and provide guidance in other places rather than the hospital. A service like this will also have implications for the way we handle real estate.

Hospitals, or I should say hospital-systems, will tend to migrate more and more into a network. From that perspective, we are migrating from a university medical center into a university medical network, with the opportunity to share facilities, high-end medical technology, and even spaces. A university medical network builds services around the patients' needs, guiding them to the best treatments in the right place.

Healthcare's Copernican moment

So, do we still need real estate for hospitals? Of course we do! We still need places to store high-end medical technology that meets specific requirements. But we need much more regional cooperation, medical networks, to share knowledge, skills and high-end medical technology.

Healthcare is facing its Copernican moment, as I point out in my lectures. In the mid-1500s, Nicolai Copernicus proved the theory that the Sun was circling the Earth wrong. Copernicus formulated a model of the universe that placed the Sun rather than the Earth at the center of the universe. I think with all the technology and the change in society that's coming up, healthcare is up to its own Copernican moment. Rather than placing the professional in the center of the universe, this new model of the healthcare universe places the patient at the center. We will witness a shift, from patients circling around the professional, to the professional visiting the patient, in real life or virtually.

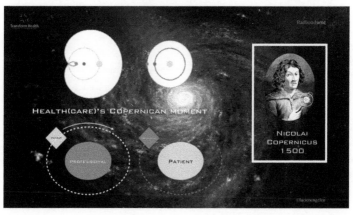

Of course, a universe that centers around the patient, requires a lot more from our healthcare facilities than what's offered today. For instance, we need safe and secure remote monitoring, collecting data continuously rather than as separate measurements. While we are still debating the advance of 5G internet as successor of 4G and 3G networks, companies like SpaceX make plans to provide worldwide Internet coverage with the launch of orbital satellites. SpaceX and its competitors are launching over 4000 small satellites that are covering the entire world. Just imagine what that implies for people living in rural areas or areas without internet, to get access to healthcare knowledge, information and the possibility to remotely contact healthcare providers.

CHAPTER 7

The impact of the fourth industrial revolution on healthcare real estate (vignette)

Rene Bleeker, project director Real Estate, Radboudumc

New technologies such as artificial intelligence, robotization, Internet of Things, cloud computing and 3D printing, form the basis of what some call the fourth industrial revolution. The consequences of this fourth industrial revolution for healthcare real estate are substantial, risky and costly. In the past, a hospital was built with an expected life span of forty years; the question now is whether we should invest in bricks anyway, given the pace of change. Who is currently able to outline the development of care in ten years' time: is it the doctor, the innovator, the manufacturer, the start-up, or the Internet giants?

A future-proof healthcare real estate strategy will be organized in a different way than we are used to today. An integrated real estate strategy rests on the three pillars - bricks, bytes, and behavior - and is staged over a period of ten to fifteen years. Due to these three variables, the outcome is different for each case. The Radboudumc has opted for the strategy of investing less in bricks, investing more in technology and innovation, and more in the development of new and location-independent healthcare processes.

Bricks

Long-term production prognoses, real-time occupation rate measurements, lean agenda planning and activity-related work will lead to less space requirements for operating rooms, beds, outpatient clinics, laboratories and offices. This requires a cultural shift in thinking about the current and future use of space. We have to get used to building less square meters, instead of more square meters.

Healthy architecture focuses on the well-being of people in a building. A healthy working environment leads to stress reduction in patients and employees and will lead to shorter hospital stays, less use of painkillers, and less work-related absenteeism. Naturally, the highest demands are placed on the sustainability of healthcare real estate. At the same time, a sustainably developed building will lead to higher initial financial investments and longer payback times than usual. This therefore leads to fewer bricks of higher, more expensive quality.

Care buildings will become more and more intelligent through the large-scale use of smart building technologies. The data from sensors can be used on many processes, such as demand-controlled heating, lighting and, for example, smart purchasing of electricity. This real-time data can also be used to analyze, optimize and improve care processes. Take for example the real-time monitoring and feedback systems to staff, to remind them of consistent washing of their hands when visiting patients. This monitoring will lead to a substantial gain in the quality of hand hygiene and prevention of contamination of patients.

Behavior

Visitors, patients and employees have a much greater influence on care processes at home, on the way to and in the hospital. Smartphones have increasing computing power and increasingly sophisticated sensors. This computing power is increasingly used in preventive and analytical medicine. Measurements that are still taking place in a hospital will take place in the patient's living room. This means fewer follow-up visits to the hospital, and therefore fewer outpatient clinics and parking places.

The same smartphone can also be used by health personnel to receive information and notifications about their patients, and where their collaegues are, and where the nearest blood pressure monitor is located. But also building functionalities such as opening curtains, controlling lighting and heating, and reserving a conference room or a workplace can be done with a smartphone. Intelligent signposting and navigation (wayfinding) will help patients to appear - just-in-time - at their appointment.

Bytes

Medical processes will change due to technological developments and impose different requirements on the infrastructure and architecture of healthcare buildings. An example of this is the continuous monitoring of large groups of patients. With the advancement of continuous monitoring, hospitals need to be equipped with care centers that analyze generated patient data in real-time and take immediate action when needed. Smart algorithms will also monitor large groups and send alarms directly to the smartphone of the medical professional on duty. This development leads to different use of spaces, and also to the emergence of new professions.

Modern medical equipment is placing increasingly higher demands on the technical infrastructure of a healthcare institution. The dependence on data is so great that temporary network outages are a disaster. It is therefore obvious to not only simulate power failures, as is currently commonplace in hospitals, but also to simulate data failures. The Internet of Things will lead to heavier demands on cabling, computing power and storage, on the expansion of cooling and redundant systems, and on the expansion of emergency power. In the past, perhaps half of a hospital was wired to the emergency power, while modern hospitals need to be fully wired to the emergency power outlet. Property owners will have to invest significantly more in both information technology and the supported hardware.

Developments in diagnostic equipment, for example for genetics, will lead to the redundancy of large surfaces of traditional laboratories. Traditional wet laboratories will have to make way for analytical robot streets and office environments for researchers. Investments in laboratories will be depreciated more quickly due to the rapid technological developments. Laboratories have therefore become risky real estate.

Designers, developers, users and owners of healthcare real estate will have to realize that the possibilities that the digital revolution brings, will change the brick and mortar world of healthcare forever. My advice is: align your real estate strategy with the three pillars I described above: bricks, bytes, behavior. The mistakes that physicians make will disappear , but the mistakes that real estate directors and planners make, will remain for decades.

CHAPTER 8

Hospital of the future (vignette)

Jörn-Ole Stellmann, partner Wiegerinck urban
architecture inspired by Lucien Engelen and Robert
Muijsers (Arbol)

The hospital is in for a huge transformation. On the drawing
boards of our firm of architects, <u>Wiegerinck architectuur
stedenbouw,</u> are designs of hospitals that will be completed
in one or two years, up to sometimes even seven years. These
designs are created in a meticulous process, based on present
policies, a broad base of support and a conservative estimate of
the developments in healthcare, in many cases coming down to
shrinkage or maintaining the status quo.

Think about those seven years completion time for a hospital for a second. If we look back in time, the <u>first iPhone</u> was
launched almost eleven years ago. The first iPhone started a
generation of new technology (smartphones), in a way we could
hardly predict back then. Only a few months later - in 2007
- the so-called <u>schillenmethode</u> (functional zoning model)
was introduced as property model for the hospital. These two
introductions are not related in any manner, but if we consider
the technological developments since that time and extrapolate
this trend within healthcare for the coming ten years – if only
from the perspective of the lifespan of buildings – we need a

new encounter between the two.

Functional model

In 2007, the now discontinued Dutch Board for Hospital Facilities presented the 'schillenmethode' as new methodology for considering investment decisions in hospital real estate. Every function in a hospital poses specific demands to the building typology. In this functional model with zones, a distinction is made between four essentially different building typologies, named 'schillen' (literally layers, i.e. functional zones). By grouping functions with the same accommodation requirements, an efficient building can be created that actually consists of four buildings. Hospitals like the Dutch Gelre Hospital in Zutphen have been created based on this property model.

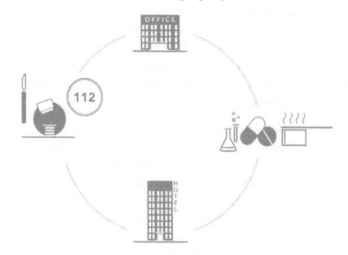

The first layer, the 'hotfloor' comprises the advanced technological capital-intensive functions. The 'hotel' houses all functions for the hospital stay of patients. The functions for consulting hours and carrying out relatively straightforward examinations and treatments are placed in the 'office' layer. It makes sense to also include office facilities, staff accommodation, administration and management tasks in this layer. Finally, there is the 'factory' that accommodates all support and facilitating functions from a medical perspective.

New technology

Physicians have many competencies. Starting with an examination of a patient, each time they go through a cycle of fact finding, diagnosis, prescription, treatment, care and monitoring. A significant part of these tasks, through both technological and social developments, will (partly) become automated. Some tasks will increasingly be performed by patients in their domestic environment. These changes concern each layer of the hospital and introduce a new functional zone.

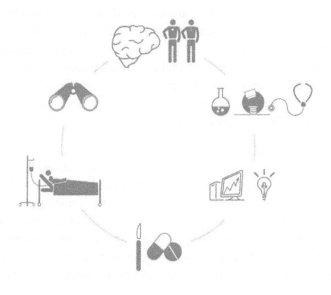

We need to reconsider these functional zones, the layers of the hospital, in order to make them thrive again. Below, we have outlined a number of developments per layer. These show that the outpatient clinic mutates, the nursing section becomes more focused, the hotfloor is reduced, the factory is sublimated and the 'home environment' prospers.

The office mutates

Despite the shift from clinical to outpatient treatment, the scope of the outpatient clinic will not increase. The widening acceptance of digital contact will reduce the number of physical meetings between patient and physician. Less examinations, more communication.

The outpatient section will become a helpdesk with an open walk-in character surrounded by an extensive (artificial) knowledge center. This will be the very heart of the hospital: the place where professionals can meet in their official capacities or in informal encounters. This heart will seek to follow the principles of Activity Based Working. There will be a balance between the open spaces for multidisciplinary observations and knowledge sharing, and closed spaces for digital contact with patients. Waiting areas will largely become obsolete. Multidisciplinary capacity is widely available both in a physical sense and online.

New entrants, such as artificial intelligence and data science companies, add an extra layer of medical knowledge to the office. Video-consultations facilitate a second opinion with a doctor in Dubai or Denver, and rare diseases can be discussed with colleagues around the world in a matter of minutes, rather than weeks. In many cases, contact between physician and patient no longer needs to be physical: digital consultations have the same intimacy and quality. We will look back at cases such as Donte Broyne (2015) with a combination of bewilderment and unease, as this future office provides the hospital - professionals and patients - a range of new technologies, in-depth knowledge and machine learning capabilities.

This 'health store' is visited by a self-confident patient, who has drawn a preliminary diagnosis and brings a large amount of personal medical data (whether or not correctly measured). Some even argue the hospital of the future is in our home, were data is collected without disturbing routines, through self-monitoring equipment that has evolved from portable devices and wearables to implantable devices.

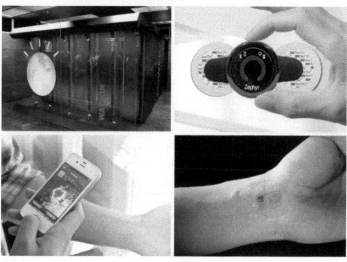

Visuals: We will increasingly be witnessing empowered patients with digital aids to draw their own preliminary diagnose. Collecting medical data increasingly takes place in the home environment and making a diagnosis is supported by artificial intelligence (supercomputer Watson, Zephyr sensors, SkinVision app , Epidermal Electronic System)

The factory is sublimated

The factory components will nearly completely disappear from the hospital of the future. Meal preparation and laundry processing have already been phased out in many cases, as external suppliers and partners can deliver better quality services and products more cost-efficiently. Analysis laboratories will become extinct. Simple analyses will be done by patients themselves in their home environment. For more extensive analyses, a limited number of national centers will be used. The hospital will maintain a small basic facility for urgent analysis.

In the pharmacy, the 3D printer is introduced to produce patient-specific medication. The first 3D-printed medication has already been approved. An automated logistics distribution point or service from Amazon or Picnic (read for instance the vignette of Picnic's founder Michiel Muller) may be the only factory aspect to remain in the hospital.

Personalized medicine has become a reality. Animal testing will be replaced by lab-on-a-chip or organs on a chip. Researchers and molecular geneticists will be able to test, with cells or with human tissue, whether or not a particular medicine or treatment will be effective for patients. So-called organoids or mini-organs, made and grown from human tissue such as intestines, will be very effective to search for the best medication.

The hotel becomes more focused

The hospital's nursing center will be filled by more complex casuistry on the one hand and patients with comorbidity on the other. As a result of the reduction of occupant days and the shift to the outpatient monitoring, the hotel becomes more focused.

The double room may not be filled by two patients any longer but offers full rooming-in for partners who actively contribute to the care and relieve nursing staff. We will see active informal care within the nursing environment. If patients prefer to be washed of cared for by their family members and loved ones, the hotel makes it possible. Parents of small children will be able to accompany them during their hospital stay.

Technology shifts from the ceiling and bed wall panel to the patient's bed, tablet and even clothing. With wearable, wireless sensors, patients will have much more freedom to move and get up from their hospital beds, as the sensors continuously collect all vital signs. Advanced monitoring techniques will detect subtle changes in data patterns, marking when a patient's situation deteriorates. Medical activities that are at present centered around the hotfloor, will shift to the hotel, including the monitoring of intensive care patients.

The hotfloor is reduced

The hotfloor is the technological heart of the hospital, the layer of technological capital-intensive functions. As technology grows exponentially, the operation room will become smaller and smaller over time. Robot surgery and hybrid operating rooms are two important technological developments on the hotfloor. Advancements in imaging and robotization will make medical procedures and operations less invasive for patients, more effective, quicker and will lead to better outcomes. The hotfloor will be accompanied by complete data centers, close to the operating rooms as well the medical imaging department.

With advancements in 3D-printing, we will see more 3D printers within the hospital. The Radboudumc in Nijmegen has a 3D Lab in collaboration with engineers, doctors and patients. This lab is exploring new possibilities and finding answers to the question how 3D technology can improve the care for the individual patient.

Two possible answers are patient-specific virtual surgery planning and 3D printed anatomical models, an example of care and treatment plans that are much more tailored to the individual patient's situation.

This hotfloor will also be enhanced by a digital layer, as medical equipment such as PET- and CT-scans and departments such as radiology are aided by clinical workflow and medical support systems. Analytics and artificial intelligence (AI) systems support clinicians with the ever expanding collection of medical data, from X-rays to pathology images. Dashboards provide data scientists, clinicians and healthcare providers access to advanced analytic capabilities to curate and analyze healthcare data.

We will see the current democratization trend expand in the future, putting medical equipment in the hands of patients, enabling technologies such as ultrasound imaging in their home environment. When we talk and think about building a hospital for the future, we notice the largest number of white spots on our design drawings when it comes to the hotfloor.

What will the technological heart of the hospital look like, ten years from now? It is virtually impossible to predict what the future will bring in ten years' time.

Visual: technology reduces the distance and increases intervention speed.

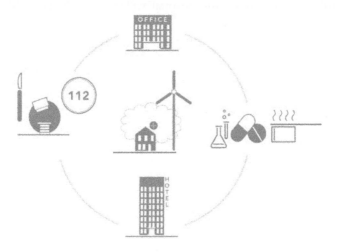

Home environment prospers

The home environment will be the hospital's new layer. Continuous monitoring of health parameters through smartphone, blood, urine, and possibly DNA analyses, self-diagnosis, digital contact with medical professionals and fellow patients, monitoring of medication use, deployment of informal patient care: it all takes place in the trusted environment of one's home. Hospitals will have to embrace this contribution from and by the home environment and even structure their building plan accordingly. In the future, the need to visit a hospital will diminish: the hospital will visit us at our homes.

And even the very definition of a hospital as an 'institution where the sick or injured receive medical care' is up for change. It no longer concerns a condition or illness but the desire to be informed, to be reassured, to take preventive action and eventually intervene with respect to our health. If you draw that line further into the future, the 'hospital' will increasingly see healthy people.

CHAPTER 9

Missing voices

Why patients and nurses are the axis in innovation :
#patientsincluded™ and #nurseincluded™

When it comes to innovation in healthcare, you'll find people working in IT or finance, doctors or the head of department sitting at the table. What does it mean if patients and nurses join the conversation?

"Aren't we all patients?". "It is all about patients." Or what about this one: "We know what our patients want." These are three often heard 'arguments' against including patients on stage or in the audience at medical conferences, back in 2010. It is great to see the change that has taken place since. Not only did patients got more verbal due to the use of the internet and social media, but they also stood up for their cause more and more, claiming their place at conferences, in meetings and online.

Change takes time. Addressing an issue over and over again, and taking action as conference organizers or speaker yourself, helps a bit as well. In 2010, I made it clear that I was no longer speaking at conferences where patients were not included, and took care for inclusion in all of our conferences we organized a Radboud University Medical Center.

Very often in the healthcare sector, We often talk about the patient and rarely with the patient is this sector.. The fact that we also do this in innovation really hit me back in 2010, when I was a keynote speaker at a mHealth conference in Dubai. All major telecom and consultancy companies were present, predicting a billion-dollar market, even in the following year. When I asked the attendees: 'who of you is a patient?', nobody raised their hand. In fact, there were no patients present at all. There was not even a doctor in the room.

That struck me as strange, I thought this was strange, since we were - after all - at a conference for mHealth and mobile care services. If you are a developer or entrepreneur with a new product or service, then it should be logical to check in with customers at an early stage. How in the world can you innovate if you do not understand what your customers (patients, physicians) want or need? Chances are you are developing something that is missing the target.

Ultimately, the patient determines what he finds good or bad care. In addition, he often only partially assesses the quality of medical care. His experience is much more determined by the rest of the healthcare process: the logistics, the treatment by professionals and the facilities. Nevertheless, healthcare professionals often remain one-sided - looking at the medical side alone, with the result that they do not ask patients for their opinion.

Often, it is assumed in advance that patients do not understand this. That is a misconception. First, the patients are the experience experts in having a disease. It would be good to combine the medical knowledge about treating a disease with the knowledge about living with the disease. And secondly, 80 percent of the healthcare consists of logistics and process management. These logistical processes can benefit greatly from the expertise patients bring to the table. And it is also these logistical processes that will make it possible for patients to receive healthcare at the moment and time that suits them, in the future.

#patientsincluded™

On the way back in the plane, I was still agitated, deciding to never speak at a conference where there were no patients on stage, in the program committee and in the auditorium. I created a logo, trademark and basic clauses. Not for commercial reasons, since it is self accreditation via www.patientsincluded. org with the help of great volunteers - but to protect misuse of it. The #patientsincluded™ program can be used by parties that involve patients in initiatives that are aimed at improving care.

The moment we launched the accreditation process and put a real logo on it, things started to go fast. You are only eligible for #patientsincluded™ accreditation if you actively involve patients. If you invite them to a conference, you should, for example, provide them with a free admission ticket and travel costs, because it is self-evident that you cannot demand a patient to pay a few hundred euros to attend a conference. I can write a whole chapter about the tricks that organizations were pulling to get out of the accreditation process. I could also write a book about the success stories that organizations have when they finally start to include patients. But I will keep that for another (new) book.

We can not have enough ways to incorporate patients into our processes in the creation of their health(care) on a daily basis. When we organized the sold out TEDx conference (with 1000 people in the audience, while 4000 wanted to get in), the first announced speaker was ePatientDave, as one of the patientspeakers, 25% of the speakers were patients.

Now the #patientsincluded™ movement is being broad-ened to also create clauses for Scientific Journals, trails, ethics etc. So you can imagine how proud I was when The BMJ started on a mission to include patients into their journal processes. As a result, we gladly presented them with the first ever Patients Included award for taking the leadership in a very traditional branche. The BMJ still keeps on track, working towards true partnerships with patients.

#patientsincluded™ was also incorporated in many processes like co-designing healthcare in 2014 healthcare in 2014 and changing our medical curriculum in 2015. We even thought about ranking conferences on a 'star' scale, but at that point choose not to do so, since it is not about rating but about creating awareness.

In this interview video I elaborated on some of the aspects of Patients Included that is completely in the heart and strategy of our organization and of my personal mission.

Still, there is a lot of work to do. Besides incorporating patients in every step we take, we need to change the system according to the paradigm shift that is erupting from the digital world we live in as well.

A chat by the bed

We often take it for granted: nurses working fiercely to make things happen, making sure the patient and family are well informed, taken care of and doing everything in their power to support a solid recovery

Mid last year, I suffered from kidney stones again (7th episode) and had to have them removed surgically (again). So I was well aware of what was ahead of me when I was admitted to the ward on the day of the intervention. At admission, I told them I had to be home next day to proudly attend the graduation ceremony for my daughter. During the whole process it was the nurse, and a physician every now and then checking in and doing the needed checklist, that 'controlled' the whole flow.

After the surgery, everything went well, nothing seemed to keep me from going home next day - unlike the former episode when it took over 10 days to get complications under control. Once the bladder catheter was removed, within 5 minutes all hell broke loose. I was in extreme pain, just like the renal colics I know so very well. As I lay crawling on the floor, one of the nurses saw this in the blink of an eye and called the physician. The pragmatic way she handled the situation struck me. The peripheral infusion was reinstalled with pain medication in an instant, and (unfortunately) my discharge was delayed until the next day.

But the next day, multiple colics kicked in, with the nurses standing next to my bed every time, giving me moral support and making sure the pain was drilled down as much as possible. There was clearly no discharge for me...

At the moment and time when the graduation of my daughter was scheduled, out of the blue two of the nurses stepped in the room with a cup of tea, and a coffee for me, making me share a story about our beautiful daughter and her graduation ceremony as proud fulfillment of her education. Besides all the great nursing work, the care and the hospitality, the careful medication regime, and the treatments that I had received, it was that moment - when they decided to step in and sat next to my bedside - that made a great impact on me, my #mangomoment!

But.... there is another side to nursing too. During my stay in the hospital, after they discovered I was actually a colleague of theirs at the REshape Center, we talked a lot about innovation and my view that nurses should be more involved in innovation, as they have a great overview and share the majority of their time with the patients. They agreed and said they were hardly ever asked about these kinds of projects and decisions, but had to work with the results of innovations they did not participate in.

#nurseincluded™

As a follow-up to the #patientsincluded™ program, I also wanted to pay attention to another often forgotten group: nurses. Anyone who has ever been a patient, knows how important nurses can be. She or he provide much more than just medical care. What patients especially appreciate, is the sincere attention that nurses give. Their involvement reaches further than just the medical recovery. It is therefore not surprising that the profession of nurse belongs to one of the most valued professions worldwide and why the story of Florence Nightingale is still appealing, even to this day.

It does not seem right to me that nurses are hardly ever represented at the table - between doctors, IT-managers and financial staff members - when it comes to innovation. Yet, the nurse's job is infused by technology nowadays. Whether it is in an intensive care ward or home care, technology plays a crucial role in virtually every nursing setting. Nurses know better than anyone when technology delivers high or low added value to the quality of care experienced by the patient. They are the experts, based on their own experiences, when it comes to adapting technology to the wishes and needs of a patient.

Nurses are also one of the few in a hospital that understands both the clinical workflow and the patient journey; who see where those two roads run parallel and where the obstacles arise. Nurses are therefore an indispensable link in every innovation team.

Ironically, nurses hardly ever receive an invitation to think about innovation. Even if they do get that invitation, nurses are often not in the position to schedule their own time. That means that leaving work to attend a conference is not facilitated easily. Most nurses need permission from their manager before they can take part in a meeting, whether it is an internal meeting or a conference. If they do find or get the time to attend a conference, nine out of ten times this is a nursing conference. They certainly do not witness their boss signing them up for an innovation conference or an event outside of their own field.

Claim your seat

Now this story has two sides, because nurses can also claim a seat at the table. They can become a bit more active themselves, but they certainly also use some help. That is why, in line with the #patientsincluded™ initiative, I set up the #nurseincluded™ program and declared 2018 the year of #nurseincluded™ in innovation in healthcare. In order to support and guide, I have been able to attract my good friend and nurse specialist Shawna Butler from Texas for a year (from May 2018 to May 2019), who coined the term EntrepreNURSE, resembling the entrepreneurial spirit a lot of nurses have.

The difference between #nurseincluded™ and #EntrepreNURSE is that the first applies to all nurses and the last applies for that group of nurses with entrepreneurial ambitions and skills, but who still lack some skills and want to be trained in gaining an entrepreneurial mindset. Because what these nurses need is a business toolkit that enables them to translate their 'soft' experiences into hard figures. With this skill set, they can exert power at the policy level.

2018 is the year in which we want to work on making nurses more involved in innovation. This is something I started a couple of years ago with Angelien Sieben, at that time chair of the Nursing advisory council at Radboudumc. Together we created some buzz and 'trouble' about it. And now we do this together with partners such as the Dutch Ministry of Health, Verpleegkundigen & Verzorgenden Nederland (V&VN), Singularity University, the Health Innovation School and others. I hope that, as with #patientsincluded™, others follow our example in this area too. Because we cannot and do not want to leave nurses behind if we want to innovate in a way that truly fits patient needs.

In 2016 I was flabbergasted to be awarded the honor of the Sigma Theta Tau International "Friend of Nursing" from the Honor Society of Nursing which is still proudly sitting in my home-office. (The way they tricked me to the celebration location, with the help of many, including a decoy meeting at the Ministry of Health, still makes me smile).

Even in our own Radboud University Medical Center it took me a while to bring nurses to the 'innovation table'. One nurse joined us at the 2013 San Diego meeting, there were 2 nurses in 2014, and 4 in 2016 (see the exponential pattern here?). However, this is still not enough, we have to, and will do, better. So I would invite you all to try and make 2018 the year of #nurseincluded™ and equally #entlepreNURSE.

I bounced the ideas at a couple of my keynotes meetings

and chats and pretty soon it started to float and buzz already. So at last year's Exponential Medicine, we sat down with nurses from the US, the Netherlands and Canada and decided to go for it and ignite a couple of events and actions to emphasize on nurse's roles in innovation, but also to be included and to boost the entrepreneurial ambitions many nurses have, similar to #doctorpreneurs.

I would like to ask you: what kind of intervention, ideas, brainwaves come across when we say #nurseincluded™ and #entrepreNURSe. How do we honor and cherish the great work our nurses are doing on a daily basis and how to embed their knowledge, pragmatism and spirit in the badly needed innovation for health(care)?

Imagine what can happen if we unleash this gigantic innovative force on the challenges we face and innovate with "the whole system in the room". Let's leverage their ideas, honor their work, their effort and passion and make sure that nurses no longer are left out of innovation in health(care).

CHAPTER 10

Patients as equal partners (vignette)

Anne-Miek Vroom MSc.: medical sociologist, patient and member of the Dutch quality council, and founder & CEO of IKONE

At IKONE, we developed a patients included maturity model. This five phases model defines the evolution of patient participation in healthcare. The first phase is defined as 'patient passive'. In the early seventies, people with rheumatoid arthritis mostly lived in institutions. They became handicapped by their condition, were bound by their wheelchair and suffered tremendously. At that time, people were relieved of their duties. They no longer had to work and had to comply with the care that was offered.

Gradually, the way we dealt with patients and disease management has changed in the Netherlands. The first homes were adapted so that people could continue living at home, rather than in an institution. The first patient organizations were established, gradually gaining more influence and creating a voice. We call this the phase of 'patient conscious'.

I was born at that stage, with a rare condition: Osteogenesis Imperfecta, the so-called brittle bone disease. Although the medical specialist was an authority for my parents and me and we listened attentively to his advice, we also experienced the first forms of collaboration. If I suffered from a bone fracture due to a fall, we were allowed to skip the GP and enter the emergency room of the hospital via the back door. In the consulting room, however, we were docile: we did not ask too many questions and walked out with a civilized 'thank you doctor'.

In the last ten years, patients are put in a central position. A new phase. I write 'put' emphatically, because I still experience this as an external movement. The patient does not do this himself but is centralized by others. There is more awareness for the importance of communication, aimed at improving the primary process. We also see the emergence of new medical opportunities during this period. Just think about biologicals. From the beginning of this century, people with rheumatism are offered this type of medication, which changes their quality of life profoundly. Patients have less pain, their limbs become considerably less deformed, and they increasingly participate in the midst of society.

However, there is also a downside to the 'patient central phase'. It is still mainly about illness, while being ill or being a patient is merely one of the roles. We also have roles as a father or mother, a partner or an employee. And that relational environment is also important in life and healthcare. For example, people with rheumatism still experience fatigue, but insurance physicians see a seemingly healthy body. With medical progress, we sometimes forget where we came from. Some patients no longer feel that there is space to be ill. Because of their grief, discomfort or pain, they take a fighting position. This often works counterproductively. That is also noticed by healthcare professionals, who feel that they are doing everything to put the patient at the center of their efforts.

This raises the question: does collaboration in health care require much more than joint decision-making? We need some serious cooperation between experiential experts in the entire health care field and through all phases of innovation. But how?

IKONE has started with this awareness, the realization that patient expertise is direly needed. Our organization facilitates and advises on the embedding of the next phase, that of 'patient equal'. A phase in which the life path is leading. We live in a fantastic time. Technology and digitization are transforming the medical domain. If we want to ensure that these opportunities are successfully implemented in our lives, we must reach out to each other, and transcending the silos.

Do not ask patients to give their opinion on an ad hoc basis. Patients must become a structural and equal partner in the healthcare sector. Avoid having to go back to the drawing board and apply different patient participation methods in all phases of innovation. Let patients within organizations be a strategic partner, stakeholder and decision maker. Work on prevention from the origins of actual illness and life experiences. And create the care together with all the patient's stakeholders: doctor's assistants, nurses, doctors, administrators, home care, general practitioners, family members, loved ones, you name it.

More than sixty patient experts are currently working within our growing organization. They are trained internally to become equal discussion partners. Together with our consultants, they work with passion and for our shared mission: the inauguration of the phase in which the patient is in the lead. A phase in which we always take as a starting point: what brings you quality of life? Knowing that we can never completely prevent disease, we work on care that is intertwined in our daily lives. Full of attention and facilitated by endless technological possibilities. Ideally, this is the end of the habit that we call hospitalization. To achieve this, it is necessary to constantly learn and improve. With an ethical view, we draw lessons from history and we have to be careful with our individual lives. We cannot rebuild the healthcare sector. However, together we can ensure a transformation that stimulates health and well-being. That is, for me, 'the end of the beginning'. Open your doors and have courage.

CHAPTER 11

The future nurse (vignette)

Shawna Butler (RN, MBA) nurse Economist and originator of the entrepreNURSEship movement

The future of nursing is rooted firmly in a rich tradition and compelling history of doing hard things, solving complex problems, and challenging the status quo. With compassion, conviction and a bias toward action, nurses have honed the skills of observation, data collection and analysis, pattern recognition, intuition, experimentation, iteration, innovation, intervention, sensemaking and solution finding to build a sound academic preparation, safe and effective practice, a global workforce, and promising future. As the most-trusted profession (with good reason and across ALL professions) nurses can be found in any circumstance -- from birth, to battlefield, to bereavement -- performing a broad range of care critical to improve health outcomes, achieve universal health(care), reduce human suffering, provide comfort, restore hope, and improve lives and economies across the planet.

With societal shifts, technological advancements, and the migration toward outcome driven and value-for-patient based care the education, practice, and influence of the future nurse is poised to rapidly accelerate.

Education

Converging technologies are radically changing how we educate and keep the future nurse current. Technologies like mixed reality remove the geographic constraints of teaching and learning so many, any, and all can learn. Animated, life-like holograms offer three-dimensional interactive anatomy and physiology views. And emotionally responsive, digitally created humans with personality and character present immersive, dynamic, and dramatically more realistic training for clinicians to learn and practice together and create unprecedented opportunities to reduce error, waste, and risk. Simulation technology allows care teams to create a range of scenarios, adjust the variables, and rehearse and fine tune the choreography, sequencing, and script of a process or procedure -- before they ever touch a patient!

Online interactive "classrooms" filled with learners, scholars, and e-patients from across the globe highlight variations in health and sick experience arising from cultural, geographic, and language differences. Studying topics such as family planning, perinatal care, chronic disease management, disaster response, infectious disease outbreaks, behavioural health, and end of life care with fellow students living in a range of locations, climates, cultures, economies, and health service infrastructure better prepares the future nurse to develop and deliver culturally relevant care, operate with an authentic and practical understanding of variation in presentation, barriers, factors, and promoters of health, and offer a much broader landscape to discover solutions and collaborators.

Virtual skills labs equipped with sensors, mixed reality, robotics, simulation technologies and patients (real and digitally-generated) can engage nursing curriculum in ways that safely and effectively demonstrate, coach, improve, and maintain technical skills and more closely approximate the actual circumstances and situations care is delivered.

Driven by the global demand to increase the nursing workforce, amplify its effectiveness, and create leaders in health, educating the future nurse will capitalize on technologies that create progressive, continuous, on-demand, asynchronous, collaborative, integrated, virtual, simulated, and mastery learning.

Practice

Technology, data, and computing power are transforming how, where, and what the future nurse will practice. Miniaturization, digitization, and mobile devices are the game changers driving health care from reactive to predictive and proactive. Digital technology converts hospitals to command and control centers reaching patients where they are and also portable enough it can travel where care is needed. Combining data gathering, surveillance, and analysis with social channels, the future nurse can scale care delivery from one person to entire communities -- whether that's tracking the immunization schedule of a specific child or the infectious disease prevalence and velocity in an entire community; or caring for a single hospital ICU patient or providing remote virtual care for the entire ICU.

Data collection and computing make it possible to visualize patterns and trends so interventions can come much earlier, are better targeted, and more specific. Mobile, handheld technologies that harness cloud computing, crowdsourcing and machine learning expand the possibilities of where the future nurse will practice. Connected to the internet and equipped with a smart stethoscope, smartphone, 3d printer, and a variety of attachments, the future nurse can turn just about any location into a healthcare clinic or intensive care unit and engage the entire the planet of diagnosticians and clinicians to reach people where the live, work, pray and play!

The portability of devices and technology contextualizes health(care) and provides a much clearer picture of the determinants that actually influences health, wellbeing, and illness. As the future nurse provides health(care) at the library, grocery store, train station, airport, and church, just as they already do in many schools, homes, and workplaces, identifying the health challenges and opportunities and creating a care plan that works within the context of a person's situation will be the norm.

CHAPTER 12

Value based healthcare #patientsincluded™

Why patients might have different priorities that physicians

In 2017, I had the honor to address the audience at the Dutch Value Based Health Care Prize. Earlier, I was invited to speak at the same time at a different event in Maastricht, about the role of patients in clinical trials in a techno-world. Since it's 2017, we decided to make this a virtual visit, so I could attend two conferences in one evening.

Speaking of virtual visits, why are we still bringing patients to clinics? Why are patients still obliged to visit a doctor physically, when we're used to speak with our friends and family virtually? Who doesn't use FaceTime, Whatsapp or Skype on a weekly, or even daily, basis?

For many of the routines done in hospitals, I would argue that there is little to no added value for being physically in the same room as the professional, currently only being binded by the not (yet) existing use of technology that brings health(care) outside of the institutions. Still, there is a lot of debate about this and other digital healthcare opportunities. Meanwhile, our friends over at Kaiser Permanente crossed the 50% mark of the ratio of virtual visits versus physical visits last year. More than

6 million of their 11 million members had e-visits, adding up to more than 23 million in 2015. Four years ago, we fixed the #1 barrier for e-visits in the Netherlands: a lack of reimbursement, and recently the Dutch government broadened the possibilities of reimbursement for a lot of digital health. But even though reimbursement for digital visits is not an issue anymore, we still don't see those ratios as Kaiser Permanente in the United States.

Year after year, data from the Dutch national eHealth benchmark (Nictiz and NIVEL), monitoring the growth of digital health in the Netherlands, shows a gap. Almost half of all Dutch patients and consumers want to make use of digital tools, but, as they state to the researchers, they are not offered digital services by their professionals. Year after year, there is a gap between patient expectations and what professionals (say they) provide. In the meantime, nearly 75% of the Dutch healthcare professionals reply that their patients are not asking for digital health solutions...

To me, this touched on a subject very near to my heart and mission. In preparing for the event, I tried to find the latest information on Value Based Health Care online. I Googled for all the submissions for the VBHC prize - each and every one of the submission was a great opportunity to deliver better health-care - and I delved deeper into the principles on which Value Based Health Care is based. Values like measurable processes and better outcomes on medical standards. I found beautiful formulas and great dashboards and VBHC-graphics. All of them extensively shared, described and debated in articles on the internet in text, video's slides and audiobooks.

But the thing I missed the most (if not completely) in this online content and in the research I found, was the role of the patient in all of this, and the importance of listening. Sure, we talk a lot about patients, but we don't talk with them. We have not yet developed a habit of listening to them. But what's important to a patient, besides better health? What matters the most to them, factors that might even be non-medical? Some might argue that these values are indeed incorporated in the principles of VBHC.

But it seems that these patient-centered believes and values are certainly not discussed nor written about a lot. It was obvious to me that this is the most important value. I found it striking to read research (Hierin B et al) that describes that in 193 of the PROMs created, only in 11% patients were actually involved in the development of the PATIËNT reported outcome measures.

In 2011, I started the #patientsincluded™ charter as described above to create awareness for having patients on stage of healthcare conferences, giving them free access to healthcare conferences and events, and incorporating patients in program committees and expert groups.

Next, I was able to help the British Medical Journal (BMJ) to take a stance in adding to submission guidelines how patients were involved in the research and creating a patient panel. Next stop in the #patientsincluded™ journey: curricula in medical schools. At the Radboud University Medical Center, we went back to the drawing table in 2015, to envision a curriculum for future doctors, where patients take a prominent place. This resulted in appointing patients on the board of curricula committees and integrating patient experiences in the class-room, with patients teaching students about the medical and non-medical aspects of their life that matter most to them.

The growing body of knowledge of innovation can greatly benefit from patients perspectives as well. That is why we worked closely with IKONE and other patient organisations in the Health Innovation School, a co-creation of the Ministry of Health and our Radboudumc REshape Center .

I think there is extra added value if we strive for a #patientsincluded™ approach as part of Value Based Health Care. Make no mistake: we often think we know what our patients want, but most of the times we actually don't have a clue. In 2011, I appointed the very first Chief Listening Officer (CLO) to my REshape team, making sure we incorporated the perspective of patients into everything we do at REshape. Most of the times, beliefs and concerns of patients are not centered around medical outcomes, but rather around the aspects of (health)care that impact their quality of life, we learned.

Patients have other priorities that their doctors. Cynthia Hofmann' PhD thesis (Geriatrics department at Radboud University Medical Center) confirmed our findings at REshape Center as well. According to her research, elderly patients value independency over pain treatment, whereas physicians - even though their medical knowledge far exceeds that of patients - are not aware that remaining independent holds the most value for their patients.

To get a better understanding of all factors that can contribute to our notion of 'health', I would suggest looking into the tool build by the Dutch Institute of positive health by Machteld Huber et al. This 'spiderweb' tool incorporates every perspective into what many say should be the new definition of health.

The majority of the new strategic models over the past decades did not incorporate targeted groups unless they were clients. In a world overwhelmed with technological opportunities, it can be a valuable and - in my opinion - necessary enhancement for the principles of VBHC to incorporate patients perspectives. We should emphasize the added value from patients own perspectives, in addition to the assumed perspectives by healthcare professionals. Technology could be very well be positioned as a tool - on a global scale - to evolve the world of Value Based Health Care into a more #patientsincluded™ world.

The world can be so beautiful and simple, if only we really listen to those to whom it matters the most: patients, their family members and informal caregivers.

CHAPTER 13

Marketing in health care - the future is bright (vignette)

Anya Kravets is Director Engagement at Cossette Health, an agency that creates and markets solutions that innovate health care

Solving today's and tomorrow's health care challenges requires not only a thorough understanding of the system, but also a 360° perspective – this is certainly true for marketing in health care.

The industry is changing at a rapid pace, accelerated by new technologies and innovations. The fundamental shifts in the ways consumers communicate and access products and services outside health care ultimately influence what they expect when it comes to health care delivery, both today and in the future.

We live in the connected age of an empowered patient (consumer) – and the health care marketing is increasingly becoming similar to retail. The patient journey has changed, starting well in advance of the first visit to a doctor's office. The journey most often starts with a Google search, followed by visiting health care information websites or patient forums for symptom and experience comparison, then more research for service providers, specialist profiles and treatment options.

Social media has been instrumental in helping patients and caregivers connect, find support, share information and inspire action.

Thanks to personal adoption of technologies in nearly every age group, health care marketers have an unprecedented opportunity to enhance and create patient and consumer experiences that are positive, seamless, bring value and build trust – for improved, measurable health outcomes.

From health care chatbots, augmented reality, virtual reality, telemedicine and artificial intelligence to blockchain, new technologies are already beginning to be applied in health care practice, including prevention, diagnosis, clinical trials, and more. Consumers have more options than ever and can select among many medical services and products, wearable trackers, insurance plans, telemedicine apps and digital drug prescription delivery services.

Health care marketers must find and embrace ways of incorporating these exciting trends into the solutions addressing their challenges – via innovation lens and digital health focus – for transformative and successful initiatives that push boundaries and exceed expectations.

With the patient emerging as the most important stakeholder at the center of the system, and shifting, changing roles of health care professionals and other traditional players (pharmaceutical companies, for example), marketers must aim for transparent, value- and education-driven consumer engagement, recognizing unique, nuanced health journeys and creating positive experiences built on respect and promoting trust. The empowered patients of today and tomorrow expect nothing less and failing to meet these expectations is not an option for any health care brand aiming to survive and thrive in the years or decades to come.

Taking a patient-centered approach will also help in addressing the current fragmentation of care and allow for promotion of prevention strategies – helping the industry move away from sick care towards health care. New emerging technologies allow access to more health data than ever, which also means better measurement of how effective marketing campaigns are – whether the message resonates, and if it leads to the desired outcomes and behavior changes.

There are a few powerful examples in other verticals where marketers leverage one-to-one strategies to solve brand challenges – and if brought to health care, this approach could truly transform the industry. The opportunity is to move the experience from an episodic relationship to a continuous and ongoing journey.

CHAPTER 14

Scientific research

Augmented Health(care)™ is changing the way scientific research takes place. Not only will researchers soon have vastly more data per patient, the nature of randomized controlled trials (RCT) will also change. The gold standard of a clinical trial still is 500 or 1000 test subjects. In the near future we will go from $N = 500$ or $N = 1000$ to 100,000 times $N = 1$. An RCT based on 100,000 unique patient datasets.

In addition, it is much easier for 'new' researchers, such as patients, to do scientific research by using new tools. What does this mean for the medical research community?

Traditionally, 'patient participation' in scientific research involves the use of patients as a study object. Patients do not really participate, they are used only as a 'data source'. To be more precise: a source of quantitative, hard data. Qualitative, 'soft' data about what it is like to live with this disease and what psychosocial effects a particular medicine can have, are usually completely overlooked. And that is a pity, because patients are the experience experts. They know much better than researchers what it is like to have this disease.

There's another group which has a pretty good view on how to deal with a disease: the informal caregivers. But they are rarely asked to participate in a clinical trial.

Finding patients who are willing to cooperate in scientific research is therefore becoming increasingly difficult. That is not because patients do not want to share their experiences. It is more likely that they have already participated in a study and were disappointed with the results afterwards. Research questions often have no true rapport to an actual life with a disability. If you are in a wheelchair because of a muscle disease, you do not want to be asked if you can walk for six minutes. That question may be quite relevant in the early stages of the disease, but it is rather hard to get a question like that if the disease is already well advanced. The reason: a researcher sees a research population as N = 500. In it there are simply 500 people - with various stages of the disease - who all receive identical questions. It's easy to understand why patients might not feel like they're taken seriously with this approach.

Another problem with many medical examinations is that they do not measure important subjects such as sleep, diet, physical activity and psychological stress such as relaxation and stress, because it is too complicated. Even though these factors often have a major impact on the course of a disease or the severity of symptoms. The beauty of current technology is that many people already record this data with their smartphone. This certainly applies to people who are ill and who want to get more grip on the symptoms. Some of them are looking for a correlation between sleep, nutrition, physical activity and disease progression, in order to better manage their disease and daily life.

We see conflicting developments occurring. On one hand, the enthusiasm among patients to participate in scientific research is decreasing. And on the other hand, patients almost plea for more relevant research - that is, research that in their view is more relevant because it is not only about finding a cure, but about how a patient can better fit his illness into everyday life, so that the symptoms become less severe and the quality of life increases.

Of course, there are researchers who would like to do research on this more holistic, human-centered view on illness, but it is usually very difficult to get funding for this. After all, the pharmaceutical industry does not benefit from this type of research. And the government is not exactly too keen on making funds available for this type of research.

It must therefore come from the patients themselves, from the patient associations. They have no money, but they have time and a great deal of involvement. They are also experts in having a disease and can therefore, like no other, come up with research questions that can have an immediate impact on their lives. That is why at REshape Center, we searched for a way to give them the tools to conduct scientific research themselves.

We took Apple Researchkit as a starting point, a software framework that supports researchers in many cases that normally cost a lot of time and energy. Consider, for example, drawing up questionnaires, collecting data about, for example, the number of steps or data from your scale, conducting a hearing test or reaction time testing, recording pain scores, and drawing up an informed consent statement that is recorded completely in accordance with the rules. Therefore we developed a platform - on top of ResearchKit - for people to easily do their own research. We named that platform REach. It is a so-called low coding platform for software development, which allows you to simply put together a number of building blocks and compile your own research into an app or in a web form.

We have now launched the REach platform in beta version at three patient associations. They are now going to work with it. Of course they also need money to process the results that will come in later, but they have come up with a smart solution: crowdfunding. They ask all patients who participate for a small contribution, for example ten euros or dollars. The idea is to not limit the research to the Netherlands only, but to expand it worldwide through the patient associations in the various countries. Depending on the condition, it is not inconceivable that you soon find thousands or even ten thousand people who want to participate. At ten euros or dollars you could raise a million euros. That is an amount that allows you to do a lot of data analyses. Analyses that lead to new insights.

Incidentally, the platform is not just for patients. It would be nice if other stakeholders, such as nurses or informal carers, came up with research questions. After all, they are closely involved with the patient and therefore have a lot of knowledge about a disease. Different knowledge than doctors have, but certainly no less relevant knowledge.

Movements such as #patientsincluded™ and #nurseincluded™ also penetrate the research world. My dream is that this will enable completely different types of research, studies that patients are looking for, but that do not take place now because the industry cannot earn anything directly. I think that the traditional research world and the new world outlined will eventually come together, with the result that we will look at diseases and disorders in a different way.

An overview of the scientific articles from or with team members of REshape can be found on the REshape Center's website and in the back of this book.

CHAPTER 15

Everyone can become a researcher (vignette)

Tom H van de Belt, digital health researcher & innovator at REshape Innovation Center

Traditionally, 'patient participation' in scientific research was mostly limited to being a 'study subject'. This is a pity, since patients are - as described by Ian Kennedy- the 'experts' in their own field, or 'the experts in having a disease', with expertise that is impossible to obtain for researchers. Moreover, they are often the end-users of new therapies or technologies.

The benefits of active patient participation in research have been well described and the leading British Medical Journal requires -as part of their effort to encourage #patientsincluded™- for researchers to describe how patients are involved during various research stages. In this article we proudly present "REach", the tool that allows anyone (patients, patient organizations, physicians and nurses), to easily set up an observational study and collect rich 'real life' data.

We are in the middle of the digital age. Billions of people use their smartphone to communicate and exchange information. Interestingly, an increasing number of people collect health data on their smartphone such as information about their mood, activity level, nutrition or vital signs including blood pressure or blood glucose levels. Medical research could greatly benefit from these 'real life' data, particularly since participation rates in observational studies have been declining for the last two decades. People may be too busy or do not feel the need to fill out questionnaires, self-measure, or complete lifestyle diaries. It's quite a challenge, however, to make this data easily available for scientific research, while keeping the user in control

In which 1) patients could actively participate in research such as by setting up their own study and 2) participants could easily share their data with researchers. First, we emphasized that patients, since they collect and own data, should also be in control. This resulted in the 'Personalized Consent Flow', that can be used by both study participants and researchers to decide what data will be shared, for what purposes, and for how long.

Then, we selected Apple's iOS as the preferred platform since Apple's ResearchKit is highly secured and allows app developers not only to create questionnaires and extract health data, but also includes a variety of validated tests such as hearing and movement tests. The challenge was - as the director of REshape Lucien Engelen already recognized in 2016 - how to create a user friendly 'drag and drop' interface, that could be used by lay people and not by 'coding experts' only. Below, you see the result. Users can select 'modules' to eventually build a study, including an informed consent procedure, open and multiple-choice questions, active tasks and health data sharing. After creating the study, a smartphone app is created and can be downloaded from the app store. This is further described in a video by my former colleague Thijs Sondag.

We have now evaluated REach and published the results in - not surprisingly - the Journal of Participatory Medicine, a sister journal of the well-respected Journal of Medical Internet Research. Dr. Marleen van Gelder, epidemiologist and one of the principle investigators explains:

"We invited young mothers participating in the PRIDE Study to test REach. They were asked questions about the delivery and their newborn such as weight and length. Subsequently, we compared answers from the app to a validated reference standard. I was impressed by the results: there were hardly any differences and correlation was nearly perfect. Furthermore, one third of participants shared their health data, which I consider as very promising, particularly as it is expected that an increasing number of people will start collecting health data. These data are impossible to collect with the traditional modes of data collection."

The full publication is available <u>here</u>. Next steps include two larger studies, that we will conduct in close collaboration with two Dutch Patient organizations. The focus of these studies is on how patients and patient organizations can determine relevant questions for scientific studies and also set up a new REach study. We expect to be able to share some preliminary results of the study this fall. If you have questions about REach or would like to discuss it further: feel free to connect!

Original post including references: https://www.linkedin.com/pulse/everyone-can-become-researcher-tom-h-van-de-belt-phd/

CHAPTER 16

Moving away from the biomedical model: systems thinking and doing (vignette)

Bert Vrijhoef, Isabelle Lepage-Nefkens and Lotte Steuten from Panaxea b.v. Amsterdam, a University spin-off accelerating patient access to bio(medical) and healthcare innovations.

The biomedical model is regarded as the traditional model of disease as well as the orthodox model of medical practice. It directs the physician to correct disease and restore normal functioning by using knowledge of basic biomedical sciences including anatomy, physiology and molecular biology. This model works fine for acute and infectious diseases. But times have changed and one may wonder whether the biomedical model of disease and practice has sufficiently evolved to keep up with the challenges that patients, care providers and society face in dealing with chronic diseases and long-term care needs.

Chronic disease increasingly challenges our way of thinking about health and health care as it affects patients' lives, including daily activities, study and career opportunities, social identity and more, beyond affecting a specific body part. Moreover, many patients with chronic disease have not one disease but multiple related or distinct diseases – called co- or multi-morbidity –

which are incurable and hence defy the old biomedical model aimed at 'correcting a single disease'. Evidence based medicine (EBM) has further defied the old model by putting evidence from results of high quality clinical and epidemiologic studies before the often-flawed mechanistic reasoning, which does not amount to evidence.

The current EBM model, however, has inherited much of the old model and can thus best be described as a model that incrementally adjusts to the new challenges. For example, patient care is still often organized around body parts instead of being directed at the whole patient in their life context. Not regarding the patient as a whole, in the context of their life, has, for example, left millions of people suffering from systemic exertion intolerance disease (SEID), formerly known as myalgic encephalomyelitis/ chronic fatigue syndrome (ME/CFS), undiagnosed and mismanaged. Regarding multi-morbidity, a patient with type 2 diabetes and heart failure receives guideline-driven care, where two separate guidelines based on separate pieces of evidence from study results are combined and applied to individual patients that suffer from both. Moreover, managing multi-morbidity by treating each of its constituent diseases, often results in fragmented care services.

Human health needs a model that disrupts the traditional one. For this, relevant pockets of knowledge and stakeholders need to be connected and become part of a systems approach towards health and the delivery of health care services for individuals and populations. For example, translational medicine represents the synergy between epidemiology, basic research and clinical trials, and employs innovation management to achieve breakthrough results. For translational medicine to be successful it needs to create value and service to the patient.

This will only happen when patients, clinicians, hospitals, pharmaceutical industries, research institutions and policy makers are all sources and contributors to the system's performance. Systems ought to become people-centric, information driven, e-oriented, and reciprocal. In doing so, systems need to shape themselves into networks proposing shared goals and diffuse value for all stakeholders involved.

Different steps need to be taken to reach a future proof model. These steps have been described before and entail:

1. integrate reductionist medical knowledge research contributions (make a whole from the parts);

2. facilitate systems oriented medical research studies (understand the whole);

3. facilitate the translation of research from researcher to clinician (information transfer);

4. facilitate the training and certification of physicians;

5. support the practice of clinical medicine (clinical support tool);

6. building the patient-clinical relationship (communication platform tool);

7. facilitate the collection of needs from medical practice. The potential that Artificial Intelligence (AI) brings to the table is unimaginable.

If we want to improve the health status of people suffering from multi-morbidity or other chronic diseases such as SEID, we need to take some bold action. The first step is to embrace innovation and adopt a systems thinking and doing approach.

In writing the above text, we gratefully took insights from the following references:

Fuller J. The new medical model: a renewed challenge for biomedicine. CMAJ 2017;189:E640-1; Institute of Medicine of the National Academies. Beyond Myalgic Encephalomyelitis/ Chronic Fatigue Syndrome – redefining an illness. February 2015; Khayal IS, Farid AM. The need for systems tools in the practice of clinical medicine. Systems Eng 2017;20(1):3-20; Polese F, CapunzoM. The determinants of translational medicine success – a managerial contribution. Transl Med UniSa 2013;6:29-34; The Lancet (editorial). Artificial Intelligence in health care: within touching distance. Lancet 2017;390:2739.

CHAPTER 17

The Way of the Dodo

Will healthcare go "the way of the dodo"?

"The Internet has revolutionized our lives!" is an often-heard exclamation. Internet has indeed added a lot to our lives and has also made a few things disappear. Think of all the things that became obsolete due to the Internet, such as letter writing, keeping encyclopedias, privacy, and all kinds of brokers and middlemen.

These developments make me think about the dodo, the notorious pigeon-like bird, almost one meter tall and unable to fly, that was last spotted by a Dutch mariner in 1662 near Mauritius. Of all the species that became extinct, the dodo has become a kind of metaphor for extinction. To "go the way of the dodo" means that something will cease to existence, is destined for extinction. In the era of Internet and technology, this applies not only to flora and fauna, but to all the stuff we use or the things we do. Many futurists have already predicted that things like post offices, taxi drivers, manual labor, and even death itself will go the way of the dodo.

So what about healthcare? What will vanish in the field of medicine? Will technology and the Internet take over like they did in music and travel industries? Will nurses be replaced by robots? Will the doctor be replaced by a smartphone app? Will we no longer go to a hospital or to the doctor's office? A shift is surely occurring, and some things in healthcare have already begun their march, following the path of the dodo. But, in my opinion, we will still need medical professionals. Real people with real compassion giving great care.

The challenges that healthcare faces are huge; that is no breaking news. Financial mismatches, doubling of healthcare demand and the shortage of skilled personnel (the Netherlands will lack 400,000 professionals by 2040) will drive healthcare systems to reinvent themselves. Moreover, there are two developments awaiting at the gate to disrupt many of the current care models: the assertive patient is here to stay, and new technologies are developing at exponential rates. The impact of new communication paradigms, such as social media and transparency of performance, is just as underrated as the role of e-health is sometimes overrated. Medical professionals need to think big, dare to fail, stop talking... and start acting now.

If medical professionals still want to be a relevant cog in the healthcare system in, let's say the next five years, they should be concentrating on these three topics, for themselves, for their institutions, and most of all for their patients:

1. Engaging patients

2. Exponentially growing technology, including the Internet

3. Social media

Guided by the three topics above, the Radboud REshape Center has initiated a range of innovations in the past years. Among these are (in random order):

- HereIsMyData™, one of the earliest prototypes of a Personal Health Record at Radboudumc, combining data from wearables and clinical systems with patient generated data.

- AED4US: Since 2009, we are crowdsourcing the locations of automatic electronic defibrillators (AEDs) in the Netherlands. We created the largest database in the world, with over 18,500 units and nearly 300,000 downloads. Since 2015, the AED database of the Radboudumc has been transferred to the Dutch Red Cross, thus becoming the owner of the AED database with around 22,000 AEDs and taking responsibility for the database.

- FaceTalk is a videoconference system we've developed at Radboudumc, that allows healthcare professionals to consult with patients and colleagues in an easy and secure way, without additional hardware other than regular computers or tablet PCs.

- AYA4: an online community for young adult cancer patients (18–35 years of age) to share, on a secure platform, intimate details about their life with cancer, about challenges such as relationship, work, finances, etc. AYA4 has scaled from a physical meeting area and digital platform at Radboudumc to a public platform, becoming available for all Dutch young adult cancer patients.

- TEDxMaastricht, TEDxNijmegen: Every year we organise a high-level conference- twice in Maastricht (2011 and 2012) and twice in Nijmegen (2012 and 2013)--to share ideas, dreams, and examples; that is, over the Internet. In 2014 we organized 360andabove, a conference that was run virtually on the Internet, connecting patient-centered innovations in a new format. For 24 hours in a row, starting in Nijmegen, traveling with the daylight one time zone at a time, to London, the East Coast and Midwest U.S., California, Canada, Australia, Japan, India, Hungary, France, and back to Nijmegen for the finale.

With these projects, we try to outsmart the dodo; otherwise we will become living (or extinct) examples in the near future for others that do succeed to innovate in a way that creates future proof health(care).

Location

One of the major shifts in healthcare is that location is becoming less important. Due to new (mobile) technology and cheaper testing methods, things are already changing. And yet, rising healthcare costs are forcing all stakeholders to become much more efficient with regards to processes, staff, and overhead. The number of mergers and takeovers is increasing. Whether or not that is the way to go, is still to be seen.

At the Radboud University Nijmegen Medical Center, we think there are other ways to become more efficient. For example, by creating a network based on collaboration instead of two organizations merging. With different points of care nearby, and with the help of new technology, a great of number of things can be achieved. We will be able to monitor our patients at locations just around the corner, or even in their own homes. More specialist procedures will be performed outside of a traditional healthcare setting, for instance at home, at work, or while traveling or at the airport. I call this trend delocalization.

Over the past decades we have tended to move healthcare away from where people are. This started with bringing people into hospitals rather than caring for them in their homes. Healthcare has become centralized in institutions rather than in networks, as it was in the old days. But new technology is enabling us to reverse that development, while keeping the same high standards. So, this means that trusted, well-known hospitals we are now so familiar with, will increasingly disappear. On the other hand, we will bring health(care) back into people's homes.

Duration of the Stay

A decade ago, some procedures required up to 15 days of hospitalization. Now, they take only 3 days. Due to new technologies, innovations in medicines, logistics, and protocols, and new insights on rehabilitation, the duration of recovery in the hospital is decreasing. An average stay in U.S. hospitals at present is about 5 days. Long stays for regular procedures will become unnecessary, and prohibitively expensive. Monitoring at home, enabled by the Internet, is increasingly assuming an important position in this field.

Individual, Unorganized Healthcare Professionals

Healthcare is becoming even more complex than it already was. This is caused by increasing legislation and severe budget cuts. There are many constraints on medical education and the overload of information that has to be digested makes it hard to keep up. In addition, the administrative burden is increasingly distracting medical personal from delivering actual healthcare. The part-time ratio for healthcare workers is increasing. The number of female professionals entering healthcare adds to this tendency (Graham 2012).

More and more tasks are delegated from doctors to nurse practitioners and physicians' assistants; next up is delegating to the patients and their network. In order to maintain quality standards and to be able to keep collaborating on complex issues, working in groups or setting up strategic partnerships could benefit healthcare processes. I believe that within one or two decades, individual, unorganized healthcare professionals will become a minority.

Two-Party Research in a Three-Party World

Until now, health research has mainly been done by the pharmaceutical industry and researchers. Patients were merely passive research objects. I often say, "Doing - or designing - medical research without the cooperation of patients is like racing a car backwards... blindfolded." Now, we have the tools at hand to involve patients.

New communication techniques have democratized the media, and we have even seen regimes forced from power through revolutions; regime change where the role of the Internet was crucial. The same tools will also be employed to organize patients around research on matters they care deeply about, namely their own health or the health of a family member. Research with patients in co-control will transform traditional research and create a pathway for (applied) research through new systems that will change the situation forever. It will just be a matter of time before these kinds of tools will become available to patients.

We need innovations for the way medical research is done. One of our earliest ventures was MedCrowdFund™, a pilot project and social platform (like a medical Kickstarter) where patients can design and find funding for innovation and research. In 2017, we launched REach, a tool that allows anyone (patients, patient organizations, physicians and nurses), to easily set up an observational study and collect rich 'real life' data. Together with patients, doctors and members of a medical ethical committee, we explored this new concept in which patients could actively participate in research (by setting up their own study) and participants could easily share their data with researchers.

What we see is that the two-party health research system - pharma and research companies - is being transformed into a three-party one. Patients will swap roles: they will go from being the object, to being the subject, acting as a partner in research.

Another good example is my friend Jack Andraka, born in 1997(!). After countless rejections by traditional institutions, and with a lot of perseverance, Jack developed a pancreatic cancer test "just by using Google and Wikipedia." It is designed as an early detection test to determine whether or not a patient has early-stage pancreatic cancer. The test is over 90 percent accurate, and is 168 times faster, 26,000 times less expensive (costing around $0.03), and over 400 times more sensitive than the current diagnostic tests. And: it takes only five minutes to work. He says that the test is also effective for detecting ovarian and lung cancer, due to the same biomarker they all have in common. Truly inspiring! So medical professionals must look carefully at these new initiatives; they need to judge them not on what they are doing, but on why and how. They need to reach out, explore, and challenge diseases together!

Being a Good Doctor Won't Be Good Enough Anymore

We have gotten used to submitting and finding customer opinions on almost every kind of service online. Reviews and ratings of restaurants, tourist hotspots, travel agencies, financial products and so on are now in the public sphere. And of course, healthcare professionals are part of this trend.

A treatment has become an experience, and the customer's satisfaction in general might be just as important as the quality of the medical procedure..

According to Pew Research, 50 percent of smartphone users in the U.S. use their device to look up health information; a recent study for the Netherlands showed that this figure was 60 percent. This means that they will probably have researched their physician online while they were sitting in the waiting room, and that they will review him or her as soon as they have left the building. "Hospital-ity" has regained its vital meaning.

Not only text-based web content, but also informational videos will become increasingly important. Healthcare could benefit from adopting the use of video as well. It offers great opportunities for providers to present themselves and their services. A caveat: The quality of medical care will no longer be the only indicator people compare in order to choose healthcare providers.

The Patient Is Not in the Center

Many healthcare providers are pivoting their service by By placing their patients in the center, many healthcare providers are shaping their services to live up to their ambition to change healthcare into a more open, co-creative environment.

Putting patients in the center, however, seems to me one of the most paternalistic approaches a patient might have to deal with. Patients are not objects which healthcare providers perform their duty. Patients should be(come) partners. They are equals in the team that collaborates to sustain or achieve their optimal health. If patients want to take control of their health but are unable to, we must teach them. If they want to but cannot because there is no system or technology, we must build it for and with them. And if they do not want to collaborate, we must deliver healthcare in the traditional way.

What I do see, in the center of all healthcare interactions, is something else: an ear. A very important organ (that's why we have two, right?). It is the sense of hearing that many healthcare systems have stopped using. As healthcare professionals know what's best for patients - at least, that's what they think - they make choices on behalf of, instead of with, the patient and their families.

We often see innovation as the big solution for everything. We start innovating without having a close look at existing procedures, without analyzing how optimizing these existing systems could bring great benefit and improvement for people. For me, that approach starts with listening - really listening - to what is truly needed. Healthcare providers need to stop assuming, they need to quit thinking they "know" what patients need; or from an industry perspective, what healthcare professionals need.

Listening is asking. I highly recommend appointing a Chief Listening Officer (CLO) into every healthcare team; I created and appointed this position back in 2009. Our Chief Listening Officer moves between the online and offline worlds. Every time we intend to change the way we deliver (health)care, the CLO will interview patients, family members, and informal caregivers. "How can we help you?", she asks them. We noticed that patients were more open to our Chief Listening Officer than they were to other healthcare professionals, like doctors or nurses. And patients spoke more candidly than they did with, for instance, focus groups or surveys we used before. Every project we start at REshape, begins with the CLO listening to what the target groups really want. Almost every project that started with an original plan our colleagues came up with, changed because we truly listened to patients and their healthcare professionals, family members, and informal caregivers. I can assure you: all of these projects benefited significantly from our process of listing and adapting

Partnerships.

Never underestimate the power of collaboration. At our medical center, we love to team up with other parties, nationally as well as internationally. In order to do so, it's necessary that healthcare providers do not suffer from the not-invented-here syndrome. They need to open up, and unlock the gates surrounding their domains. Sure, it is hard to find like-minded collaborators, but they are out there!

In the Netherlands we mostly come across the usual suspects, and thus we broadened our horizons and contacted numerous international innovators. Other countries have different healthcare systems, different cultures and different mentalities. We are impressed by the pace we are able to maintain in our international teams, and a bit ashamed that it is quite clearly impossible to develop and implement quickly in our own country.

The importance of the Internet in this respect is also crucial. Connections are being made through social media, based on slideshows we have put online, with people often reflecting on photos of the things we are doing we have published in social media. Entrepreneurship, leadership, decisive action, and speed are important assets for implementing innovations successfully. Without them, one cannot evolve. And the fate of the dodo is one step closer.

Rules and Regulations

The thing with exponential developments is that they take little time to develop, but laws and ethics do not develop exponentially. These systems need time to catch up. How should regulatory agencies prepare for an ever-changing world in which technology is growing exponentially and changing the arena? In the old days, it took big companies years of innovation before they could launch a new medical device. Nowadays, with the time to market dramatically shorter, new devices are released on a daily basis. Does this actually change the way regulatory agencies should act?

In the Netherlands, regulatory requirements for digital healthcare innovations are hot topic at the moment; it is at the center of attention of the Dutch Health Care Inspectorate. And that's a good thing. The certification of medical applications will contribute to a rise in quality. I do not think, however, that this is enough. I strongly believe that the appliance of open technical standards, standards, for information exchange or the reuse of existing and proven applications for instance, mandatory by policy makers. The software industry has powerful interests. They operate defensively and are far from eager to open up their systems and thereby implicitly grant access to competition. Furthermore, the financial system must be improved. If developers and producers of (digital) healthcare innovations cannot find a sustainable business model, either by reimbursement, the dodo will soon be joined by many talented peers.

e-Go Systems

At the moment, huge amounts of data are being generated by information systems, medical records, tracking devices, laboratory and imaging equipment, etc. What we need is the ability to mine these different types of data and to understand their meaning, the relation between them, and how they interact. We need a central repository where anyone (not only patients, but any citizen) can access their own data in a comprehensive way. I'm not only talking about health data, but also about other types of personal data, such as financial data. The patient (or citizen) must be able to decide with whom to share it. A patient could share data with his physician or siblings, so that they may both use it on relevant occasions.

The reality is that almost all healthcare information systems are focused on the healthcare professional. It is not an open system, but closed, with data stored in hidden silos. These systems are characterized by poor user experience. I call these e-Go systems. They are egoistic, hierarchical systems that do match up with contemporary demand, and mostly do not connect to other systems in the healthcare chain outside of their own. They somehow still manage to profit from business models that have already failed in other markets. These systems should have gone the way of the dodo a long time ago, but still manage to survive.

We have to work on open, transparent, user-friendly, and cooperative systems based on open technology standards that actively promote interoperability. We have to move on from e-Go systems to e-Co systems. Now is the time for an e-Co system that sees and treats the patient as the linchpin: a system that is the constant factor in any health-related action and intervention; a transparent system that services patients and their networks independently.

Putting people in charge of their own personal health data, of course, also creates co-responsibility. I believe - and have also witnessed it - that a lot of people are able to and want to be in that position. Giving patients control over their own data is an important step in making patients partners.

Here Is Your Data!

This is exactly the reason why we at the Radboud REshape & Innovation Center decided to start a non-commercial service to boost the process of creating these e-Co systems, setting them up, validating them through scientific research, and making them widely available. Just like our other tools - such as FaceTalk, MedCrowdFund and later REach, and our AYA4-community, we sometimes set up services or products ourselves if the market acts too slow or prices are too high.

In 2013 we've created a vision e-Co system HereIsMyData™, based on our ambition that we need more e-Co systems instead of e-Go systems. HereIsMyData™ is a noncommercial service, developed at REshape to test and validate a Personal Health Record (PHR) and a community system that gives patients, caregivers, and families the opportunity to talk about a specific disease. HereIsMyData™ also functioned as a testing bed for connecting all kinds of personal health devices like Withings, Fitbit and Jawbone and great data visualization tools. To enable video-consultations, we connected our FaceTalk™ application to it as well.

HereIsMyData™ is not a platform; it is more like a service combining the best of three worlds. This service will give people the power to combine a lot of their personal health (measurement) data in one place. If this data is needed for one's health(care), it also can be used in one's own Personal Health Record (PHR).

The difference between HereIsMyData™ and many other platforms and systems, is that the users of HereIsMyData™ decide for themselves who is granted access and who receives a subscription to their data. In addition, it is possible for a health-care professional to subscribe to connected services of patients, such as weighing scales and other medical tools to gather clinical measurements. In our eCo-system, patients can subscribe to data from the hospital, such as blood values or clinical notes (from their electronic medical record [EMR]). Outside of the hospital environment, patients can grant healthcare professionals like their general practitioner or family caregivers access to their personal data as well.

REshaping Radboud

In almost all of my keynote presentations, I emphasize my mantra "stop talking, start doing." By living up to this mantra we have been able to realize many innovative projects at Radboud University Medical Center. Inevitably, not all of them were successful, but we always ran a number of projects simultaneously. So quite a few managed to survive evolution (so far). We incubated these projects in our Radboud REshape & Innovation Center, and when they reached adulthood, we let them go - back home, to the Radboud University Nijmegen Medical Center, where they could be implemented and incorporated into regular process flows. Of course we stay in touch, to perform maintenance and to evaluate. You can read more about this process in Taking part is the only way, theme 3 in this book.

I find great joy in seeing projects finding their way into the daily routine of nurses, physicians, managers, and board members. We collect evidence by researching the effectiveness of new technologies scientifically, and we incorporate our vision, experience, and innovations into the curriculum. Last summer, upon discovering that the viewing angle of Google Glass prevents surgeons from using it optimally in the OR, our REshape Center provided the Google Glass team with valuable feedback -- and continued receiving and implementing ideas from inspired medical professionals worldwide on how to use Google Glass to improve quality of care.

Our innovation flywheel is in perpetual motion. This gives us the opportunity to keep innovating. Because we refuse to go the way of the dodo!

This chapter is an adaptation of a chapter I've written for BBVA's 2014 annual book-essay. To find more about the essay-book please find the <u>website about "Change" of BBVA</u>

THEME 2:

Cracks in the systems

CHAPTER 18

The digital (r)evolution

Parallels between innovation and digital transformation

There is not a single sector that can escape a digital transformation not even the healthcare sector. Digital transformation is, for many, an abstract word. For some, it might be hard to make a concrete impression. I have discovered that it is a lot easier to think about digital transformation when you draw the parallel to how innovation progresses. Because both an innovation process and the digital transformation that healthcare institutions go through, take place in three phases, which have many parallels.

Three phases of innovation processes

An innovation process consists of the phases awareness, groundswork and upscaling.

Awareness

Those who are not aware of the need for change will not change. After all, people are creatures of habit, and we prefer to continue to operate in our fixed patterns. That is why it is important that everyone in healthcare becomes aware of the fact that their world is going to change. Without that awareness, they themselves will never take the steps to change.

We do this in different ways at the REshape Center. We organize conferences, provide lectures, use Twitter and blogs, and we ensure that the doctors and nurses in the Radboud University Medical Center come into contact with new technology and with ideas to improve care with the use of technology. We often start with a small group of, for example, one doctor, two or three nurses and a maximum of ten patients. We let them them brainstorm5about new applications. We will make a mock-up, a kind of prototype that does not yet contain IT, but that gives an idea of how an app, website or process can improve communication between care providers and patients and impacts the outcomes for the patient.

Groundswork

If all those involved are aware of the opportunities for improvement that are available, then we will really start working on creating. We investigate the business side: is there a business case to be made? What does the development of this product or service cost and how do we recoup those costs? If the business case is positive, we make a first working version of the product or service. In doing so, we involve the IT department, because the product must be embedded in the existing IT landscape and of course everything must be set up AVG / GDPR compliant. In other words, governance is an focal point in this phase.

At this stage of the innovation process, very different people are involved than in the first phase. The creative minds flourish in the awareness phase, and spark enthusiasm amongst others as well. In this groundswork phase, you need more structure and project management. This requires different knowledge and skills and a different type of people.

Scaling

If the product or service is ultimately a success on a small scale and if the lessons from the first users have been translated into improvements, it is time to scale up. Scaling is possible within the hospital or organization, in a region or even world-wide. The route you choose depends partly on the application. A service such as a video consultation is suitable to scale up within the hospital and within the region. But an app for better self-monitoring of a rare disease may be a valuable service for patients on a global scale. It goes without saying that governance plays an even more important role in this phase. In addition, the technical support and back office functions must be in order. What happens when a patient or users has urgent questions on Sunday afternoon, what do you do in the event of a breakdown over the weekend?

All successful innovations have gone through these phases. The product or service improves at every stage. This is due on the one hand to feedback from the users, who come up with good ideas for additional features and, on the other hand, because the dataset is growing. Whether it is a website, an app or another digital application, every time a patient uses it, he or she leaves data behind. By analyzing that data in an anonymous way, we can gain insights into the possible needs of patients or other users, or into data on characteristics of the disease.

Take for example Skinvision, an app to distinguish benign and malignant melanomas by analysing photos uploaded by users. The first publicly available version of this product might give false positives: people who were advised to go to a doctor, while it was an innocent birthmark. Meanwhile, the app has been greatly improved and the number of false positives has been reduced considerably, without leading to false negatives. The database now contains 3.5 million skin photos from patients worldwide. A self-learning algorithm determines whether or not there is cause for care. If the algorithm is in doubt, a dermatologist will examine the photo within 48 hours. The accuracy by which the algorithm can indicate today whether it is skin cancer or not, is amazing. The threshold for people to take a picture of a suspicious spot is low - an analysis is possible for 2.99 euros. This allows more people to control a spot on their skin early on, while at the same time fewer people visit the general practitioner. A win-win.

Another example is the automated analysis of MRI scans, mammographies or pathology sections. In common disorders, self-learning algorithms can be quickly trained with historical data, which means that they often perform better than a radiologist or pathologist within a few weeks. Hospitals that use this technology always do so in combination with a radiologist or pathologist. The AI support-system then states: "I have looked at these forty images and I am certain that I have seen cancer cells in numbers 5, 16, 17 and 34. About MRI or section 21 and 28, I am doubtful. The other images are all clean." With the help of these AI-based systems, radiologists or pathologists can thus better determine how they spend their time and on which particular scans, resulting in better diagnostics in less time. The algorithm learns from each image that is provided by the radiologist or pathologist, so that the next diagnosis will be even better.

We are currently in the groundswork phase, where labs or radiology departments all train their own AI model with their own data. But in the end, there will be a few AI models that hospitals will use worldwide. Not every hospital needs to invent its own algorithms and systems: they can benefit from the much larger dataset that arises when data from patients worldwide is shared and used for intelligent decision support systems.

Three phases in digital transformation

As we have seen, innovation can be characterized by three phases, from awareness and ideation, to the groundswork and eventually scaling. I see similarities between these phases, and the digital transformation that all modern organizations - including healthcare institutions - are experiencing at this time or in the near future. This digital transformation will take place in three phases as well: digitization, digital transition and finally digital transformation

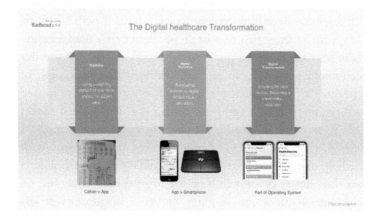

Digitization

The first phase is digitization, where we go from physical to digital recording, processing and storing. Something that we previously put on paper, we now record in a digital system or an app, for example in the notebook on your phone. There is no real intelligence behind that, it is purely the digital recording of what was previously recorded analog. The advantage of this is that you only have to record it in one place to make the data available to several people at the same time and to use it in more than one physical place. It goes without saying that the privacy of users and the data must be guaranteed, especially if several people can access these data.

Digital transition

The next phase is that some intelligence is added to this digitized layer, such as a graph or a visualisation with the historical course of what you record in the app. This involves, for example, combining multiple types of data, such as weight, blood glucose levels, blood pressure and amount of exercise, which ends up in one app, but does not yet interact with other apps. In that case the patient sees the interaction between the different types of data in one graph. For example, he can be urged to make lifestyle adjustments, through the insight that more exercise has a positive impact on his blood sugar level.

Digital transformation

The final phase is that of the digital transformation to its full extent. In that phase, a healthcare consumer not only records the data for himself but shares it with all healthcare providers in the ecosystem. We are talking about a personal health record (PHR) in which the patient, as the owner of the data, determines who is allowed to view certain parts of his personal health record.

In this phase of digital transformation, healthcare institutions can use artificial intelligence to relieve the burdens and simplify some workflows. For instance, caregivers automatically receive a signal when the vital signs of a patient go outside of a predefined bandwidth. The PHR is also part of the 'operating system', just like the notebook or the calculator. Who still uses a separate calculator nowadays?

There are various examples of companies that have initiated a digital transformation with these three successive steps. One of the most successful companies is Apple. Initially people could record information about heart rate, exercise, weight, etc. on their iPhone, in third-party health apps. Apple currently has its own review board that evaluates all apps with a medical research claim: is that claim valid and proven? Do they comply with the GDPR (European legislation)? If not, they will be removed from the Apple Store. With this review board, Apple wants to maintain a high quality of apps in its stores and at the same time protect its users.

The second phase - that of the digital transition - was the introduction of Apple HealthKit, ResearchKit and CareKit, an app ecosystem for users of health and fitness related apps and software developers. At Radboudumc, together with Cambridge University in 2014, we were the first two institutes that set to work with HealthKit outside of the United States. Data from a digital weighing scale and sphygmomanometer ended up in our electronic health record (EHR) from Epic via HealthKit.

HealthKit is a platform that enables companies to create health apps aimed at consumers, with health, exercise and nutrition functions. Apps developed with HealthKit automatically exchange information with Apple's own Health app. This Health app is now part of the Operating System (OS) of the iPhone. Every iPhone user therefore has this app as standard. This makes Health (Apple Health) the central point where all data about a person's health comes together - from both iPhone and Apple Watch users.

Apple also introduced ResearchKit shortly after HealthKit, a software framework aimed at medical researchers and developers. With ResearchKit, researchers can easily create apps for specific patient groups and thus collect data via the built-in sensors in the smartphone. A good example is the mPower app for Parkinson's patients. More than 10,000 patients have signed up for the largest Parkinson research study in history. It has already led to various new insights into this disease, although the final number of people who finished the study was of course much lower.

The third element in the ecosystem is CareKit, an environment in which developers can develop self-monitoring apps for specific patient groups. An example is a diabetes app, in which patients can keep track of how they feel, what they have eaten, how much they have moved and where they can compare this data to their blood sugar measurement. They can add their caregivers to the app so that they can provide remote advice. Apple is already cooperating with many university hospitals worldwide in this area.

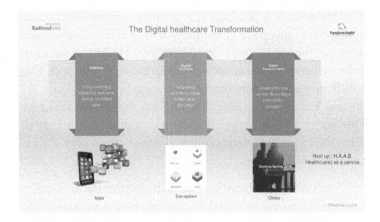

Now that all health data comes together in one central location, the next logical step is that Apple will also offer medical services. And they have already taken that step. The company announced in early 2018 the start of Apple clinics, initially only for their own staff and their families. Of course, these are clinics in which the digitization of remote care has been implemented and in which prevention and early detection take center stage. You can guess what the next step is. This has made the digital transformation a reality.

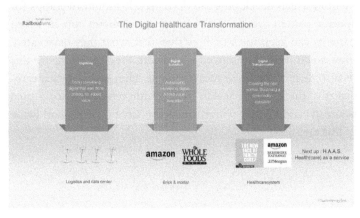

Amazon is also following these three steps to digitally transform healthcare. Their strategy looks slightly different than Apple's, though. Amazon first plunged into the distribution of medicines and other medical products such as wound care and stoma care, purely aimed at pharmacies and other medical service providers. Every year the technology company (re) considers when it is the right time to take the next step again.

The second step was the purchase of the American supermarket chain Whole Foods (similar to Albert Heijn in the Netherlands). This move lead to a lot of debate and confusion: why did this 'king of online retail' need 550 brick and mortar stores across the United States? One possible explanation is that, in addition to supplying medication and medical supplies to pharmacies and healthcare institutions, patients may also be able to use Amazon's services and products directly at those locations. At former Whole Foods supermarkets, Amazon wants to create an accessible GP or nursing post where you walk in and, for example, take a diagnostic test, give urine or pick up your medication. Couple this walk-in clinic with digital items such as home monitoring and video consults, and Amazon would really bring the (health)care to the American consumer. And since Amazon is the king of logistics, you do not have to leave your door for a new prescription. You just get your medication delivered to the front door.

The third step is similar to the step that Apple is taking: the technology company is planning on organizing health care for its own employees. Amazon has teamed up with two other major employers in the US: JP Morgan bank and Berkshire Hathaway, the investment company of Warren Buffet. These companies will jointly offer primary health care to the more than one million employees and their families, with the aim of reducing the costs of care, improving the quality and improving access to care.

Parallel paths between two innovations

I see a clear parallel between how innovation progresses and how newcomers in the healthcare market - Apple, Amazon - experience a digital transformation. The parallel is that new developments starts small, so that nobody is aware of the impact that the initiative will eventually have. The second phase is always a very logical next step on the first, so that only a few people can oversee the impact and the overall picture. That awareness only comes into the third phase, when the system change takes place and a whole new business model has arisen.

What I hope to achieve with this description is that from now on, you will look differently at developments that you see happening around you, whether it is a new entrant from outside the healthcare sector entering our market, a new app or an initiative to communicate between patients and to improve informal caregivers and health care providers.

Take a look at this innovation through the lense of these three phases and remember: if this is the first phase you are witnessing, what could be a logical second phase? There is a good chance that you will devise different directions or scenarios for phase 2. Then consider for each of these directions what phase 3 could look like. You can also think of several different options for this. This way you develop different scenarios. Then in each scenario, consider what the role of your organization could be. And carefully consider what you need, if phase 1 and 2 are to take place. The chances are that when you do nothing, someone else will claim the role that you would like to fulfill.

CHAPTER 19

4D's - Bird's eye view

These four D's determine the changes in care

The changes in healthcare are driven by four D's: I call them Delocalization, Democratization, Digital and Dollars. What do I mean by that?

Delocalization

Many people will think about the relocation of care from intra- to extramural, which moves from within to beyond institutions. This care can take place at home, such as dialysis, home chemotherapy or simply a video consultation instead of a physical appointment with a doctor (Just think about how many parking spots would be available if only five percent of the consultations would be made via video from now on).

But delocalisation also involves care that is transferred to the general practitioner. For example, the Philips Lumify, a portable ultrasound device that can be used in situations where speed and simplicity of diagnosis is more important than the most high-quality images.

These developments will continue. Where the Lumify can now only be used by trained medical staff, you do not have to be clairvoyant to predict that the next step is a device that you can operate at home and that can be used by pregnant women with pre-eclampsia. Increasingly, using the latest technology, clinical care will find its way to the general practice and then to the home situation..

There is also a development: more and more 'consumer equipment' gets an FDA quality mark. Consider, for example, the Apple Watch, which can accurately monitor the heart rate. Also think of smart scales, pedometers and blood pressure monitors for home use. Previously there was a very strict boundary between consumer devices and medical equipment, but that boundary is fading.

Consumer devices are increasingly being used together with medical applications. Consider, for example, the Freestyle Patch from Abbott, a patch that diabetics can stick on their upper arm and that continuously measures the glucose. There is no need for finger pricks and the patch also measures 24 hours a day. The beauty of the patch is the ability to capture all measured values. Combine this with the fact that more and more diabetics monitor their lifestyle with, for example, a diary app and smart-watch that measures their heart rate It can provide them with insights on how their eating and exercise patterns influence their required amount of insulin.

This makes it possible to regulate the glucose level much more closely than with the traditional method of finger prick.

Democratization

Today, data is still in what I call eGo systems: the EPD of the hospital, the HIS of the GP, the AIS of the pharmacy and so on. And then we have not even mentioned data that patients increasingly collect themselves with the devices mentioned above. That growing amount of data is nice, but nobody has a total overview.

Fortunately, we are beginning to realize that we need to go to an eCo-system: a place where all that data comes together and is directed by the patient. This means that the patient determines which healthcare provider has access to which data.

This development is receiving a tailwind from the GDPR, the new European legislation that gets a local effect in every country. In the Netherlands in the form of the General Data Protection Regulation (AVG in Dutch). This law states, among other things, that people get control over their own data. They get the right to see all the data that organizations have about them and are allowed to decide who can do what with which data.

This means that the relationship between doctor and patient will change. Where previously the doctor always had more data than the patient, it will now be the patient who has the most data available. He sometimes needs help from the doctor to interpret that data properly, but he also receives more and more help from technology that is able to coherently analyze data and to give an opinion about it. This creates an equal playing field between doctor and patient. Marco Derksen, in his vignette, describes the shift to what he calls co-operative care. Not only do the data from all healthcare providers finally come together and can be viewed in an integrated way, the patient also becomes part of the cooperative relationship. Healthcare professionals no longer decide for the patient, but in collaboration with him. In fact, the patient determines which healthcare provider he gives access to which data. In short, the patient is at the helm.

Digital

Of course, digital refers to the technology, but also to the speed with which information and knowledge can be shared.

To start with the technology: digitization makes it possible to make devices smaller and smaller. We used to have a telephone, a camera, a calculator and a typewriter. Nowadays all these functions are in one device: our smartphone. And the word smart says it all: there is also a lot more intelligence added to those traditional functions of, for example, a camera or telephone. And the number of functions increases hand in hand. The smartphone is slowly becoming a medical device.

In addition to the reduction of technology, digitization also enables an acceleration with which knowledge and findings are shared. In the past it took years before a medical discovery finally found its way to the clinic. Not to mention the speed with which we could bring medical care to third world countries. We sent a missionary to Africa by boat.

How different is that in the internet age. Because the internet not only makes democratization of healthcare possible but also of knowledge. This happened even much earlier, for example by a party like Wikipedia. The purchase of a physical encyclopedia was only reserved for wealthy people in Western countries. But today even the poorest in the world have access to knowledge via a smartphone.

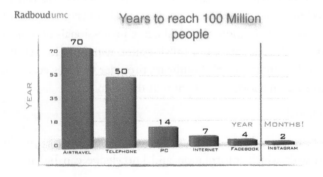

The graph above shows how long it took for 100 million people to benefit from a new invention and how fast it is today. This also applies to new inventions in health care. Companies that come up with a new application, such as the Freestyle patch, can immediately serve a global market.

Dollars

And so I naturally arrive at the fourth D, that of Dollars. Because they are necessary to really tap into the world market. Of course, there are also small start-ups that make inventions that are interesting for the world market, but they often lack the financial strength to address all patients and / or caregivers worldwide. But big companies do have that financial strength. It was therefore a completely logical choice from Philips a few years ago to focus on healthcare and to divest other divisions. Philips realized that it is important to dominate a market. Because in most markets there is room for two, at most three parties, and perhaps some niche players in sub-areas. To acquire such a position, Philips could no longer afford to invest money and energy in consumer electronics, it required focus.

In addition to focus and perseverance, money is also important. Large companies are generally not afraid of a few billion to open up a market. Take Amazon's innovation strategy, described in the introduction of this chapter. Originally a web shop, this company also became an IT company, threw itself into the distribution of medicines and then took over super-market chain Whole Foods to get a foothold in the supermarket world. That world is incredibly interesting with a view to health care. Because place those supermarkets now with a kind of doctor's office where people can get blood, can give urine or have their blood pressure checked. Because Amazon is also an

IT company, they do not have difficulty with the analysis of large amounts of data, which is also crucial in the new world of Augmented Health(care)™.

Amazon paid 13 billion dollars for the acquisition of Whole Foods. The stock market price rose by as much as 200 billion dollars the next day. I would not be surprised if Amazon will later take over a party like Ahold Delhaize in Europe. This company, which also owns drugstore chain Etos and webshop Bol.com, now has a shareholder value of approximately 27 billion dollars. It is a perfect complement to Amazon's current proposition in Europe. And the financing is no problem; an investment of 27 billion is peanuts for them.

As I started this chapter, the four D's developments that take place independently of each other, but they also reinforce each other. If you want to place the impact of new developments, it would be a good idea to lay them next to the 4D's. The stronger the four D's are represented, the greater the chance that the development will become a (worldwide) success.

CHAPTER 20

Exponential change is coming gradually

But don't miss the opportunities

One of the remarkable things of this era - an era some like to call the fourth industrial revolution - is the exponential growth of technology we are witnessing. Over and over again, things change exponentially. We as human beings, on the other hand, are programmed to think linear. If I take 30 steps, I can be at the other side of the room. If I take 30 steps exponentially, I am able to circle the world almost 26 times. It is hard to wrap your head around exponential growth.

So, what often happens is that we find it difficult to sense the small signals we see happening within our branches, or that we even forget or neglect these signals. And all of a sudden, it seems like new initiatives start to pop up everywhere. It almost looks like somebody has put a magnifying glass on this fertile ground. One by one, the seeds start to grow. One announcement may even lead to another announcement from another company or organization, because nobody wants to be left out.

By now, it's obvious technology companies like Google, Amazon and Apple have spent the last years working on solutions that could be beneficial for health and healthcare. However, healthcare is a very regulated market. So, the entrance strategy of these tech giants has been to address consumers and corporations via the much less regulated market of (corporate) wellness, prevention, nutrition and coaching. Gradually, they are blurring the lines between health and healthcare, between medical devices and consumer devices, as technology is providing opportunities that up until now were only available and accessible to medical professionals. We are witnessing the consumerization of healthcare, where consumers and patients use their everyday technologies - smartphones, fitness wearables and tablets - for their healthcare needs. Delocalization of healthcare is adding to this trend of consumerization.

This new generation of technology - and all the data points that are created with it - are going to provide helpful insights and tools for medical professionals to create even better health services. I am not talking about the digitization of healthcare, the process of turning what was once analogue into a digital format, for instance turning a bunch of X-ray images into one digital image. This digitization is happening all around us.

What I am talking about are the massive amounts of data that are collected continuously, as opposed to the spot measurement that is often healthcare's standard at this moment. Take, for example, the current routine for hospitalized patients at the nursing ward in our hospital. During their eight-hour shift, nurses take three spot measurement when they visit hospitalized patients, taking their vital signs (sometimes even on paper!) and registering this data in the EMR. What if we could move from three separate measurements, to a continuous, noninvasive method of measuring patients vital signs? Instead of three measurement during the day - let alone the workload and responsibility for nurses - we would gain a better understanding of the patient's progression or deterioration, we would notice the tiniest changes that might happen inside their body before we even become aware of it.

These amounts of data can and will be analyzed, processed and used for pattern recognition. This will in turn affect medical research, open up new rules and standards for treatments and prevention of life events such as an infection or a heart attack. The proliferation of data and meaningful clinical support and AI systems based on data will affect all aspects of healthcare. It is hard to think of one specialty that will not be affected by this.

Technology is going to help medical professionals and healthcare systems more than ever before in history. We are entering the era of what I call "Augmented Health(care)™", healthcare augmented or supported by myriad technologies. Keep in mind that Augmented Health(care)™ will not only be impacting hospitals, the traditional brick and mortar bastions of care. Augmented Health(care)™ reaches beyond the hospital walls, and makes no distinction between treatment or medical interventions, and prevention. Augmented Health(care)™ is not limited by time nor distinguishes between pre- and post-operative phases.

Augmented Health(care)™ will change how we care for people who have underwent a procedure. Homecare and post-operative care are equally as important as taking care of people before an intervention, to make sure that they are in the best possible condition, since we know this will increase the impact of and the recovery from the treatment.

In the future, hospitals will not be the center of the healthcare universe anymore. Delocalization has a profound impact on the way we deliver care to people in the comfort of their own home, or at their work, or in the car or even on a plane.

During my keynotes, I frequently ask my audience to answer this question: where do you think healthcare will be delivered in ten years from now?

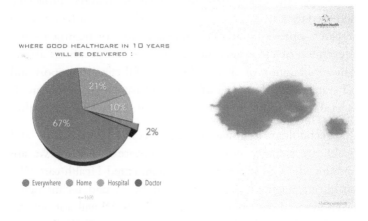

Almost 2000 people have answered this poll. Do you know what is most interesting about their answers, in my opinion? Only 2 percent thinks healthcare will be delivered at the doctor's office, ten years from now. About 10 percent thinks this will be done at the hospital, twenty percent thinks healthcare will shift to our homes. And most respondents, 67%, think healthcare will be delivered everywhere and anywhere in 2028.

Sure, you can say that there is a bias in attendees at digital health conferences I usually visit to deliver a keynote. But I used this poll at all sorts of events, with audiences ranging from doctors and nurses to entrepreneurs, students, legal experts, designers, etc. To me, the notion that things are changing and shifting is clearly present with the general public, it seems.

All of this brings a couple of challenges, but most of all opportunities. Opportunities to do things differently, to remove friction from our current logistical systems in healthcare, to cope with the challenge of a steep rise in demand and a decline in budgets and personnel. We need to deliver more, with the same (or even a smaller) budget.

Let's look at this from another perspective than you usually hear: maybe this exponential era and tech corporates stepping into the international healthcare arena, could be a blessing in disguise. Let's look at the changes. Let's test, and pilot and valorize new technology with an open attitude. Let's form new partnerships, let's reach out to new organizations to make these things happen.

I've always learned that if people are talking about me at the dinner table, and I am not sitting at that table, it means I'm on the menu. I don't say that in a defensive way, for that is not my intent, but as a motivation. Become part of the dinner table company, take part in the discussion. I really think we should collaborate and by that, be able to steer these current technological, financial and social debates into the right direction.

CHAPTER 21

"The paradigm 10 years from now has to be digital health based" (vignette)

Harold (Hal) Wolf is the President and CEO of the Health-care Information and Management Systems Society (HIMSS). HIMSS consists of HIMSS North America, HIMSS International, cause-based, global membership societies; HIMSS Analytics, the market research and data services group; HIMSS Media, the diversified media and publishing division; PCHAlliance, the Personal Connected Health Alliance; and most recently Health 2.0 the Digital Health Conference--all focused on better health through information technology.

Lucien: We witness a tendency with different kinds of legislation to bring healthcare data from institutions and healthcare systems into the hands of people. From your position within HIMSS, what is your perspective on that?

Hal: "Data is created at multiple layers and the amount of data in the world doubles every 18 months. So literally, twice as much data will be available in the world 18 months from now that exists today in companies or institutions. That's just inevitable. Information is the second part of this development, because data and information are not the same thing. Data is 1s and 0s that sit inside servers. Information is when we collect packets of data for comparative analysis or into packets of like genres we can turn back into information. Information is then compared in order to create knowledge management, and then from knowledge management we are able to create clinical utilities which are the applications that are used either by the individual or the clinician. The merging of these two developments - the proliferation of data and the advancement of data into relevant information and knowledge management - that's ultimately where the strength of healthcare from a full ecosystem will come into one."

Lucien: Exactly, I like to call this Augmented Health(-care)™: data will be turned into information, into visualization and then augment the choices and the way that we deliver and receive care. If you extrapolate these developments, how does the international healthcare landscape look 10 years from now?

Hal: "We will continue to have, certainly in Western nations, the influx of what I call the "silver tsunami". We will have a huge number of people that are moving into retirement age. And they are going to live longer and bring with them more and multiple chronic diseases, which will cost money and demand services in terms of healthcare. These are, amongst others, the economics that will drive the next 10 years. And you will see financial stress continuing on all of the single payer systems or any country that has a significant course of its GDP tied up in healthcare, which is basically all of us. The ability to take care of people - which is largely still an encounter base paradigm - will change: ten years from now we won't have the manpower, we won't have the positions and we won't have the bed capacity to take care of the healthcare needs that simply are going to exist."

"And so I think the difference between a consumer's piece of data or a clinical piece of data and the information and the applications goes away over time. The institutions that are responsible for supporting individual patients are going to continue to build applications that do outreach. Consumers will continue to get a hold of applications that are part of their health and will be provided by institutions. It is no question in anyone's mind, that the paradigm 10 years from now has to be a digital health-based platform by which we will be managing people's care, because we simply will never have the resources to take care of the aging silver tsunami."

Lucien: That paradigm change you describe leads to the question: is the current approach IT-vendors take valid enough to the things that are needed for it or should they change their perspective?

Hal: "Traditionally, healthcare has been an inside out type of approach and largely IT systems inside healthcare providers have been truly an internal facing space. Let's take one example from the Netherlands: there has been a lot of data exchange with the government per se but not necessarily with the individual patient. We can argue that the information available to primary care, to a GP, to a station is very limited. And yet there is a rich amount of information collected from a population health standpoint. But at the individual hospital level and at the individual level of an institution that has to take care of people, IT systems have to be prepared to be an outside in facing entity as opposed to inside out."

"In other words, it is the expectation that their systems will have to be interfacing with those devices and external databases and knowledge management in order to participate in the newly established currency of information in healthcare and information management. Organizations that are not already on that path, are falling behind. Organizations that are already thinking about the architectural impact of that - certainly in the United States - probably won't even be in business in 10 years. It's that critical. It is happening that fast. And I think in the European environment and other places around the world, packets are absolutely moving forward with the understanding of the information currency. So the healthcare IT platforms have got to be focused outside in and recognize the full ecosystem participation."

CHAPTER 22

Is digital health a different planetary system?

As the use of information and communication technology evolves, new definitions erupt, including a debate about this terminology and new uses of technology.

One of the fields is healthcare, where new devices, data, algorithms and knowledge are creating a new paradigm. I often use my 4D approach to describe the upcoming shift. Healthcare is changing under the influence of 4 global, driving forces: Delocalization, Democratization, Digital and Dollars.

In healthcare - as well as other branches - we are experiencing a debate about terminology as well. Often heard terms are e-health and m-health (or eHealth and mHealth). E-health is often described as healthcare practice supported by electronic processes and communication (Wikipedia) and m-health in terms of practice of medicine and public health supported by mobile devices, or simply mobile health.

Some simply say: if you are mobile, it is m-health, and when at home we speak of e-health. For me, that shift and definition do not cover the two at all. We have seen a convergence of consumer technology, both at work and at home, and we have become almost inseparable from our mobile phones. So, if you use your smartphone at home to enter of transfer your blood pressure data to the hospital with the use of your WiFi-network, is that m-health or e-health?

To make matters more complicated, I coined the term i-health somewhere in 2016. I see i-health as the practice of medicine and public health supported by (artificial) intelligence, deep & machine learning. There is indeed a lot of fuss about terminology, and I have done my share in creating that fuzziness ;-)

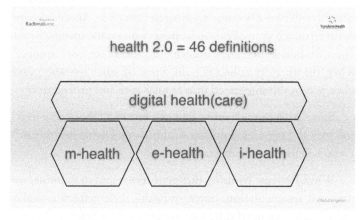

Our healthcare systems consist of eGo-systems, as I coined them: hospitals, pharmacies, primary care facilities all use different, often non-interoperable IT-systems. The most value would be created if all of these separate systems would be integrated seamlessly, not as jigsaw-pieces connected at one or two sides, but really fitted into one system.

Most value would be created if healthcare systems move towards an eCo-system, rather than separate eGo-systems. At the same time, with the proliferation of all kinds of e-health, m-health and i-health solutions, new systems are added at the outer side of healthcare IT. Often adding an extra layer of complexity and separate, non-interoperable systems.

Our professionals need to open as many as 4 to 5 different browsers and programs to log into separate systems. On the one hand we try to decrease the number of systems by offering as many functionalities in the hospital's electronic medical record (EMR), on the other hand we encourage to add new stuff, as planets circling the Sun (the healthcare system).

By treating it as a separate aspect of healthcare, ehealth or mhealth will never become an integral part of it. All this debate about terminology makes you wonder: when is the turning point where m-health becomes e-health or the other way around? When do we stop calling certain types of care 'e-health', and when is e-health integrated into regular care and procedures?

Since 2016 I urge people: let's just regard all these new technologies and services simply as health(care). Digital health(care) if you will, but just health(care).

Why? Become by using different terms and definitions, we stimulate fragmentation. Since m-health differs from e-health and i-health, we need different governance, policies and reimbursement-systems for it.

That is a very tricky evolution, if you ask me. If we see ehealth or mhealth as a service on top off regular care processes, insurers and payers will be reluctant to pay. If we come up with separate departments, separate ways of financing and separate business units, digital healthcare will never fully integrate in our system. Promising ehealth and mhealth services will be like planets circling around the regular processes, the "way it is always done".

I see strong resemblances with the introduction of quality systems and safety programs in healthcare. Quality and safety programs were the work of 'those colleagues on the second floor'. "That's not my job, it's theirs". As an effect, quality and safety regulation became a separate movement that did not work effectively. Only when quality control and safety protocols became embedded in everyday practices, thinking, processes and systems, things started to take off.

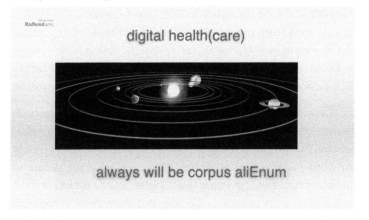

As long as we are doing ehealth/mhealth/ihealth on top off regular care, we are offering a way out. A way out for insurers and payers, a way out for our colleagues and a way out for policy makers, a way out for medical directors and the educators responsible for curricula. Why not make these new services and products part of regular health(care), so digital health(care)?

CHAPTER 23

Crossing the boundaries of our sector

As more and more branches in society get digitized, the notion we can learn from other branches and from each other increases. Of course, every industry has its specific contexts, customers and constraints, but I would argue you can find more similarities than differences, as this digital era is changing into every sector.

Let's take my branch, healthcare. We tend to approach almost every process in my sector completely as a medical process. We do that for the best reasons, amongst others, safety for both patients and providers. However, what we define as medical processes, are often 'just' logistics, or communication or administrative processes. So why not learn from companies specialized in those areas? Companies that are not (yet) working in healthcare but bring tons of experience with logistics, business intelligence or supply chain management.

As we are facing a doubling in healthcare demand - with aging populations and growing number of multi-morbid and chronically ill patients - with a fixed or even declining budget, we really can use every help we can get to come up with smart solutions. It was Einstein who said: "We cannot solve our problems with the same thinking we used when we created them."

So, I took the stage at the leading tech event in The Netherlands, called The Next Web conference in 2017. The Next

Web is an online community and an awesome group of people, reaching up to 12.500 souls (it is sometimes even referred to as "LowLands for geeks"). On stage, I applauded all the attendees, coming from communication, research, AI, finance, marketing and data backgrounds. I asked them to come over and join us, to help cope with the challenges we face in this great sector that has a profound impact on people's lives. Here's a link to my TNW keynote on where opportunity and responsibility collide.

We need all the brainpower and passion to take on the opportunities and challenges of our healthcare systems and our communities, I argued on stage. My goal was to encourage others to come over and help the health(care) industry with their own expertise and knowledge, because it's badly needed.

As I got off the stage, people were lining up in person and reacting on social media. They shared (very) personal stories and offered their help, or asked where and how to make a start with their contribution. I hope calls like these will truly help in the shared effort to make "Planet Healthcare" an even better place, with a sustainable future.

After my talk, I stuck around at The Next Web Conference a bit longer. One of the other keynotes I visited was Ben Hammersley's presentation, who talked about why innovation is so hard. His story really resonated with me, and the great part is that Ben's story is not industry specific: all organizations are struggling to prepare themselves for the digital transformation.

I think we really should "cross the crossing" more often - to speak with Ben Hammersley - and reach out to each other. When we are crossing the boundaries of our sector, we will experience that there is so much to learn.

In fact, why don't you get out of your chair right now, walk to the company next door - or a block away (if you want to reach that 10.000 step count today) - and ask what your sector could learn from theirs? You'll be amazed, I promise you.

CHAPTER 24

"We need to optimize the chain with the use of data" (vignette)

Why healthcare needs to go from a supply-oriented to a demand-oriented system

Michiel Muller is founder of the online supermarket Picnic. Earlier in his career, he introduced the concept of unmanned petrol stations in the Netherlands with Tango and he broke the monopoly of the ANWB with Route Mobiel.

Lucien: Even as healthcare in the Netherlands is of high quality, we can still optimize the way care is delivered: there is still some profit to be gained in the logistics field. How does entrepreneur and logistics expert Michiel Muller view healthcare in 2030? If you look at the care through your glasses of logistics and technology, what do you see?

Michiel: "Industries are currently undergoing enormous change. Some sectors have already been turned upside down, others are on the verge of major changes. Technology is the solution for everything in 15 years, and also in healthcare. Problems such as a shortage of employees or waiting lists are only temporary. Technology offers a solution for virtually all challenges. You cannot stop that."

Lucien: My point is: healthcare is 80% logistics and only 20% real medicine. Given that distribution, what could you improve in healthcare?

Michiel: "A lot, especially because of course, the logistics in healthcare are currently quite badly organized. You are in the waiting room for three quarters or one hour because there is always an urgent case in between. While in every other industry, the urgent cases are separated from the non-urgent cases, to get their service levels. There is still a world to be won. I am convinced that in health logistics, the logistics will be organized and taken over by technology. You only come to a hospital for examinations and treatments that require expensive equipment, such as an MRI scan, surgery or radiation. All other care takes place digitally or can be organized very close to the patient."

Lucien: How can you compare that scenario with your world, that of the online supermarket?

Michiel: "Today, we are still trying to persuade people to do their shopping online, whereas you will have to persuade people to go to a store physically in 2030. The care will go through a similar development and nobody goes to the hospital for fun. And you can eradicate the majority of those visits by offering care in a different way, much more focused on convenience for the patient."

"This, however, requires a very different way of thinking. I recently did an exercise during a training session. "Pick up a pen and paper", I asked the attendees, "and write down which six things you need at the minimum if you want to start a restaurant." Then I asked everyone to erase number 4 on their list. One suddenly had no premises, the other had no cook, the next one didn't have waiting staff anymore. This urges you to think creatively: what does this mean for your concept or business? It would be nice to also do this exercise for care. What does the model look like if you no longer have physical premises? Or if there are no more doctors or nurses?"

Lucien: At the moment, the supermarket is still the only bastion in the neighborhood. There is a cash machine, post office and pick-up point. It is also a place of social contact for many people. You could establish a stripped-down GP station where people can take blood and urine tests, and pick up medicines. The logistics flows can then be integrated with those of the supermarket. But if supermarkets will no longer physically exist, that model will not hold in the future. How could you integrate this idea into Picnic's model?

Michiel: "We see ourselves as the milkman 2.0. The milkman used to visit his customers at home. He knew exactly who ordered what. If a housewife was not at home, she put the basket next to the door. The milkman filled it and the payment came the week after. Our delivery people have the same trust relationship with our customers. They bring the groceries to the kitchen, sometimes they even put the groceries in the fridge."

"Pharmacists can see that too: we are currently in the first round of talks with pharmacists to explore the possibility of delivering medication as well, in addition to the groceries. We can cool pharmaceuticals, and we have the relationship of trust with the customer."

Lucien: So, your role in healthcare therefore starts with the delivery of medicines. Where does it end?

Michiel: "We do not know that ourselves either. But to give you another example, we are also talking to a local municipality about elderly people and loneliness. Many of our customers are older people with limited mobility. As we visit them every week, we notice that some people are just overjoyed that someone rings the doorbell. We had been philosophizing with our team already: what if we start selling more social services, such as changing in a broken lightbulb, drinking a cup of tea together? We would be the first to see it when a person starts deteriorating; we would notice if this elderly man or woman becomes a bit forgetful, not only because of old age, but because of incipient dementia, and so on. This specific municipality is interested in this social service and wants to pay for it too."

Lucien: Your idea sounds a bit similar to an idea that we at Radboud have, where we want to create a digital avatar that can visit all patients who have not been to their GP in a year. The avatar asks a few questions about a person's health and can identify - from a distance - if there is a change in someone's personal situation that can lead to a demand for care, such as loneliness or stress.

Michiel: "That is very smart because you create data points that you did not have before, which is also the secret behind our business: we collect as much data as possible about our customers so that we can predict in the best possible way what our customers need next week. Data is incredibly important in logistics. Without data, you cannot forecast and you do not know how to organize your supply chain in the most efficient way. You also need data to enable the chain as a whole to function better, to go from supply-oriented to demand-oriented. Care must also make this movement, because the system is still fully supply-oriented. This requires openness across the entire chain: you have to share your data and together with all suppliers you have to ensure that your client - in this case the patient - is served as well as possible. There is still a lot that can be gained in healthcare."

CHAPTER 25

Resistance

On 5 April 2016, the Dutch Ministry of Health, Welfare and Sport (VWS) conducted a meeting with experts about the proposed bill on client rights in the electronic processing of data (wetsvoorstel cliëntenrechten bij elektronische verwerking van gegevens). These expert meetings are intended to examine the opportunities and risks concerning new legislation, as the invited experts provide different perspectives. As I contributed to this meeting, I was eager to point out the importance of giving patients easy and safe electronic access to their medical records. That should be, in my opinion, the most important driver for change (but is met with resistance).

As of 1 July 2017, the law on the right of clients for electronic processing of data became partially effective in the Netherlands, but most of the changes for patients will only be effective from 1 July 2020. In the meantime, European law (GDPR) also requires an obligation to legally regulate digital access and data portability. Below is a somewhat summarized account of my contribution to one of these expert meetings with the Commission for the Ministry of Health, Welfare and Sport (VWS)of the Dutch Parliament on the law of client rights in the electronic processing of data:

"The parliamentary debate on digital access to patient data is currently underway, including the digital access right for the patient. I will not discuss the techniques or safety in terms of content, as other people are better at it me. But I do ask myself the question: why were we going to do this anyway again? 'That will always be my first reaction when we talk about the patient's right of inspection, to see his or her medical details. All arguments against can simply be positioned as arguments for the benefit of the professional. While: wasn't it the right to promote the patient's safety to regulate digital access, as well as to see what others have recorded about him or her in the most intimate details?

We have access to our own records of our energy consumption, to our banking data and the data on our tax situation (not a small job) and all of that online. So why do we still talk about this (access patiënt records) today?

Data has become a currency, from which you can derive power, which you can earn money with, and which makes you relevant, and remains to stay so by holding on to it. is about and belongs to someone else is apparently (or has become) subservient to the interests of the professional, the institution or the companies keeping the data 'hostage'. Healthcare is the only sector where I still have no (digital) access to all my own data. Obviously through the right to (non-digital) access, but may I ask you to try this yourself! You'll be amazed. With some six practitioners you have to request access and pay six times, sometimes even per department level. Not to mention the plethora of copies you get, as they will offer it to you mostly on paper!. Apart from the ever questioning looks and asking for explanations if you asked your records at the desk. "Shall I call the doctor for you? No, I just want my data!"

This discussion isn't new, and no one can say that they did not see this one coming. Nevertheless, the institutions and professionals have not been adequately proactively acted here and the introduction of the law that regulates electronic access for patients now seems to be postponed for a shocking three years. I think mainly because the stimulus is lacking for the institution and the professional: you do it for the someone else (hence the patient) and it just makes your work more difficult and it also costs money to make it happen. I am convinced that if the funding / payment of interventions would have depended on it, we wouldn't have had to have this discussion today.

As Radboudumc, we opened up the data as the first UMC in 2012, and at the end of last year our colleagues over at the UMCU added the real-time component. Not the smallest organizations you would say, so obviously it is possible after all, and there are several good examples. It is important to give the patient access, from the various eGo systems (EPDs, HISs and KISs etc) in what I am going to call eCo systems. My wish would be to arrange through those who have the most interest in this: patients themselves, especially in the first place, and not as proposed now in the last place.

Better make the start date of 3 years the end date by which access must be arranged. Make it legally mandatory that within a year the terms (eg NEN standards) must be clear, tests have takne place in the following year and in the last year the national implementation must be completed. Otherwise they will be discussed again in The Hague in three years 'because it is all so difficult'.

In particular, link the payment of the treatment: only treatments for which the patient has access to the data qualify for (full) payment. In the other case, an insurer may, for example, take "hostage" 5% of the going payment rate until that issue is resolved, which will also reduce fraud sensitivity.

I have been surprised for years why we still do not use existing and available high-quality authentication methods and means to grant access to invent something new again. After all, we all have a bank card and a random reader or scanner, and according to the usage figures of internet banking (more than 90%) they can all handle this perfectly. Here, too, the company's interests as well as the institution's interests are paramount and not that of the patient. He just wants to use his bank card.

What amazes me the most is that the insecurity, lack of clarity and inequality for the patient in 2016 continues. And that while we live in a time where scientists are able to cut and paste pieces of DNA, and thus repair a defect (CRISPR). We are also currently preparing missions to Mars, and yet what would not be this simple technical part of digital inspection we cannot do?!

This subject is politicized and became part of the lobbying, thereby making it so complex that the original goal became almost completely marginalized. We should be ashamed of ourselves!. When I look at our neighbour countries, I notice that I apologize. I apologize for the endless debates, lobbying and political hardship, while just a 100 kilometers more North this has been arranged for more than 10 years. In Estonia, Sweden, Finland, and Andalusia (already 10 years) but also in Israel, Arab Emirates and Singapore everyone has digital access to (parts of) their medical records.

All of this because we supposedly 'take good care' of the patient, which is the least heard group in all discourses btw often mainly conducted by healthy people, While people with a chronic disorder often have completely different opinions and just want access to their data as soon as possible.

But please let's not stop, but above all start: adopt the bill, take phased steps, with clear deadlines, and so to speak make payment dependent on it.

Why now and not in three years, you will wonder. At the risk that it sounds somewhat populist, I paraphrase the Prime Minister of Canada, who answered the question why he had installed a gender equal cabinet: "because it is 2015".

For the completely full text see the website of the Senate. I would like to refer once again to the TEDx talk of e-patient Dave who at our first TEDx congress in 2011 talked about the care, which we organized as Radboudumc in Maastricht at the time: 'Gimmy my Damn data".

CHAPTER 26

It's the trust, stupid! (vignette)

Prof. dr. Dr. Bart Brouwers is Professor of
Journalism and Media Studies at the University
of Groningen and owner of Media52 and
Zeelbergmedia.

Discovering an abuse or unlawfulness - whether in society or in someone's body - is important work. The job of a journalist is similar to that of a doctor in that sense. But the similarity goes further: however important that signaling function is on both sides, without coming up with or linking it to a solution, it is only the perfect recipe for distrust. That has everything to do with the changed role of the public.

Or rather: from what we used to call the audience. Thanks to the internet, this 'public' has developed from a passive news (or care) receiver into a practically full participant in projects that were previously reserved for professionals. You don't need much fantasy to see how much good this has brought society. The almost limitless accessibility to knowledge, as well as the ease with which facts and opinions can be shared, is absolutely a blessing for society. What was previously hidden in the hands of the 'haves', is now available and manageable for virtually everyone.

The best example of this journalistic development is perhaps Elliot Higgins, a fired bookkeeper from Leicester. Higgins succeeded in exposing a complete war industry with his ever-expanding Bellingcat platform. His recipe? A combination of smart crowdsourcing (together, we know everything) and the use of artificial intelligence to underpin the journalistic story. With this method, Higgins succeeded in taking steps that classical journalism did not succeed in taking until then. Bellingcat did not only became a value in itself, but also functioned as a wake-up call for journalism as a sector.

Higgins is by no means the only one who has succeeded in this, but the examples of newcomers who made their entrance in a less constructive manner are more numerous. Some 'old values' are dearly missed there. Education, experience, an organization where professional colleagues keep each other sharp, a shared ethical awareness: it all helps to approach the requested quality requirements as well as possible. And indeed, a lack of these values can actually cause accidents.

At the moment that professionals and amateurs have virtually the same sources and means of distribution (which is the case in 2018), it becomes much more difficult to estimate the value of both sides of the information spectrum. Those who are not educated or 'literate' enough, may find it difficult to assess how certain information should be weighed. They might not even care for such an assessment or weighing of facts in the first place - and that has an influence on the further distribution of information.

The more fluid the transition between professional and non-professional becomes, and the more 'realistic' the incapable or deliberately misleading author makes his or her message, the more difficult it becomes for the public to recognize the difference between real and fake. And I am not even talking about governments or presidents who deliberately infiltrate or mislead the system with their own messages, facts and opinions.

The labeling of a fact - whether that fact comes from the news or from a diagnosis - as real or fake, does not mean that it is actually real or fake. And the more confusion about real or fake, the higher the distrust against the bearer of the news. Which, in turn, makes the impact of a subsequent diagnosis even smaller.

What facts are needed to label an undesirable situation as an abuse? What are the characteristics of a disease, how does a condition look like? Every Internet user is able to determine his or her own definition. Moreover, every person has a platform at his or her deposition, to spread their own definition of reality, ranging from "it's a Zionist conspiracy but editors refuse publish about it" to "my child clearly has ADHD but that doctor does not want to prescribe pills!" These and similar messages stimulate further distrust, not only for the bearers but also for their recipients. And the difficulty is that they are hard to distinguish from the valuable contributions.

A lack of trust is a direct attack on the raison d'être of journalism. But of course, the same applies to the raison d'être of doctors. It is therefore useful to look at two recent developments to encourage trust: cooperation between old and new, and a more constructive attitude.

Collaboration

Many traditional newsrooms have now found out that the Bellingcat methods are of added value, just as many new organizations have broadened their professional digital skillset. This leads to collaborations that aim to bring the best of both worlds into a new, professional structure. The best example in the Netherlands is De Coöperatie (The Cooperation), a platform that offers space for new and old journalistic talent, that explores new business models alongside the existing ones and links solitary individuals with traditional organizations.

Constructive

Not necessarily positive, but always focused on solutions: that is the description that best captures the rise of 'constructive journalists'. In the Netherlands, De Correspondent (The Correspondent) is the best example of this worldwide trend. The platform prides itself on not focusing on the stream of daily news and deviations of the normal, but rather wanting to show how society really functions. Of course, it is no coincidence that De Correspondent is also a platform that attaches great importance to the substantive contribution of the public.

Trust is decisive. Journalism starts to show that this can only occur if we work on solutions for the identified problems, and if we show respect for the contribution from the non-professional voices. In medical terms: in the logical treatment process after the first diagnosis, every meaningful contribution from patients or patient organisations will have to be weighed seriously. Crowdsourcing and tech sourcing like a true Bellingcat really helps: even a doctor is not omniscient, and his patient - with the help of Google - knows that too.

THEME 3:

Taking part is the only way

CHAPTER 27

The Day after tomorrow

Why solely focussing on the daily operations distracts us from long term, strategic vision

Everyone knows it: the issues of the day deprive you of the time to be busy with your long-term goals. This happens in our private life, in our work and it also happens to organizations. This focus on the things of today also leads to a certain business blindness. Because you are so busy with the here and now, you cannot form a good picture of the future. It remains blurred, you never get a sharp focus. This is one of the main reasons why innovation is so hard in most organisations. In this chapter we offer some tools to focus on 'the day after tomorrow', as my good friend Peter Hinssen calls it.

Three planning horizons

Health care is under heavy pressure. There is a shortage of staff, budgets are inadequate and the demand for care is growing. The pressure is so great that it is not possible to finish all tasks today. With our workloads increasing, it is hard to find time to sit down and think about tomorrow. We see that we are sailing down a cliff, but it is 'all hands-on deck' and we do not take the time to change the course of the ship.

In this respect, consultancy firm McKinsey talks about three planning horizons. The first is the short term: which bottlenecks should we solve now? The second is about the medium term: what changes do we need to make in order to meet the requirements of the various stakeholders over the next two or three years? And the third horizon relates to the strategic direction of an organization: where do we want to be in five to ten years? What does the world look like and what role does our organization play in this?

The essence of a good strategy is that it connects the world of today with that of tomorrow and the day after tomorrow. The reality is that companies hardly dwell on tomorrow, let alone think about the day after tomorrow. I like to use Peter Hinssen's chart, entrepreneur, consultant and thought leader in the field of radical innovation.

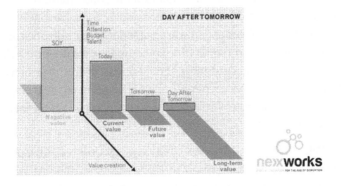

In an ideal situation, 70 percent of leaders' time is spent thinking and making decisions about the current situation. This involves issues such as: what can we do to improve the flow of the emergency care? How do we prevent under-occupation in the coming holiday period? These issues are often internal in nature and have the characteristic that you can make decisions directly and act accordingly.

Leaders should be able to spend 20 percent of their time on the medium term, so on decisions that will affect the next two to three years. This involves, for example, the introduction of a new care concept, more intensive cooperation with primary care or another form of cooperation with the health insurer. These decisions are characterized by the fact that it often takes some effort to reach agreements, but that the benefits in the long run are quite high, especially in relation to the low-hanging fruit that you pick from the first category of decisions.

In the last ten percent of their time, leaders should use to think about future scenarios. This third horizon is the farthest removed: you cannot see it exactly, you can see at most the contours of the new world. There is still a lot of uncertainty. And despite this uncertainty, it is necessary to consider the possible roles that your care organization could fulfill in that new world. What does the care ecosystem look like? Which different forms of cooperation are possible? What role does my organization want to fulfill? In what competencies do we excel, as an organization? And what should I start today to achieve these ambitions? These types of major changes need on average seven to ten years to really land, so it is vital that you act on them as soon as possible.

Peter Hinssen observes that virtually no organization achieves an ideal distribution of 70% - 20% - 10%. At best, they reach 7% time for the problems of tomorrow. Hardly any organization is busy with scenario planning for the long term. Which means that 93% of our time goes to the problems of today. The worst thing is: those problems often arise from "the shit of yesterday".

"The shit of yesterday" (SOY) is everything that has happened in the past, but which creates negative value today.

Take for example a data breach, that has already taken place, but that takes up a lot of time. Wrong decisions have been made, that have a different effect than you thought and which have to be reversed. Clearing "the shit of yesterday" does not only take a lot of time, it also draws energy from people. And that energy is so badly needed to think about "the day after tomorrow".

Marketing myopia

This focus on the short term leads to something I call corporate myopia, or corporate short-sightedness. Everything that is close to you can be seen sharply, but things in the distance become blurry. The point is: people often find out only how bad their short-sightedness is when they go to the optician for the first time and see the difference between their hazy own vision and the sharp vision that arises when they put on glasses.

We see that effect in organizations too. Organizations do not know that they are nearsighted. This realization only comes into being as a new entrant on the market, often with a whole new business model, turns the existing world upside down and removes a substantial part of the turnover. This has happened, for example, in the music industry, the travel world and the taxi industry. By the time the traditional companies in these sectors got their prescription glasses, it was already too late.

Take Kodak, the inventor of digital photography. Rather than acknowledging that this invention would radically change the market, Kodak went bankrupt because they did not embrace digital photography. Kodak stuck to analogue film rolls, even though the demand was decreasing rapidly.

Nokia is also a good example of an organization that was once very innovative, failed to adapt to changing horizons. The notion that the smartphone would change the market

169

for mobile telephones for good, came too late. The iOS and Android operating systems had already divided the market when Nokia choose Windows as its operating system: a clear case of corporate myopia.

An important part of corporate myopia is marketing myopia: a blurred view of what customers really want. This phenomenon is very well described by Theodore Levitt in Harvard Business Review. He states that organizations often have a one-dimensional view of what customers find important. For example, they only think in terms of product quality and barely reflect on the impact of the service provided on that product.

Companies that sell consumer products were the first to notice that product quality alone was not enough, due to the rise of the internet. If someone else can deliver faster or has better conditions for exchange, then that is enough for many people to switch to a new supplier. The product remains the same, what changes is the service or experience around it. The emergence of the internet has even created completely new business models that better meet the wishes of consumers. Who will buy a CD if you can also stream as much music as you want at a fixed monthly fee? And why would you book a trip with an intermediary if you can have direct contact with the owner of a holiday home online?

In healthcare, these developments seem light years away. And that is because there has never been a shortage of 'customers'. They come naturally, especially now that we are getting older and are suffering from welfare diseases. This may have made marketing myopia one of the biggest problems of healthcare. The top clinical and general hospitals do slightly better than the university medical centers, for the simple reason that medical specialists working in a partnership (maatschap) have a slightly more business minded vision. I consciously write 'business' because they mainly think about how they can improve and accelerate their own process using technology, they do not dwell on what this means for their patients.

Hospitals do patient satisfaction surveys afterwards, but never before in the sense of: what do you expect from our care? Moreover, these patient satisfaction surveys are so generic and uniform, that patients can hardly express their real opinions. Perhaps the medical treatment was a success, but the trajectory left its mark psychologically, because there was little room to talk about anxiety and additional problems such as loss of income or relational problems. Patients would like to talk about this with their caregivers and other patients, but we have limited them to assess the received care purely on the clinical outcomes of the treatment. Those patients who do start talking about the impact of their illness on their life, are all too often told: "But you are doing well now, right? That's all that matters."

The power of listening

This is why I appointed Corine Jansen as Chief Listening Officer (CLO) at the REshape Center in 2010. Her main task is to listen to patients and their informal caregivers: what do they find most important? What topics do they struggle with? And how can we help?

The first major project for Corine was our Adolescents and Young Adults (AYA) project, for young people with cancer. In oncology, there are actually two distinct worlds: the world of children and the world of adults. Young people in the age of 18 to 30 years, fall in between these two distinct worlds. They struggle with very different questions than people who are already settled and mature when they get cancer. At the same time, they are no longer children.

Corine listened to the questions, hopes and anxieties of these young people. Based on their input, we developed a community together with them, with a corresponding website, entirely focused on the topics that concern them. In this way, we offer young people help to fit their illness into their lives. We focus on their lives instead of their illness. The Adolescents and Young Adults (AYA) did not stop at the Radboud Medical Center: this community has now been scale up nationwide.

The AYA project formed the basis for how we still work in the REshape Center. The outside world often thinks that we are 'that department of the apps and websites'. Because that is the visible part of what we do. But the core of our work is that we put patients and their lives at the center, and that we redefine care from there, creating a new culture and approach. Changing care starts with listening to the target group. Doctors may then be experts in diagnosing a disease and devising the best treatment, patients are the expert in having a disease. You must use that knowledge.

Another initiative is to change our medical curriculum. In 2015, the curriculum for the study program in medicine and biomedical sciences in Radboudumc was adapted. There is now more awareness of what a disease means to the patient and more attention to technology. Like Peter Bennemeer in his vignette ("Hospitals are internally focused, while the change comes from the outside"), you cannot expect people who have been trained and educated in a certain way to think differently from one day to the next. If you want them to think and act differently, you will have to give them intensive attention during a lecture or training program. That is our motivation to get the curriculum up and running.

The impetus to that change was given a year earlier, when we traveled from the REshape Center with a group of people to the annual conference of Singularity University in San Diego, in the United States. Every year about fifty people come with me from the Radboudumc and from our network: , medical specialists, nurses, general practitioners, people who work in long-term care, health insurers and so on. In 2014 we consciously took into account a proportion of more people from the educational side. During the congress, what happens every year happens: at a certain moment the group collectively realizes that the change in care concerns them all. All aspects of care change, and that has an impact on everyone's role. In San Diego we decided on the spot to jointly look at the curriculum, so that in any case the doctors and biomedical engineers are trained in a different way. A year later, the new curriculum was a fact, even though we still had to start with the real work, it seemed.

New doctors are entering the labor market in 2022, seven years after 2015, they will have a better fit with the rapidly changing world. They will cause a lot of commotion in the hospitals where they will work. Because their colleagues and the directors do not yet have that new view. And that is why at the end of 2016 I made the proposal to set up the Health Innovation School (HIS) in collaboration with the Ministry of Health, Welfare and Sport: a program for policy makers, administrators, doctors, nurses, patients, politicians, health insurers and other stakeholders in the Netherlands. ensure that they train in the mindset, skills and behavior that you need to shape innovation. To this end, the HIS offers three Cs:

- Content in the form of teaching materials and tools;

- Competencies in the form of training how to deal with the tools;

- Community because HIS brings the entire system together in one room: patients and their families, industry, doctors, nurses, regulators, insurers, etc.

In short, HIS makes people in healthcare innovative-skilled. It gives them tools to stimulate innovation in their own organization and in the cooperation chain. Because nobody can innovate alone. You will always have to do it in collaboration with others.

Transformation is all-encompassing

What the HIS people learn is that there is not one way to Rome. And that there is certainly no easy-to-use model that guides healthcare organizations through the digital transformation. The change process will be different for every organization. What is the same everywhere is that large-scale change takes years. The literature assumes that cultural changes last at least seven years, often even longer. And that is why healthcare needs to start changing today, if we want to design the model differently in 2025.

There is another reason: history shows that successful companies reinvent themselves when they are still doing well, that they are still growing. "You have to repair the roof when the sun shines", they say sometimes. Companies that only start to change when they are over their top have a much lower chance of success. That makes sense because with falling sales and profits there is no budget, but also no time to be busy with tomorrow, let alone with the day after tomorrow.

Care is still in a phase of growth. Long-term care is beginning to feel budget pain, but hospitals are not ready yet, if you look at what is approaching them, in my view. This is the time to take change seriously and to consciously get started with 'the day after tomorrow'.

Of course, that is not easy. Because nobody can predict exactly what the world will look like in 2025 or 2030. But there are contours. We describe these contours extensively in this book. It is easy to say: by that time I can see how I react to this. Because in the issues of the day there is little time to work on that now. But chances are that you are too late, that others have already taken over your role.

If your healthcare organization does not want to be the next Kodak or Nokia, make sure that you now create a clear vision of the future. So go and sit together with other stakeholders in your organization and in your chain. Design different scenarios and think of possible strategies for your organization per scenario. You will see: the more intensively you deal with this, the sharper your view of the future becomes.

The beauty is: you do not have to constantly involve the entire organization. Of course, the more people participate, the better it is. But start by naming a Chief for Innovation (M/F). I am always talking about a KSG (Klein Slim Groepje in Dutch) a small smart group, that has the space and the time to explore innovations. Every department in a hospital has a focus on patient safety, and also one for quality. But virtually no healthcare organization makes people free to think about innovation. Someone who goes off the beaten path, who comes up with disruptive ideas and who also gets the freedom to work out those ideas.

I had previously contacted Peter Hinssen. He compared traditional organizations, such as hospitals, once with plantations. Anyone working on a plantation thinks in fixed processes and working methods. All improvements are only focused on how you do things.

The innovation in a sector often comes from start-ups. Look at the impact of Spotify on the music industry or of Uber on the taxi industry. Start-ups operate in the rainforest. There are many dangers lurking, the chance that you survive is at most 1 percent. They are not so much concerned about how they do something. They mainly look at what they have to do to be successful. There is a focus on: do we do the right things, instead of everything that matters: do we do things right? That is a fundamental difference in rules, people and culture.

Anyone wishing to incorporate something of the start-up mentality into their own organization must dare to let go of traditional forms of organization and dare to turn over the hierarchical corporate 'structure'. At the top there are no longer the drivers, but the patients. The task of the management is to optimally facilitate healthcare providers in the best possible way of serving those patients. That is a fundamentally different view.

Those who want to still exist in 2025 will have to start today to incorporate this view, knowing that it takes at least seven years to shape such major changes. Again, there is no manual and there is no fixed route along which the change should take place. There is only one advice that applies to everyone: go looking for the glasses together to correct myopia and get a sharp look at the future.

[i]. https://hbr.org/2004/07/marketing-myopia

CHAPTER 28

To REshape or not to shape
(2010 - 2018)

Just like the rest of society, health(care) is changing. Although medical innovations usually get adopted very fast, changing the health(care) model is lacking the same velocity. With huge challenges of doubling of healthcare demand, declining budgets and shortage of skilled personnel we need to find a pathway into a sustainable (business) model. Meanwhile digitisation of society makes digital the default for many activities like banking and from it a digital transformation will derive. The search for a sustainable health(care) model continues as demand is increasing and budgets declining. At the convergence of technology and patient empowerment, new (business) models in health(care) will evolve that could provide solutions for current challenges. Just as in other branches like travel industry, easy access to data, or well designed technology like tablets that brought computing into the hands of many elderly, technology shifted some of the existing paradigms. Often this has been called 'disrupting' or 'creative destruction'. Either way it brings change to health(care).

Over the past 7 years I have been working alongside Gartner's Hype Cycle[1] model.

Their description of the model is :

---

1   http://www.gartner.com/technology/research/methodologies/hype-cy-cle.jsp

Gartner Hype Cycles provide a graphic representation of the maturity and adoption of technologies and applications, and how they are potentially relevant to solving real business problems and exploiting new opportunities. Gartner Hype Cycle methodology gives you a view of how a technology or application will evolve over time, providing a sound source of insight to manage its deployment within the context of your specific business goals.

I have not only been using the model to predict the breakthrough moment of technology. But as I noticed at our REshape Center, every project was going roughly through the same phase of the Hype Cycle. I started to try to influence a specific portion of it, more as a guidance of how projects evolve. Speeding up the Hype Cycle in my opinion could increase the actual access to and use of innovation and adoption of the #patientsincluded™ model.

How Do Hype Cycles Work?

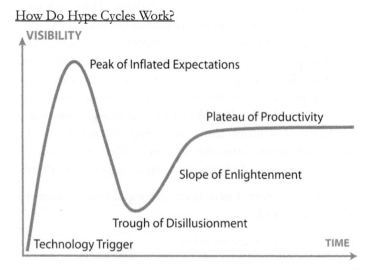

Each Hype Cycle drills down into the five key phases of a technology's life cycle.

Technology Trigger: A potential technology breakthrough kicks things off. Early proof-of-concept stories and media interest trigger significant publicity. Often no usable products exist and commercial viability is unproven.

Peak of Inflated Expectations: Early publicity produces a number of success stories — often accompanied by scores of failures. Some companies take action; many do not.

Trough of Disillusionment: Interest wanes as experiments and implementations fail to deliver. Producers of the technology shake out or fail. Investments continue only if the surviving providers improve their products to the satisfaction of early adopters.

Slope of Enlightenment: More instances of how the technology can benefit the enterprise start to crystallize and become more widely understood. Second- and third-generation products appear from technology providers. More enterprises fund pilots; conservative companies remain cautious.

Plateau of Productivity: Mainstream adoption starts to take off. Criteria for assessing provider viability are more clearly defined. The technology's broad market applicability and relevance are clearly paying off.

I've been using this next to the yearly updated estimated status but moreover as a guidance for how innovations develop during their flow. This model can have steep peaks or flattened throughs. One of the reasons to start the REshape Center (2010) at Radboud University Medical Center was the notion things started to move fast outside of healthcare. It seemed like there was a different clock-speed in healthcare and outside of it.

My hypothesis was and still is the sooner the peak of inflated expectations is reached, the sooner the next phase of the Hype Cycle will start. By speeding up the process, the actual time needed to reach the plateau could be decreased.

That is why much of my work has been focussed on shortening the phase from the 'Technology trigger' to the top of the 'Peak of Inflated Expectations' and to explore if this could impact the actual adoption of the innovations.

Many initiatives or ideas are being 'killed' right here, due to the fact the uptake of the idea and enrichment of it is only been narrowed to the own inner circle. By broadening the reach, being open to feedback engaging with the targeted group the end result will be more sustainable for the next phase.

By explorative studies of using different technology, methodology and channels (i.e. social media) for sharing the knowledge, measuring the impact of those and relate them to i.e. citations in scientific papers. Creating a pathway : "Digital First, Physical next" as the new default mindset could help people comprehensive the new paradigm.

30-day projects

In the REshape Center we've used the model of creating serendipity of coincidental meetings, that often evolved into project. Most of our projects typically would run for 30 days. In those 30 days, we investigated concepts, the probability, the use case and the adoption into daily practice.

By placing it into the broader perspective of tackling huge challenges with radical approaches, we also tried to inspire others with conferences, books, lecture and next tried to create access to startup knowledge and capital in a 180 day accelerator program for health startups, together with Rockstart Digital Health Accelerator Nijmegen.

Accelerating projects by starting in them 30-day project including patients from the start, by using the methodology of service design we ensured to incorporate everyone's needs and vision. Also we bypassed the often long processes of 'talking' instead of doing about innovations and change.

With the use of 'new media' channels we built a network to inform and be informed, from early stage innovations and ideas to delivered products and services including as research. The latter usually only is being 'marketed' via scientific publications, poster-presentations and presenting at (peer)conferences, of which the content hardly gets beyond the scientific community. Using Pecha Kucha, conferences, lectures and social media we 'broadcasted' the developments to a broader audience also taking stand in the globalisation of media and health(care). Wouldn't it be great if every PhD candidate prior to the defence mandatory would have to publish a YouTube video, explaining in 'plain English" what the thesis is all about and what society benefits from the work being done.

We have been testing this hypothesis in several projects listed on our website a partial list of REshape projects is in the back of this book.

The use of Social Media or modern channels can possibly increase awareness, adoption, and geographical spread of innovations and knowledge. Writing blogs i.e. about the process of innovation , new technology via LinkedIn, spreading content on Facebook, and Twitter does not only serve as 'marketing' for the ideas, but also as a low threshold peer review from people across the world. While the general population of users of Linkedin are to be found in the higher educated groups, this also increases the cross fertilisation from other branches. In face it becomes Social Peerreviewed Knowledge, I coined SPaRK, added the a for the acronym only).

Corporate neglect

One of the main reasons for existing business to fail is often neglect, in all kinds of variations. Neglect to (re)act on the changes in their surroundings or by competitors inside or outside their branche. Neglect as a result of maintaining the status quo, not accepting there is a 'new order' coming up.

History has some strong examples of companies who neglected what happened around them. Companies like Kodak who, by neglecting the fact that the market was ready for digital photography, eventually put themselves out of business. This example is commonly referred to as 'a Kodak Moment', based on their own marketing tagline. Take Kodak Moments, photograph your life events. Who knew this tagline would become a metaphor for Kodak's own major 'life-event'.

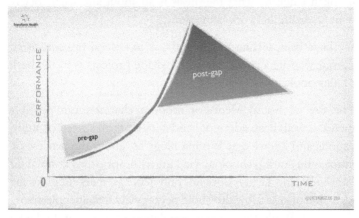

But not only corporates struggle with neglection: there is a lot of 'neglect' in healthcare as well. I have described this as a "pre-gap" phase. We tend to think technological and societal change only affects the jobs and professions of others, outside of our branche. Healthcare is 'too complicated' for these changes, some say. Or: people will never want to replace healthcare in real life by real humans, with digital care.

More than fifteen years ago, my friend Jeroen Tas lead the transformation into electronic banking for Citibank. Next stop after the financial sector: healthcare. After being CEO of Philips Health Informatics, Jeroen is now Chief Innovation & Strategy Officer at Philips.

In his Citibank era, people called them 'nuts', he revealed to me recently. Why would anyone ever want to do their banking online? According to Jeroen, he has heard the same arguments in healthcare now, as he heard at Citibank at that time. Critics tend to oppose the digital transformation - whether it's in finance or healthcare - with identical arguments, it seems.

By playing it right and making digital care available for those who want to handle their (health)care online, we could improve patient's experiences. Experiences that people already have in different branches, such as e-commerce and online banking.

Take a step back. Analyse your own behavior in society, see how digital technology has impacted almost every aspect of your life, from dating, communicating, to travelling and shopping. When you take these experiences into account - if you think about your digital journey in life - how can you relate that to your own professional healthcare practice?

And history repeats...

Is the "funeral" of the telco's coming up ?

As an example, I was recently interviewed by a government agency doing research on connectivity in the digital age. I got asked some thoughtful questions and had great discussions about where connectivity would be heading in the next, say 10 years. So we talked about 5G networks, WiFi and how mobile connectivity could change, and what would be needed for my field: the domain of health(care).

When we talked about terminology (see chapter Is digital health a different planetary system?), I argued that m-health (and also eHealth) are virtual silo's that we keep creating, while digital care and health services should just blend in with our regular processes. mHealth and eHealth are 'just' ways to deliver health(care) to people in need for it. That's why I rather talk about digital health, because it really should be part of our regular healthcare model, and not be added at the outer-side of our current system, as is often happening nowadays. Adding a digital layer on top off existing care is not only driving costs up but also brings in new interoperability challenges.

We tried to picture the impact on connectivity and bandwidth for the amount of data that is gathered in the medical field. We are living in an era of smartphones, smartwatches, and patches that measure your vital signs continuously - an era where the patient soon will generate more data himself than the professionals will. More cell-towers with bigger bandwidth seems to be the most obvious conclusion.

When I noticed the interviewers were going to wrap up, I asked them: "When are we going to talk about space-based internet?"

That question was not only not on their list, it also invoked sort of an uncomfortable situation and even a bit of laughter. The reply was "not really, this is a long way ahead of us, right". I was flabbergasted.

Trying to forecast the future of digital connectivity, and not taking the current developments of Google, Facebook, Tesla's Elon Musk, OneWeb and others into account, to me seems like a missed opportunity. Let's face it, the recent explosion of orbital internet initiatives that claim to be operational ultimately by 2020, Musk aiming to have his 4000+ satellites operational by the end of 2019, need to be taken seriously.

To me this development is bringing great opportunities for health: having an internet-connection, especially in rural areas where it makes the most sense to use digital health, is a must. With internet coverage on every inch of the world, just imagine the impact on global health, when 3-5 billion (with a B) people will come online in the next 10 years. With more and more delocalization of healthcare by new technology to do things remotely, this is a huge chance.

One step further we could even discuss the future of the current telecom ("telco") operators in a world that is always connected, everywhere. Already in my life the number of WhatsApp phone calls will very soon surpass the number of regular calls I make in a day. Sure enough, at the start these orbital internet services will be very expensive, just like satellite phones-calls or the first mobile telephones were when they were just launched. But very soon - with this 21 first century 'space-war' going on right now - prices for space-based internet will drop, while the number of people you can sell a bundle of internet to triples with the current numbers. Probably running an ads based business model, making it free. Hora est!

Blast from the past

The Jetsons - a popular TV-series from the creators of The Flint-stones - were way ahead of us in the sixties and seventies. They had belt conveyors, mobile phones, automatic toothbrushes, video conferencing, remote monitoring and ready-made 'meals' from a kind of oven.

The creators undoubtedly weren't aware of their competence of predicting the future, just like the creators of Star Trek did not intend to predict the future with their format: they just wanted to make great content for TV.

Looking back to these nostalgic 70's TV-series, it is astonishing how right the creators were in depicting a future where people would be using portable communication devices, making video-calls via a network and putting food in a oven with electronic waves. Even the Medical Tricorder of Doctor McCoy from Star Trek serves as inspiration for companies like Scanadu and participants of the Tricorder XPRIZE, an international competition to design a device that fits into the palm of your hand, a 'real-life' tricorder. The only 70's invention that is not possible yet in 2018 is matter-transmission, but I am sure that somewhere in a lab, some bright minds are figuring that out at this very moment.

Now that we got used to video-calls, microwaves and using a mobile phone, the question arises: will we be ready for the future, and what will that future look like? My guess is that we will have our blood taken in supermarkets. And yes things will turn out not to work from the start, projects, companies and ideas will fail (read the chapter: How one case can set a whole sector back). Or will a small microchip in our veins do the blood analysis? And does that same microchip also measure the amount of medication that is released into our bloodstream, coming from our medication tooth? That's right, wouldn't it be possible in the future to have a smart, connected tooth, filled with medication, that releases an adjustable amount of medicine, depending on our treatment? We could easily adjust the dosage via a Bluetooth connection with our smartphone, whenever more or less medication is needed.

How about that ambulance driving up to you driveway, automatically dispatched to you to prevent the heart attack that was predicted by the latest algorithm, based on data from remotely monitoring your vital signs. And what about your groceries? Will they be delivered at your fridge, based on your diet, your health parameters and the predicted risk of running out of certain groceries, such as milk, fruit or eggs?

Based on your schedule for the next weeks, you will be advised squeeze in some extra workout time this week, because there will be no time for that next week. And based on your habits, working out is not necessarily one of your priorities, so technology could offer you personalized support to stimulate healthy behavior.

And what about your smartphone? Will your phone be always on, listening not only on your conversations on the phone, but also recording your voice tremors and voice patterns in meetings and chats? Will you smartphone be able to sense that you are feeling a bit annoyed, that your stress levels are actually going up? If so, it can be your phone that will suggest to your secretary or PA to keep your schedule free for this day. Now that that morning meeting is cancelled, you feel like you have more room to breathe. In the future, there will be a time where, all of a sudden, it will be retro to have your blood pressure taken by a human again.

Will all of those developments above make health(care) better? Yes and no, I think. I would say 'Yes' because it can free up valuable time of healthcare professionals: they can stop performing the mundane routines that really do not tickle their intellect. They can invest time in the challenging problems, or turn their attention to specific cases that need extra time and energy.

I could answer 'No', because we could run the risk to dehumanise healthcare. What if the human touch is replaced by an algorithm, by a machine that takes your blood pressure and prescribes your medications? But at the same time, new technological advancements have a profoundly democratizing effect, by lowering the threshold and making knowledge and personal care available at a greater scale, for instance in rural areas, or regions with dire healthcare needs.

Changing mindset

If we take the spectrum of medical grade devices on one end and low-cost consumer level on the other end, we will see the emergence of the pro-sumer device. These pro-sumer devices will be validated into 'serious devices' as <u>Prof Bart de Moor (KU Leuven)</u> coined it. Low-cost devices will hit the market, giving consumers access to technology that was previously only accessible to professionals.

We are now living in the decade of 'wearables', all kinds of wearable technology we can wear around and on our bodies. Next stop: insideables, digital technology we can 'wear' inside our bodies. Think: medication with a microchip built in, safe for consumption of course. With the help of wearables and insideables, patients will be able to create data 24/7, allowing professionals a subscription to their data.

We are in the midst of the Fourth Industrial Revolution, where everything will be connected to everything. The Internet of Things (IoT) is taking shape around us. As <u>Swaab pointed out at the WEF</u>, innovations will come as a tsunami, a giant wave, instead of small waves. These giant waves will accumulate and we'll go from product innovation into system innovation. Entrepreneurship and agility will become key-factors of success and survival in a world where the fast fish will eat the slow ones, as opposed to the big fish that will eat the small ones.

Impact

Radboudumc

- Will come as a **tsunami** in stead of small waves
- Innovations will **accumulate**
- is a **System innovation** as opposed to product innovation
- Entrepreneurship & Agility
- No more big fish eats small fish, but **fast** fish will eat **slow** fish

(Ex. Schwab WEF)

We have to innovate our way into a sustainable future, built on three pillars: consumer, technology, and business models. From a medical point of view, academic medical centers are the experts on the medical aspects of innovation. From a business perspective, we should partner with leading business schools like Nyenrode, Tuck School of Business or Harvard Business School. And of course we need patients front and centre, since they are experts in living with a condition or disease.

Meanwhile in healthcare, we keep trying to become better, cheaper and faster. I honestly don't think this is the way to go. Sure, we will have to continue to get better, but our mindset has to change. We have to take bigger leaps.

As with any branch, health(care) will also become a software 'business' within the next decade. We will face a huge digital health(care) transformation on a global level. By starting with formulating the ambition to run everything 'digital first, physical next', we could steer our medical centre in the direction that many other 'businesses' like hotels, air travel, banking and music have gone.

Of course, we will not create a digital only policy, thereby leaving groups of patients or people out. Rather, we aim to flip the coin, from adding 'some' digital options like we were used to, into a two-sides approach by default. Digital first, physical next. Encouraging people to start their health journey digitally, whenever possible.

Essential in this vision is the aim to become obsolete. It might sound strange to put effort and energy in becoming obsolete. What I mean by that is that it should be our goal, with the help of digital technology, to serve that part of our population that is empowered and willing to use technology. In that way, we can free up time, resources and energy to serve those who are not able to go digital first, or are in need of 'in real life' visits.

I hoped to inspire a sense of urgency, even though it might seem 'artificial' in the sense. I hoped to encourage our thinking beyond 'doing the same a bit differently'. What we need is an 'artificial' sense of urgency, to take bigger and daring steps. We need to think bigger than the current process improvement, these incremental improvements that are some mistaken for innovation. We have to leapfrog some of these processes: thus my rationale for "we have to become obsolete" as a strategic direction.

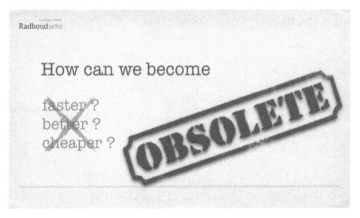

And we need to act now. Because "if we won't, others will". By that, I referred to new players in the healthcare market, startups and corporates that will not only talk about new business models but set up new ventures, products and services at lightning speed.

We now see the eruption of new technology that will have to be processed through all kinds of validations, certification etc, but for the majority of that it will only be a matter of time.

We can learn from these new entrants as well. Healthcare lacks a true start-up culture. Luckily, we started the <u>Rockstart Digital Accelerator Nijmegen</u>, to bring a startup ecosystem into our region and into the hospital.

Come to think of it, sometimes I envision us to act as a actual startup. A huge one though, with 1B$ in revenue and 11.000 people. But what I mean is the never-ending quest for learning, reinventing every step, asking questions, starting from scratch, and trying to create our own competition and competitor. And that is exactly what we are doing in our REshape Center.

This all will not only affect our delivery model, but it will also strongly impact our research models and even existing business models. You could for instance think about alternative research models, such as crowdfunding, collaborating with patients organisations and open access publishing. Luckily, we are moving towards a future where data from publicly funded research is (digitally) accessible for other researchers and organisations. Non-public-access will hopefully become a think of the past.

At REshape, we are working hard to make sure that the physicians, nurses and engineers of the future have the appropriate skill set when they finish their education. We worked on the educational models i.e. curricula for freshmen in medical and nursing school. Next, we have to train our current ánd new leaders into an era that will be characterized as what I coined "the era of never-ending change". For that i pitched an idea to the Ministry of health to create a program across healthcare, cross geographical spread in the Netherlands to pre-charge' the leader of the future with current tools for innovation. In co-creation with the Ministry we developed the Health Innovation School (HIS) aimed to strengthen my 3-Cs : Content, competences and community.

To be honest I had some worries if we would be able to find the first 50 people to be part of this "alpha' version, but 380 people applied and the same was true for the second round we did early 2018.

Everything that we do at REshape, starts with patient. I would argue that #patientsincluded™ should be the default. "Do not look at me, but see me. Do not hear me, but listen to me". This powerful quote is from Rene Tabak, patient advocate and part of our REshape Center's network for years. At one of our TEDx conferences, organized in 2012, Rene shared some of his own experiences facing a heart disease. I think Rene's quote is extremely important, as it points out that healthcare starts and ends with the needs of patients. The ongoing digital health(care) transformation we are facing right now, could really help to incorporate these real patients needs.

"Do not look at me, but see me. Do not hear me, but listen to me". Sometimes, there is a mismatch between medical expectations and real patient needs. Research over and over proves the average patiënt gets interrupted by the doctor in 18 seconds, while telling their story. In addition to Rene's experience, there is another point I would like to make: not only listen to what is 'out there', but really adapt and translate that into your own daily practice. Go out and stop attending only conferences you are familiar with, organized by your peers. Step out of your comfort zone: that is where the magic usually happens. If you want to know more, just read the chapter Crossing the boundaries of our sector in this book.

Reinvent yourself

We have to reinvent ourselves as well, over and over again. As I pointed out in From the valley of disillusionment, organizations often expects their innovation team to guide the implementation of their innovation as well. However, innovation is not interchangeable with implementation. Sometimes, you will learn that the hard way.

Organizations that stick to the maxim that the inventors of an innovative idea must also implement it, have a problem. That is why we came up with a seperate team, or a business unit in corporate jargon, to separate the innovation team from the implementation team. At REshape, we research scout new technologies, design new concepts and create visions, since the early days in 2011 we're using a human centered design approach.

REshape Center
Radboud umc

CONVERGENCE OF TECHNOLOGY AND PATIENT EMPOWERMENT

Explore the World   Create solutions   Share & discuss

TO SCOUT, EXPLORE, RESEARCH AND ADVOCATE (THE USE OF) NEW EXPONENTIAL GROWING TECHNOLOGY IN A DISRUPTIVE ERA, TO DESIGN A MORE PARTICIPATORY AND SUSTAINABLE HEALTH(CARE) SYSTEM, WITH A GLOBAL PERSPECTIVE.

Challenges for healthcare are enormous: increasing demand, decreasing budgets and shortage in skilled personnel puzzle many healthcare administrators. Next to that we think the next decennium should be the era of the rising self-empowered patient, where we will embrace the patient, their family and informal care into the healthcare team. Technology is changing possibilities and lowering in costs of it faster than ever, sometimes even exponentially. To cope with these aspects, Radboud University Medical Center launched a program called the REshape Innovation Center.

We nurture the movement by setting up conferences to exchange thoughts, visions and listen to each other. But also by doing research on the different aspects of participatory healthcare which helps to move forward. As a vehicle for the (needed) changes we are scouting, inventing and sharing innovations (inter)nationally to improve healthcare.

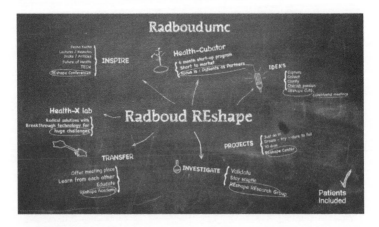

We explored innovation models and frameworks. Having been challenged many times in projects we ran, I can clearly see a pattern, also in the uptake of numbers of posts, articles, investments, and research being done. While mostly the out-called barriers are 'money,' 'technology,' 'government' or 'the board' the elephant in the room is 'us.'

It's us who are the real problem in blocking change, although we all want change, almost nobody wants to change their work, their behavior and indeed not their job. In reality, it is often the 'other department' that has to change, because 'we' are doing the stuff correctly.

Where innovation is often seen as the solution to many of our problems it often distracts from facing the real problem: culture. Most people do not need change, they actual benefit from the status quo and want to keep it that way.

So if there is no need or a 'burning platform,' it comes to the will of people to change or from the leadership painting a horizon that people want to be part of. The vision of the horizon needs to be supported by strong, authentic leadership securing that horizon as the way to go and make subsequent decisions into that path. That requires a layer of strategy that people can adhere to, brief, compelling and with simple logic. The majority of the strategic plans require tons of 'artistic lingo' to explain what we do and why we do it, that the bulk of the people cannot buy into.

To innovate you need a clear pathway and model you can use. I often describe innovation into three phases : (creating) awareness (by show and tell), (doing the) groundswork (for more solid scaling) and (building) breakthroughs (by making it the new normal).

Once that has been in place then it comes to the real challenge; the culture to make the change happen. This comes not easy and should NOT be part of your innovation process, but should've happened long before. It is part of your HR approach, of your leadership, the training. Often i see companies struggle during an innovation process, with a backlog of work on the aspects of 'trust,' 'feeling valued,' and lack of a clear vision. Culture is an ongoing part of your business and should in no way be the reason to start an innovation process. Innovation, however, can help to support cultural change, if played right.

And lastly, often significantly overestimated is processes and technology. Even though I use technology often as my 'Trojan Horse' (boys and girls still like toys) to me it never has been the goal, but nothing more than a tool. Some colleagues of mine try to change healthcare & medicine by doing research, or improving the quality & safety. My approach (actually my Trojan horse) is through innovation, supported by the technological opportunities of this era.

One of the things that strike me over and over again is that we fail after a successful innovation the final step to 'kill' the old way we were doing things, or the old technology is kept alive. While giving the laggards a choice and a tool to avoid working through the new normal, we also 'punish' the ones fiercely working and using what has been achieved. My call is therefore to next to the innovation team create a 'demolition team" that clears away our old 'habits' and perhaps puts them in a particular room to conserve to later be placed in a museum. You know, things like a fax, paper records, You know, things like a fax, paper records, and email (just kidding ?)

As we've gone through our tasks as REshape Center, we'll decide together with our board (our so called MOC's Moments of Choice) the next steps for that specific project : stop, on hold (waiting for future changes or change of conditions to implement) or to pursuit the next stage this possible innovation will be brought to.

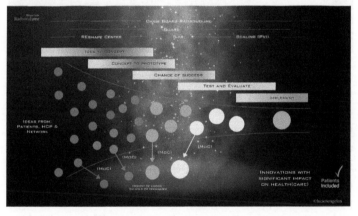

From there on, often the newly created Radboudumc iLab will take these innovations a step further. The new lab was created mainly due to the lack if implementation capacity in our organization for these innovations. Although the REshape Center wasn't created, equipped and staffed for implementation, 'the organisation' wrongly expected us to do so. So we're proud the board boldy decided to also take the next step into investing into a solid innovation climate by creating the iLab. With that making sure could go back to the original intent of 'scouting' the third horizon and the rest of its task you read in this book.

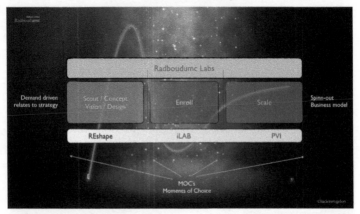

Next to that we also started the iBoard. The iBoard oversees the projects coming into the iLab - out of the REshape Center or other pathways of the organization - and guides the exit of these projects, for instance as a separate spin off company or as a solution/method, ready to implement for 13.000 people within Radboudumc. The iLab prepares for the next level, makes IT compliant, does next level business development, creates an implementation approach again based on human centered design, and implements in one or two departments, This can be done at a ward, or in a team or across the whole organisation or even in the network.

As you can see in the graph of the three labs, we also projected Gartner's Hype cycle in the background, as many of the project we take on have that samen trajectory. IF we choose to pursuit a project after the hype we know we'll face another heavy lifting phase of making things fit in the present operational model.

From a simple tweet to remote monitoring: a typical REshape process.

Anna Jacobs (SmartHealth) interviews Lucien Engelen and Bas Bredie from the Radboud University Medical Center on a "typical REshape case", as the two call it: it all started with a tweet, eventually leading to continuous monitoring patients at the hospital and even remotely.

It's November 2012, at the Exponential Medicine conference in San Diego. Lucien gets in touch with a startup called Visi Mobile. A few months earlier, Lucien saw a tweet from the Palomar Medical Center, about a device they are developing that supposedly could measure vital signs via the wrist of patients. This little device would even make it possible to monitor patients at the nursing ward. The contact is made via Twitter, and Lucien gets redirected to the headquarters of Sotera, a US company.

A visit with a Dutch delegation of 50 persons to the Sotera headquarters is a coming at a unsuitable time, but since it's Exponential Medicine 2012, Sotera is around at the conference as well. Lucien: "A number of other colleagues from the Radboud University Medical Center were also very enthusiastic about the system. At Exponential Medicine, we laid the foundation for our later collaboration. In February the next year, together with my colleague Ronald Lolkema, I visited Sotera's office for the first time."

REshape wants to be the first to test the Visi-Mobile – as the wireless device is called - outside of the US. However, Sotera is cautious: the company is still in its early stages and the technology is going through extensive testing. Lucien persists and returns in April, this time together with a whole camera crew from the Dutch VPRO, who broadcasts a behind-the-scenes documentary about the work of Lucien and REshape. "I'm not sure whether that last "raid" with a complete camera crew was the turning point", he says with a smile. "We will never know, but during that visit we not only received two devices to test, but we also got the green light for a large-scale test later in the year." In the Tegenlicht broadcast, Lucien calls department head Professor Kees van Laarhoven with the good news about the collaboration.

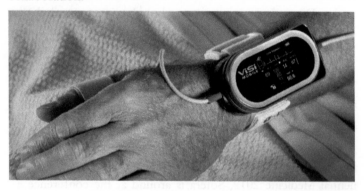

Later that year, both return to receive the test devices from Sotera and take them back to the Netherlands, because Sotera cannot send them directly to the Netherlands. Upon arriving home, two physicians are enthousiastly taking over: Bas Bredie, internist at of the department of Internal Medicine, together with Prof. Harrie van Goor, surgeon from the department of Surgery. Both Bredie and Van Goor work as a REshape Fellow one day per week, besides their daily work at the Radboud University Medical Center.

What's the problem? Internist Bas Bredie explains: "The monitoring of the vital signs of patients in a nursing ward is currently done three times a day. Nurses have eight hours shifts in which they take these measurements. That manual monitoring not only costs a lot of manpower, but also involves risks: the measurements have to copied manually to our EHR and that is not always flawless. Moreover, the measurement is periodic. That means that you do not have the ability to predict what the expected outcome will be for a patient or the development in the next two hours." According to Bredie, this clinical problem can be resolved with technology, for instance the Sotera devices. "It is now technically possible to monitor patients with smaller devices and smart software at the regular hospital wards, even outside of the intensive care unit (IC)."

REshape started a small-scale pilot by using and testing the ViSi mobile, a little device (box) that measures vital functions such as blood pressure, heart rate, breathing rate, temperature and oxygen saturation. The ViSi Mobile collects this data continuously and transmits it wirelessly. The REshape team and the fellows dive into the technology: what are the functions, how does the data collection and integration work? The ViSi Mobile is tested extensively with users, both patients and nurses, to understand how this novel technology can be used in the care process.

Bredie: "You really create added value if you can analyze and predict trends, based on all those data points from patients. If you can see that a patient is deteriorating, and you can respond to that much quicker than we usually can." To achieve this, the ViSi devices are linked to predictive software. This software comes from OBS Medical, the manufacturer of the FDA approved Visensia. That AI system was developed for the early detection of a patient's deterioration. "We have agreed with OBS Medical that we will continue to develop jointly through the clinical validation of Visensia," says Bredie. "The technology is changing at a lightning speed: the device that we use today will look very different in five years' time. Therefore, we want to invest in the development of software and clinical validation, which is the most important basis for us."

Although this REshape project reads like an adventure story, the road was far from easy, according to Lucien. "You can definitely say we went through peaks and "valleys of disillusionment" in this project. But more and more, things were taking a solid shape. The challenge for me is to be able to eventually move to remote monitoring outside the hospital via continuous monitoring at home. For that, we need newly developed standards and parameters that fit these new possibilities."

"By being able to let a doctor of internal medicine, Bas, work at REshape as a fellow for one or two days a week, we are creating a basis to integrate novel technology into the 'normal' departments at the hospital. So, we go from REshape to the hospital's wards. When the departments take over, we hope that continuous monitoring will become the new standard, especially in the new hospital building that will be built. The next step, that we are planning to take with the same team, is to go from 24/7 continuous monitoring to remote monitoring, outside the hospital walls, at home and outside. By following this approach, we ensure that we keep both the progress and doing things carefully at the same time. At REshape, we also take the time to write peer-reviewed articles about these developments (these can be found at the end of this book)."

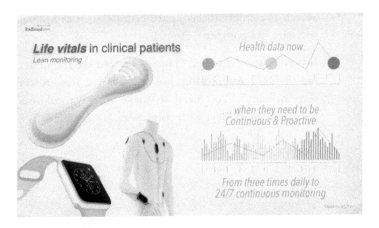

The case of ViSi Mobile is a good example of a successful digital health project, that moves from an innovation department into the regular wards and eventually (hopefully, according to Bas Bredie and Lucien Engelen) into the whole organization. Bas Bredie: "What started as a small idea at REshape, become a thoroughly tested concept, that grew with the passion of our professionals and the network we deployed. Now, as of 1 June 2018, we will start with monitoring patients 24/7 at 60 beds in the departments of Surgery and Internal Medicine"

Five REshape Learnings, from the Visi-Mobile-Sotera case:

- Start small with an enthusiastic group of like-minded people, to test the technology

- Use the power of your network

- Be patient/persistent: it might take a while to convince your managers/board/colleagues

- Search for (international) partnerships, such as Sotera, software/AI company, etc.

- Involve nurses! Lucien: "Nurses say: we see the benefits of 24/7 monitoring, but we also see the greater responsibility". You need to make sure you address these points and test with your users.

CHAPTER 29

"Hospitals are internally focused, while change comes from the outside" (vignette)

Peter Bennemeer, CEO of Dutch hospital Bernhoven, lead the Zinnige Zorg project at Bernhoven.

The Dutch hospital Bernhoven succeeded, with the help of health insurers, to move from volume based financing to outcome based financing, removing the stimulus of volume and production. What did former CEO Peter Bennemeer learn from this process? Can this approach be translated to other hospitals, or does the transition that we need to make from volume to value based healthcare require a different approach?

Lucien: At Bernhoven, you have turned a complete business model upside down. The incentive for more diagnostics and treatments has been removed, resulting in a sharp drop of turnover for the hospital. However, the current healthcare system is not yet structured in such a way that we can translate this model to other hospitals in the Netherlands. Where do you think we will be in 2030?

Peter: "Of course, something is going to happen to the way we pay for healthcare, which is now focused on volume and segmentation. The chain as a whole cannot function properly because every healthcare institution only optimizes its own part, without taking the total value chain into account. We need to start rewarding for quality, so that the entire chain focuses on the patient. All stakeholders - health care providers, insurers, politicians - keep each other in a lockdown."

"Most caregivers do not feel the need to change. And health insurers - the directors of funding in healthcare - still do not look at the patient. That is why I think the government should take a central, organizing role."

Lucien: Bernhoven managed to put quality at the center, replacing production volume. How can more hospitals follow this route?

Peter: "Bernhoven has sought a strategic cooperation with health insurers, who smoothed out the system errors behind the scenes. This approach worked in a regional setting however not at a national level, so you really need a system change."

Lucien: Bernhoven received a lot of media attention, with its decision to move some treatments out of the hospital, into a primary care setting. And the choice to refrain from treatment, instead of always opting for a medical treatment, isn't something you hear daily as well. What happened behind the scenes at Bernhoven?

Peter: "My drive was to create a decisive organization, that can move along in a rapidly changing environment. Most hospitals are not agile enough to fend off new entrants. Also, most hospital leave all uninsured care out, but with relatively low extra costs you can generate a lot of extra turnover if you do take up uninsured care as a hospital.

Look at it like this: I have transformed the messy internal financial systems, the administrative spaghetti as I like to call it, into asparagus. One of those care pathways, or asparagus, was chronic care, which we organized in a separate path. By isolating care for chronic patients outside of all the other activities of a hospital, it becomes easier to organize chronic care differently. Outside of the organization, for instance, and with a much closer integration with the general practitioners in our region. Also, a large part of the care for chronic patients can become digitized. If your digital proposition and model works, it is ease to scale to the whole of the Netherlands or even worldwide."

"Another asparagus or lump of care is the care for people who are uninsured. Corporations have an interest in vital employees. So, they are prepared to pay for the wellness and care of their employees, to reduce absenteeism due to illness. As a hospital, you can generate millions of extra income by investing much more in prevention and early signaling. Another stakeholder in this uninsured care are local municipalities, that formally have the responsibility and care for vulnerable elderly people in their region (Wmo). If we can ensure that their vulnerability diminishes with targeted care programs, that leads to diminished costs as well."

Lucien: How do you see your organisation in 2030? And what about traditional hospital that do not make a transition?

Peter: "If you do not undertake action right now, your hospital will probably be diminished to a supplier of acute care. In my vision for 2030, the entire chronic care part has been taken over by other players by that time."

"At the same time, even for hospitals that do have a clear mission and vision, it can be challenging to find the funds to invest in digital health and innovation. When I was still working at Bernhoven, we were having talks with Philips. Eventually, we could not come to an agreement; they were not yet willing to co-invest in technology and data knowledge. I'm no longer working at Bernhoven right now, but if I were still there, I would have called a party like Apple at some point. Because Bernhoven has something that Apple really wants to have, and a technology company like Apple has the knowledge and technology that Bernhoven needs."

Lucien: You just indicated that you think insurers and hospitals are not moving and that you see a role for politics. How much perseverance does The Hague have?

Peter: "Not very much, I'm afraid, because before you know it, the opposition repels the plans. So even if the minister and the secretary of state want something, it's still a problem to get it done. The interests are so scattered and everyone is so entrenched in their position, that politicians find it difficult to make concrete decisions or policy for these issues. Yet that must happen. We need more debate to create awareness. But I'm a little worried that it will not work without outside forces.

In any case, I do not see hospitals changing quickly themselves. Conservatism runs so deep in healthcare. Doctor Watson can make a better diagnosis than a doctor, but radiologists do not see this. They really think that in ten years from now, they are still needed to assess radiology images. Most management and directors in healthcare don't see the digital future either, because they are often coming from the same background. These are people who think in classic, hierarchical models. Convincing management in healthcare is perhaps the biggest hurdle we have to take."

Lucien: Looks like we need a destabilizing force - preferably from the outside - to act as a crowbar. I see four of those destabilizing factors:

- people who know that the current situation is no longer an option;

- the increase and use of technology;

- healthcare consumers who are waking up (I consciously use the word consumer, as we become accustomed to same day delivery and maximum service)

- a society that is hardening

And all of the above destabilizing factors reinforce each other. For a long time, I thought we that we would not experience a disruption in healthcare and that it would be a soft landing, but now I actually believe that we cannot avoid a disruption.

Peter: "You can be right, because I do not see any signs of change yet. In international ratings, the Dutch healthcare system is always in the top 10. Our care is qualitatively very well, so why would you want to change that? We do not look at the world around us, while the change comes from outside."

"Doctors need to reinvent themselves, but that does not happen yet. I remember that in Bernhoven we asked the doctors: how would you organize care for chronic patients if we put it in a separate organization? Their idea was: we are going to work at this new organization. But most people are already ruined by the system. You need new people with a new vision. People who understand that as a doctor, you will no longer care for a few hundred patients, but for a hundred thousand, or perhaps a million. Patients who you no longer see physically, but whose data you analyze and who you inform based on real-time data and completely customized information. That was too much to take in for most doctors: they found the small movements that Bernhoven made already very disruptive."

Lucien: What can we expect from new entrants, non-traditional companies that such as Apple and Amazon that are going to provide care to their employees and their families? You can expect that they will soon enter into partnerships with hospitals. What is your vision of the future?

Peter: "You will have to provide integrated care from cradle to grave: through that integration, you can achieve a big profit. My dream is that we bring acute care and planned care back to the right proportions. And that we will tackle chronic care with digital healthcare via a subscription model: with a fixed reward per patient. This model stimulates collaborations. The question is: who will become the care director? I'm afraid that is not the hospitals, but rather corporations like Apple.

Hospitals simply never had to fight for their clients. Their customers came naturally, and with that also the money and the growth. But in today's world, you need to be ready to minimize your business, to become obsolete. This requires that you think in very different dimensions: in terms of added value, in terms of innovation. As long as hospitals do not feel the pain of a lack of income or less patients, they will not change. Then they continue to see digital health as an app, as a gadget, without truly seeing what's behind it. Until a new entrant comes along."

CHAPTER 30

From a doodle to a mission

Marco Derksen (founder of Marketingfacts) and
Lucien Engelen draw out the paradigm shift from
health 1.0, and 2.0 to health 3.0, and the need for
#patientsincluded™

Healthcare has come a long way when it goes into creating an equal level playing field of patients and professionals. In 2010, I was trying to tackle and explain the change of the paradigm shift in healthcare, based on the same principles as web 1.0, web 2.0 and so forth. (created by Tim O'Reilly)

Around 2009, I tried to figure out what the added value for healthcare and the role of the internet could be. We organised the first Dutch "health 2.0 event", organised by and for health professionals and patients. With trial and error, I started using social media myself, learning about the opportunities that lie ahead with social networking sites. I sat down from time to time with Marco Derksen, who created a huge online marketing community called Marketingfacts, and our newly appointed Chief Listening Officer, Corine Janssen.

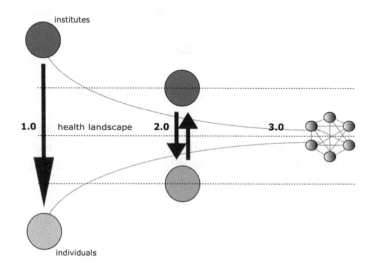

We envisioned a model that could help us in healthcare, and we started doodling around on a whiteboard, while talking and sharing our visions and experiences, but also the loose ends that we saw. Eventually, a figure emerged on the whiteboard. My drawing turn into a funnel, that we tried to turn into a coherent model. Credits to Marco for making this as simple as possible, but not too simple (tongue in cheek referring to Einstein's quote).

This is how our model turned out. Our great friend ePatient-Dave started using this model as well, with his own explanation on how he envisioned this evolution. We've made a 3D video about it and Dave was kind enough to create a narrated version.

I have been using it for years to explain to both colleagues and the world outside of healthcare, how we could transform healthcare with the use of the internet and technology, to create a better working system. The animation was used in an article

<u>in the British Medical Journal</u>, in an issue that was filled with patient contributions. With this issue, BMJ clearly showed they are leading the flock on #patientsincluded™ publishing, and why they earned the <u>first ever #patientsincluded™ award</u>.

CHAPTER 31

Towards collaborative care (vignette)

Marco Derksen, consultant for digital transformation
and founder / partner of Upstream

"It is now clear that healthcare shifts the focus from illness and care to health and behavior, making the functioning and participation of people a focal point. This leads to a different care landscape and a different way of organizing care. A care landscape that does not necessarily consist of formal care institutions, but can be organized informally, close to the client or patient, supported by technology. "

This quotation comes from an article I wrote in 2011, shortly after I worked with Lucien Engelen and Corine Jansen of the Radboudumc on a model in which we tried to outline the future of care.

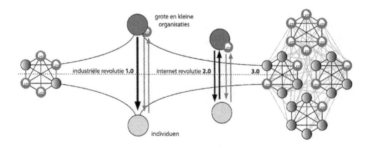

216

We concluded that healthcare, under the influence of internet technology, had progressed from a 1.0 model - where formal care institutions are central - to a reciprocal model (which we called care 2.0) and ultimately to a more collaborative care system (3.0). As we progress from a institutional system to a networked system, supported by technological possibilities, there will be more involvement of patients. They will share their experiences and knowledge in a networked model.

My vision on the future of healthcare has not changed much since 2011. I do realize now that these developments are going slower than we thought at the time. What is the reason for this inertia, and what can we do we to speed up the change?

I still believe in the transformation to care 3.0 or collaborative care, in which we see a shift from the traditional to the online and the connected patient or client. By this I mean the shift from a patient who listens unconditionally to his care provider (1.0) to an increasingly well-informed patient who uses digital resources and the Internet to become an equal discussion partner of the care provider (2.0). We will eventually see a patient who works together with all those involved - from family and informal care-givers to insurer and healthcare provider - in the care network, and who puts health and wellbeing in the center, rather than his or her illness and care (3.0). This is a shift from the physician who decides which is the best treatment for a patient, to the doctor as an equal discussion partner of the patient. It's s shift from the nurse as an intermediary between doctor and patient to nurses as an equal partner in the treatment team. And it is a shift from organizing care by illness and medical specialism, to organizing care around the needs of the patient.

This shift to collaborative care is a result of demographic, economic, social, political and technological changes. For example, technological developments have ensured that we have more and more access to knowledge and people. Technology has also ensured that we can communicate and work together in a completely different way.

At the same time, in retrospect we have overestimated the role of technology. Technology strengthens the speed and power of economic, social and political changes, but it is these underlying changes that will shape and direct technological development and applications. Roy Amara was the first to point out that we tend to overestimate the effect of a technology in the short run and underestimate the effect in the long run.

In order to speed up the necessary transformation to collaborative care, we will first have to look at the non-technological developments. Yes, technology is a vital part of a collaborative care universe, this care 3.0 scenario. We need to develop care platforms to easily exchange data between different healthcare systems, making the patient the owner of his own health data, with applications that enable us to communicate faster, easier and more safely and collaborate. But at the same time, collaborative care is about people and the way we work together.

Sometimes, it seems like we lost sight of the preconditions for the successful adoption of these technological developments in recent years. Collaborative care requires that responsibilities are shared at certain times, giving patients or other parties involved more responsibility and autonomy. Collaborative care requires personal leadership from all those involved, the ability to explore yourself and your own (professional) responsibilities. Collaborative care requires a set of digital skills that are necessary to work in this interconnected world.

And perhaps most importantly: collaborative care requires participation, and the will to constantly adapt and continuously improve yourself to be able to participate. Working together equals learning together. That goes for patient as well as health-care provider. Sometimes it seems like we have forgotten that in recent years.

CHAPTER 32

Innovation distinguishes between a leader and a follower

So the question is: where do you want to be?

The late Steve Jobs once said "<u>Innovation distinguishes between a leader and a follower</u>." And "The computer industry shifted from mainframe to personal computer, next from personal computer to interpersonal computer."

Right now, we will go from interpersonal computer to the internet of everything. Almost 23 years ago, Windows 95 was introduced. The iPad is only 8 years of age. Your grandchildren will grow up in a world that is always connected, everywhere they go, and they will laugh when you share your stories about having to charge your phone every day. The speed of change is accelerating at an (almost) exponential scale.

And still, the way we basically deliver healthcare hasn't changed much for over a hundred years. Although we all clearly see the change in society around us, we tend to think that the impact of technology and societal changes will not be so quick in our branch. You often hear statements like "what I do in my profession is so complicated that it can't be done differently" or that technology will not really affect "my" job or profession.

The why, or the need to innovate

Einstein said "If you always do what you always did, you will always get what you always got." Fact of the matter is that society simply will not have the resources to treat the number of people who will need healthcare in the future. We will fall short, both in terms of professionals and financial resources. In contrast to today's linear innovation process, driven by functional experts in a specific technology or field, we have to move to a more systemic process driven by cross-functional facilitators that never stop and always try to find innovative ways to improve.

As Radboudumc, we partnered with Philips and Salesforce to find new pathways to better health(care). Together with patients (#patientsincluded™), we created a prototype of a mobile app that patients can use to track their blood glucose levels, insulin use, nutrition, physical activity, mood and stress and get data-driven feedback and coaching. Most importantly, we built the app with the need of diabetes patients as a guiding principle: the app combines information from a lot of siloed systems into one digital platform, combining personal health data and clinical data. We built the app on the Philips cloud-based HealthSuite digital platform and the Salesforce App Cloud. New technology brings new options to the table, which could solve issues we've had for ages

We are realists and we don't know for sure if this really is going to work the way we envision, but that is exactly the point here. Working with these global giants - Philips and Salesforce - brings in technology and knowledge that, combined with our academic and clinical expertise and our #patientsincluded™ approach, makes rapid prototyping and iterations possible, creating a truly scalable solution.

If we stop wanting to improve and innovate with new models in healthcare, we actually would stop wanting to make patients better. I would even argue that it is the innovation in healthcare that fosters new solutions to increase our lifespan and eradicate illness. In the end, innovation is what makes us live longer and longer.

Medical technology and pharma have historically been two fields with a fair amount of innovation, focused on the development of new products. But when it comes to healthcare delivery and organization, things have been static for a long time. When it comes to healthcare delivery and service, the need to innovate has not been high - until a new entrant will come along that brings a new service or experience, procedure or device to the healthcare market. Something as new as Uber, for instance.

If we look at the spectrum of medical grade devices at one end and low-cost consumer level devices at the other end, we will see the emergence of the pro-sumer device: validated, low-cost devices that will hit the market, giving consumers access to clinical features or medical tools that were previously only available to healthcare professionals.

If you look at the Fortune 500, the list of the biggest companies in the United States based on their annual turnover, you will notice something interesting. Some of the biggest companies today did not exist 50 years ago. Some companies, like Facebook, didn't even exist 15 or 20 years ago. The Fortune 500 list is testimony to the fact that new international companies will come out with great innovations and surpass the traditional industry giants. In ten years from now, the deck will be reshuffled again, with only organizations that "live innovation" in the top of that Fortune 500 list.

Yet some 100+ year old companies, like Philips, seem to embrace these new waves of innovation, restructuring their company and their product range. Existing companies have to come up with strategic solutions for this new world order.

Types of innovation

We often define innovation in healthcare in three kinds; Consumers, Technology and Business Models (HBR 2003, Herzlinger).

The consumer perspective will evolve from quality care at a fair price to quality, costs and service. Ease of use will be the real change in healthcare. Consumer innovation will lead to improvements in the "use" of healthcare. People expect their healthcare experience to be as smooth as shopping online, searching for the best flights or ordering their everyday errands. These - online of offline - experiences can be translated to healthcare as well.

On the technology perspective, data and interoperability become a focal point. It is a challenge to connect every bit of data in this fragmented healthcare landscape. The lack of a connection between all the islands of information keeps this current fragmentation alive, obstructing what people really need for their health. Technological innovation will tackle this problem with solutions for system integration and data connections.

These solutions will probably be made by companies from outside of the healthcare sector. Companies that have already transformed other businesses, will also democratize healthcare by creating transparency of costs and outcomes, by connecting the dots and data. As healthcare will innovate through better information, it will become more of a software business.

On a business model perspective, we will move away from the fee for service model to an outcome-based business model. With the use of the latest technology, clinical care will find its way outside of the hospital walls, from local health clinics eventually to the patient's home. This delocalization spurs business model innovation. New players with innovative (business) models deliver a higher quality of care, with similar or even better outcomes, and a higher customer satisfaction, that will eventually be reimbursed by payers. This impact will be especially big on the preventative side, as all kinds of new devices and data solutions will shift the focus from diagnosis, care and treatment to prevention and healthy living.

These three types of healthcare innovation that Herzlinger defines - Consumers, Technology and Business Models - are impacted by globalization. Healthcare is an international market, and one of the biggest markets for that matter. At one point in time, every one of us will become a patient and start using healthcare.

Convergence of patient empowerment and technology

As Radboudumc (Radboud University Medical Center in Nijmegen, the Netherlands) we have come a long way. April 2006 was a turning point in our hospital's history, accumulating in the Dutch health inspectorate closing down one of our wards. At the same time, that event defined our mission to innovate. There was a clear need for change, and the ambition to improve was felt everywhere.

Radboudumc, with 13.000+ employees (including our students) , carefully constructed a culture with room for discussion and debate. The board welcomed all feedback on the way the teams, wards, organization and hospital were run. Everyone was given a chance to be heard. There was room to experiment, to innovate and to create. It was in this period, after all the turmoil, that the <u>REshape Center</u> was founded, an innovation cell at the convergence of patient empowerment and technology.

We (re)discovered patients, started listening and talking with them to discover the real needs patients and healthcare professionals have. At REshape, we started to redesign our way of work, making bold choices both in terms of IT as in terms of transparency. It all comes down to our mission: we want to have a significant impact on people's lives.

Change is the new constant in every step we make. Constantly discussing the way we do things, makes us aware of the room for improvement and opportunities. It helps us to understand and test if technology - as a tool - can help us. Technology is never a goal in itself, but a means to an end. All the while keeping in the back of our minds: how can we make ourselves obsolete?

With their clinical expertise, international network and highly motivated professionals, academic medical centers could take the lead in healthcare innovation. Together, with patients, we can really move mountains. If we keep leading in innovation - together with entrepreneurs and people from other industries - we will find new ways of delivering better (health)care. But if we passively wait to follow others, then we have chosen to stop becoming better tomorrow. We will always be behind in what we offer to our patients.

We will not know everything that will cross our path, and we might have to do things we have never done before. Einstein said: "It's called 'research' because we don't know what we are doing". We have to innovate our way into a sustainable future with all three pillars as foundation: consumer, technology, and business model innovation. Moving away from siloed and frag-mented healthcare (information), together with all stakeholders (#patientsincluded™) at the table, to find new delivery models that embrace new technology, thereby creating the chance to set stage for a sustainable future for health(care).

So the question is: If 'innovation distinguishes between a leader and a follower', where do you want to be?

CHAPTER 33

The future of healthcare: human-centered and tech-enabled (vignette)

Chris McCarthy, former lead Innovation Consultancy @ Kaiser Permanente, now VP Strategy & Design Hopelab.

One of the most confusing words for healthcare systems is "innovation". It can mean anything to anyone. With enough verbal acrobatics, everything looks like an innovation and everyone is an innovator. And while there are truths buried in such statements, they have clouded the past two decades of innovation in healthcare. But let me be clear: there are bright spots, major transformations, and even paradigm shifts. And it's these things that signal what the near and distant future might hold for innovation in healthcare.

Signal One: The Digitized Basics

Many of the basics of primary care (and even specialty care) are now virtual/digital. Massive increases in telephone and video appointments, asynchronous online care, prescription refills by text and app, booking lab appointments and receiving results without physician review, and even online mental health services are changing the landscape of primary care. These technologies are enabling a much higher degree of self-care and allowing physicians and nurse practitioners to practice at the top of their licenses. This signal is loud, pervasive, and probably the most recognized as "innovation."

Signal Two: Deeply Human-Centric

And yet, with the all the digitization happening around us, there is a yearning for real connection, authentic interactions, and a good old-fashioned hug when things are not going well. While controversial, concierge medicine is a bellwether of what is to come. Right now, this is only available to the affluent, but even that is changing. The price point which was once tens of thousands of dollars has moved into the low hundreds in the past 5 years. These services are incorporating old ideas in new ways, and those who deliver and receive care like it. House visits, a thing of the past, have re-emerged, enabled by handheld medical and care technologies. Across the board, healthcare institutions are 'warming up' their everyday interactions with patients and their families. This signal is medium strength and more commonly recognized as 'design'.

Signal Three: Institutionalized Innovation & Design

Finally, the way we innovate and design in healthcare is becoming smarter, faster, and more pervasive. While there was confusion, distrust, and even in-fighting among the healthcare transformers in the last two decades, the convergence of signals 1 and 2 clarify what our healthcare institutions will look like ten years from now. More and more, healthcare leaders are taking on the innovator's mindset, organizations are normalizing their innovation and design approaches, employees are demanding 'joy of work', and patients/families are becoming sophisticated in their consumption of care. No longer will IT, delivery, and facilities be allowed to design separate systems. What emerges is a robust, multidisciplinary, and integrated approach to innovation that becomes the de facto standard. This signal is the weakest of the three and recognized as 'transformation'.

And so, the future of innovation in healthcare is bright. It is human-centered, tech-enabled, and feels just right for both the deliverer and receiver. There is no shortage of challenges that our institutions are facing, but the tools of innovation will systematically and comprehensively bring integrated, novel solutions to life.

Onward!

CHAPTER 34

What is Moonshot Thinking?

Astro Teller is Captain Moonshot at X (formerly Google-X, Google's R&D factory). X is 'a moonshot factory': its mission is to invent and launch "moonshot" technologies that we hope could someday make the world a radically better place. Astro leads a team of engineers, scientists, and creatives developing solutions for the world's toughest problems. Peter Diamandis (Singularity University) has interviewed Astro several times, and published some learnings on <u>Medium</u>, we publish it over here due to its relevance:

"What is Moonshot Thinking: A Moonshot is going 10 times bigger, while the rest of the world is pursuing 10 percent bigger. When you try to do 10% better, you're putting yourself in a "smartness" competition with everyone else in the world - a competition you're unlikely to win. When you instead try to go 10 times bigger, you're forced to approach the problem in a radically different fashion. The result is 100x more worth it, but it's never 100x harder."

"Ideas Are Easy, Culture is Hard: Creating the ecosystem for rapidly evaluating and testing ideas is much harder than finding the idea. Filter weaker ideas early by running a "pre-mortem" - predict in advance why an idea is likely to fail - and celebrate and reward ideas that the team kills early."

"Experiment, Experiment, Experiment: How can you encourage your team to experiment and pursue audacious goals? X has a "Get Weirder Award," which rewards the best experiment the team runs based on a crazy idea. Instead of strictly incentivizing successful experiments, X focuses on progress, learning and asking the right questions."

Moonshot thinking: ten commandments for radical innovation

When president John F. Kennedy shared his ambition to put the first man on the moon in the early 60s, no one had an idea how to realise that ambition. Many even declared the president insane.

But Kennedy's outspoken ambition, this unlikely goal, worked as a catalyst, releasing so much energy that all conventional ways of thinking were thrown overboard. People knew: we need to do better than our regular way of thinking. We must radically innovate, go beyond the beaten track. The rest is history: what everyone considered impossible for years became reality when the first man landed on the moon in 1969.

If you strive for 10 percent improvement, you will get incremental innovation or - in my opinion- what we often call process improvement. But if you strive for ten times better than everything that was before, you get radical innovation. We need radical innovation to meet the challenges that healthcare faces. And that requires that we challenge our existing culture.

Healthcare is a heavily regulated environment. And rightly so, as we do not want to take risks with the health and lives of people. At the same time, 80 percent of the most healthcare processes consists of logistics and process management, rather than actual medicine. While this is arguably the most important part in healthcare, it is usually only 20 percent of our daily operations.

Yes, we have to be careful with innovating medicine. But do we also have to be careful on the process management side of healthcare? Everything that has to do with logistics, with processes and with communication can be organized exactly ten times better.

Kennedy elicited a self-fulfilling prophecy by expressing his dream. Let us also provoke such a self-fulfilling prophecy in healthcare. We can use the ten rules for success of Astro Teller, who is Captain Moonshot - yes, that is really his job title - at X, the semi-secret development agency of Google, responsible for innovations such as Google Translate, Google Glass and the self-driving car. Astro Teller formulated these ten commandments for radical innovation:

1. Make the world 10 times better

Do not focus on incremental improvements - making an existing model work 10 percent more efficiently - but think about innovations that make the world work ten times better. Formulate an appealing dream, a vision of the future that makes people enthusiastic because it removes all the obstacles we now know. Do not get stuck in small (process) improvements to make existing obstacles a bit less irritating, others do.

2. Go big or go home

The point with incremental innovation or process improvement - the stuff that we have been doing for years - is that no one is excited about it. It is very difficult to convince people to participate in a project that reduces the administrative burden for nurses by 10 percent, just to name an example. But if you say that you are working on a project to eradicate all registrations, so that caregivers only can devote their entire time to their patients and no longer have any administrative burdens, that's an inspiring message. This is called moonshot thinking, creating the energy that is needed to radically innovate.

People who do not feel this energy are better off if they are not in your moonshot team. That doesn't mean that you do not need critical voices in this team, because you obviously do need critical thinkers. Align these critical voices at a later stage, for example during the implementation phase. Within your moonshot team, try to avoid people who put the handbrake on beforehand.

3. Fail fast

A plethora of things can fail in any innovation project. In most innovation projects, we often tend to start with the so called low hanging fruit, with those components that are simple to achieve. Starting with these relatively tasks means that the really complicated issues have to be tackled when a project is already well underway. The complicated issues drain you team's energy. So much was invested in this project, that no one dares to pull the plug. The work drags on, eventually resulting in an innovation that nobody really expected and that is hardly used.

Start with the most complicated and daring part of your innovation! Do not go for the low hanging fruit, but start with the part that will be most time consuming or most complicated. Astro Teller gives a great example of this behaviour in teams and corporations. Let's say you're trying to teach a monkey how to recite Shakespeare while on a pedestal. How should you allocate your time and money between training the monkey and building the pedestal?

Hint: <u>tackle the monkey first</u>. According to Astro Teller, the right answer, is to spend zero time thinking about the pedestal. The hardest and most urgent challenge in this example is teaching a monkey how to recite Shakespeare, not building a pedestal. But most people will rush off and start building a really great pedestal first. "Why? Because at some point the boss is going to pop by and ask for a status update- and you want to be able to show off something other than a long list of reasons why teaching a monkey to talk is really, really hard."

His point: it takes a lot of careful cultural engineering and long-term commitment from managers to get teams to run cheerfully at breaking their prototypes and proving their ideas wrong.

That is example what X tries to create on a daily basis. Chances are that you will fail, because the idea was actually too crazy to put into words, and nobody could imagine that it would ever work. Try to see failure as a lesson, as a means of improving and learning. In a culture of failing, fast and often, you might be lucky somehow come up with a crazy, out of the box solution to realize the most complicated part of the idea. Then continue with the second most complicated part of your innovation, and so on, and so on. Who knows if one day you will put that man on the moon. And everything fails, you learned a lot.

4. Perspective shift

Invite people from very different sectors who think about innovation the same way as you do. Chances are that this different perspective will bring you new ideas. For example, the Bioinformatics department at Erasmus Medical Center (Rotterdam) invites data scientists from the business world twice a year to think about medical data issues. The results are overwhelming. Data specialists from Dutch ABN-AMRO bank, for example, found a previously unknown group of genes that proved to be predictive of whether or not a specific treatment was effective for children with leukemia. These financial experts used techniques that are used to predict whether or not a particular financial transaction is fraudulent.

A change of perspective can make it easier to think out of the box, to aim for moonshot ideas. The trend in healthcare is the opposite: professionals tend to specialize themselves further, and that's great for the quality of care and research. The drive to become the best in your profession is great.

At the same time we have to realize that we might only create incremental improvements by specializing, by keeping a narrow focus. Of course, incremental improvements are essential and indispensable, but let's not forget to dream of 'a man on the moon' every now and then. Put the specialists and domain experts together, let them work on a topic or domain that is completely new for them. At REshape, we invited experts from ING Bank and the Royal Dutch Air Force, for instance.

5. No excuses, you can't lose

Remember learning 3: failing equals learning. Anyone who launches a moonshot idea, cannot actually fail. That is why there is no excuse not to start today.

The feeling of not being able to fail is familiar to the amateur club who has managed to get through to the last rounds in the soccer cup. Here is this local amateur club, suddenly finding itself in the competition against a professional soccer club. Public and press are all in favor or the underdog, the amateur club, and for a moment they seem to be the center of the world.

Nobody thinks the amateur club has a chance of winning against the professional athletes. So: they cannot lose. A counter goal is celebrated as if the amateur club won, even if they are defeated with 10-1. Every now and then, it happens that the amateur club wins. The energy and pride that the victory brings is often felt years later: it inspires all members, from the smallest junior teams to the club veterans.

And the victory pays off in terms of new membership registrations as well. The profit is therefore much greater than just the score from that one match. You see the parallel here with moonshot thinking? It inspires the entire organization, including people outside of the team, and it gives a direction and a shared goal. So I would urge you: put all your objections and excuses aside, just start working on your innovation, enjoy the journey together with colleagues or your team, and profit from these learnings. Who knows, your moonshot project might even turn out to be feasible.

6.Take smart risks all the time

Entrepreneurship is about taking risks. This philosophy is still not part of the culture in healthcare institutions. Yes, we see most Western healthcare systems as markets, yet we avoid the corresponding way of thinking about entrepreneurship and risks. Of course you should not take risks that you cannot overlook, and that is why it is important to apply lesson 3: fail fast. Try to continuously take calculated risks, small/big enough you still dare to explain if anything goes 'wrong'.

7.Believe

Having faith, in yourself and in your vision, is crucial for success. Whether it's about completing your studies, winning a sports competition or keeping up with a good habit, you need faith in your own abilities to get the most out of yourself and to dedicate yourself for something. So go for it!

8. Swim out of your element

Exit your comfort zone. The most important way we develop ourselves is by doing things that we find exciting. As we do them more often, the tension wears off and we get better and better at that seamingly scary or exciting task. Radical innovation is exciting and scary as well. You know one thing for sure: you will fail regularly. Failing might not be fun and it might sometimes even hurts. But you also know: no pain, no gain. Release the fear of failure and take a deep dive.

I also advise people to visit a conference once a year that does not cover their own specialty or work at all (see chapter Crossing the boundaries of our sector). Get out of your comfort zone: as a healthcare professional, visit a conference on engineering or stock trading. Who knows, you might find unexpected inspiration, something that you could translate to your own field or work.

9. Don't build a ladder to the moon

Want to reach the moon? Then don't built a ladder: it would take you decades to reach your goal. This is in line with the first commandment: don't focus at incremental improvements, aim for a moonshot project instead.

Yes, small steps are important, especially when it comes to medical innovations. But most of our healthcare systems are merely logistics. Aim for the moon: develop solutions or alternative care models in which logistics no longer yield any friction. A solution where patients can receive the care they need, at the place they want, at the moment they want it. This requires a different way of thinking than for instance negotiating with health insurers, or discussing a new partnership with the taxi company that provides wheelchair transportation. Again, there is nothing wrong with incremental improvements, but they will never take you to the moon.

10. Figure it out as you go

Radical innovation requires an iterative approach. When Kennedy expressed the wish to have a man on the moon within ten years, he did not provide a concrete development and implementation plan. He formulated a dream and thereby set people in motion, who gradually figured out how they could make that dream come true. You will have to work in very new ways, making it impossible to predict in advance how things will go. You will have to embrace that uncertainty. Colleagues that try to avoid uncertainty and doubt, you might not fit in the moonshot team, the team that shapes radical innovation. But these colleagues play an important role in a later phase, at the time you start scaling up your innovation (see the chapter The Digital (r)evolution).

Values of innovation

At the Radboudumc, this method of innovation is the foundation for the REshape & Innovation Center that we established in 2010. REshape acts as a sort of free state within the academic hospital, with the aim to try things out, to think about "the day after tomorrow" as Peter Hinssen calls it. It is a place where people are allowed to experiment with new technology and new models, a place where we encourage trial and error because we know we will learn from those mistakes.

We (have) experienced that the hospital finds our approach difficult at times, simply because this way of thinking does not fit in with the medical culture that aims to prevent errors at all times. This makes sense, considering the fact that the values of innovations are fundamentally different than the values of 'production'. For that, I like to use the <u>Bromford scheme</u>:

Values of Innovation	Values of Production
1. Openness	1. Excellence
2. Diversity	2. Loyalty
3. Serendipity	3. Dependability
4. Fairness	4. Success
5. Experimentation	5. Quality
6. Play	6. Precision
7. Giving	7. Reciprocity

B.

See how values as openness, experimentation and play are opposed to values precision, dependability and excellence?

At REshape, we also noticed that patients are more than willing to cooperate, even though we cannot give them any guarantee of the results in advance. Patients understand very well that (radical) innovation can fail, or leads to other outcomes than you hoped for. Of course patients hope for a positive outcome, but we noticed that they also want to share their experiences with experiments that are less successful, simply to let us learn from those experiences and events. This approach in turn inspires us, gives us the energy to work on future innovations. Energy to keep looking for moonshot ideas.

The innovation approach of 3M

An organization that is incredibly good in moonshot thinking is 3M. They work with three teams that fit the three phases of innovation that I have described in chapter The Digital (r)evolution. The 'Scouts' look for a big (moonshot) problem that is worth solving. This team then talks about this problem with hospitals, doctors, nurses and patients. They read all the studies that are published on this topic. This is how the Scout team develops an idea: their moonshot. This Scout team includes people from different backgrounds and with different visions: by combining these visions and experiences, they come up with fantastic ideas for innovation.

The Entrepreneurs team takes over when the innovation idea is formulated. It is up to them to come up with a prototype that shows that the initial idea works. Fail fast and fail often, is the adage for this team. And yes, many of those ideas also fail. But sometimes an idea survives this phase, with a working prototype as the result. At that moment, the Implementation team takes over. They ensure that the prototype is developed further into a product, and that processes are set up for production, distribution and sales.

At 3M, the roles in the teams are not fixed. People can change teams. Moreover, the type of challenges and areas that someone is working on, also change frequently. This creates a constant change of perspective, which is so vital to come up with new ideas. In addition, this method ensures that the knowledge that employees gained from earlier projects is not lost, but is being reused in other projects.

If you compare this 3M approach with EastmanKodak, you notice a incredible difference. Kodak (founded in 1881) was once one of the largest photography companies in the world, selling the first photo cameras and photographic films. Eastman Kodak stood at the cradle of digital photography in 1975, but failed to market this invention out of concern about the "classic" photo products. The competition eventually took over this "discovery" of digital photography, even though it was aKodak engineer who developed a working prototype in the most basic form.

This first prototype was still far from market introduction, but with this innovation Kodak had already made the leap from moonshot to a working prototype. Compared to our modern digital cameras, it was a huge device, that could take a digital image of 0.1Mb that could be rinsed on a cassette tape, which took 20 minutes. You would say at first glance: the most difficult part of the innovation work had already been done, with a working prototype. But the management of Kodak did not share the view that digital photography would completely change the market. After all, wasn't Kodak market leader? Was there even a business model if people no longer buy photographic film?

Eastman Kodak's competitors left the company behind, nearly bankrupt, when they took over the idea of digital photography. The business concepts that have emerged from it are very diverse, yet all have one thing in common: digital photography became big business.

CHAPTER 35

Eleven small learnings that will boost your innovation

Just as Chris McCarthy points out there are many definitions of 'innovation' in healthcare. I would like to add that 'innovation' is often seen as a process where someone else has to change. Everyone wants to innovate, but nobody really wants to change, it seems.

'Innovation' is almost a magic word: in every three sentences of business writing, the term 'innovation' drops in, most preferably 'disruptive innovation'. But <u>what innovation</u> really is, and where innovation ends and <u>regular process-improvement begins</u>, will probably always remain a fuzzy line. And in my honest opinion, the definition doesn't matter much, once an idea hits your brain and you want to work on it.

I have been 'in innovation' in healthcare for the last seven years. And while you could write entire encyclopedias on healthcare and innovation, I decided to share some of our learnings in these 11 bullet points:

1. Failure acceptance is one of the basics of innovation. We might even learn more from our failures than our successes. Honda founder Sochiro Honda said: "<u>Success is 99% failure</u>."

2. Opposing, but equal forces, cancel each other out according to <u>Newton's third law</u>. So, there has to be inequality in play in innovation - just like any other process - to create movement. Without movement, we will experience a standstill. This inequality might concern quality, cost, or the impact of the innovation. Without some inequality or friction, you might say that there is no innovation.

3. Set a beneficiary feedback loop for innovation. Everything starts with listening, as I pointed out in <u>my first TED.com talk</u> back in 2011. Take the opinions and experiences of your customer or target group(s) into account. Create a methodology to gather, analyze and evaluate their authentic voices and feedback. It appeared we stopped listening to our targeted groups, which led all kinds of problems, especially at the implementation phase. At REshape, our Chief Listening Officer program evolved into what we call a Human Centered Design approach. By using the principles of service design, test if your innovation really provides a solution to a problem. Often, ideas are merely a problem looking for a solution. With this feedback loop and focus on the customer or target group, you should also take the ethical aspects of innovation into an account (often said but seldomly done).

4. Make Small Smart Groups. Or KSG-tjes, as I called them in Dutch (Kleine Slimme groepjes). These Small Smart Groups unite all targeted stakeholders at the table. Don't make your groups too big. Amazon CEO Jeff Bezos calls this the Two-Pizza Team: the perfect team is small enough to share <u>2 pizzas</u>.

5. You know about what I call the Idea and Innovation killers, right? Notions like 'It can't be done', money, legislation and privacy are all (mis)used as barriers and contra-arguments for innovation. When I started the REshape Center, I promised colleagues I would take care of these innovation killers at a later time. We even declared "It cannot be done", "Money", "Legislation" and "Privacy" as forbidden words in the ideation phase. Using these barriers prevents us from getting to the real point and thinking creatively. Take care of them once you have figured out your idea, opportunity and need.

6. Luck is part of innovation, just as serendipity is. Don't wait for finding your luck, or expect serendipity to occur at an instant, nor build your company on one of both. Both luck and serendipity are part of innovation: they come in the form of sudden unexpected pathways that surface, developments in the world that happen, and can be part of making your innovation a success.

7. Start working with the ones that DO believe in your innovation. This approach is called the Coalition of the willing and it can be vital for your innovation process. Do not waste time persuading critical colleagues to become members. Do not wait for others if they are not willing or skeptical. It will cost you more energy to convince 1% of them than to get a lot of others on board if your innovation really is worth it.

8. Although innovation has to occur in every department, it might pay off to organize or create a separate unit working on specific topics or approaches. This can be a

head of innovation, a team, or a completely new business unit or company, either working under the wings of your organization or separately. This approach will also prevent the risk of "discussing the x-mas menu with the turkey". Always aim to report to highest authority in the company: this is crucial. You might even end up creating your own competitor in your own company.

9. Try to make a projection of the gap between having the innovation in place and the current situation. Take for instance the model for cash streams from Clayton Christensen of Harvard.

10. Take a long deep breath and just start! It's easy to talk for months and months about what could happen, but you can learn how to cycle only by getting on a bicycle and just starting. Sometimes, getting started is the greatest difficulty. But only by starting to really work on your idea or innovation, will you gain experience, test your assumptions and create a dynamic interaction with stakeholders, customers and team members.

11. And last but finally not least: have fun! I find this one of the most important lessons: innovation should be fun. It's about exploring new worlds together. Discovering new options and endeavors together is the most beneficial when it is a playful experience.

As I said before: you could write entire books on innovation do's and don'ts. I hope these eleven small learnings will spark some creativity and enthusiasm. We've talked about luck and serendipity. Here's one last learning that I would like to share as well: create serendipity.

Gaining innovation ideas? Create serendipity

New discoveries can arise in two ways. One way is to try to find a solution to a problem that you experience. So you become very focused on looking for innovation. The other way is coincidence. Now people often think that you can not trigger inventions that happen to occur; you have to wait until it happens to you. Nothing could be further from the truth. You can come up with great ways to help the coincidence.

Many accidental findings often arise because 'something' that has been developed for one problem can be applied to a completely different problem. That 'something' can be a ready-made product, but also a concept or idea. The famous yellows of 3M are a good example of this. The company 3M wanted to develop a new type of glue. The 'yellows glue' was initially a rejected test result, until someone from outside the innovation team devised a completely new application. The <u>Post-it</u> was born.

This form of innovation - the creation of chance encounters or discoveries - is also common in the medical world. An example is Erasmus MC, where internist immunologist Prof. Martin van Hagen 'shops' at pharmacies for anti-cancer medication that is not strong enough to attack the cancer, but which is very promising for some rare immune disorders. Because the degree of aggression needed for cancer therapy is not desirable or even contraindicated for immune diseases. But such a non-aggressive drug can be ideal if you just want to slow down processes that work too hard and do not completely shut down..

These are examples of coincidence that arise by looking for other applications within the own world of glue or medication.

A step further is to look outside your own world for ideas or applications in completely different sectors. I always advise my colleagues to go to a congress in a totally different field at least once a year. So I am not talking about a dermatologist who attends a cardiology conference, I'm talking about a doctor who goes to an event about supply chain management (see also the vignette of Michiel Muller, founder of online supermarket Picnic). Or about a nurse who attends a congress on space travel (see the Space Health contribution from Jules Lancee).

The REshape Center organizes an annual group trip to the Exponential Medicine event. Last year, the innovation boss of the Royal Dutch Air Force was one of the participants. The conversations that arose between him and people from the care sector provided all the inspiration for innovation.

The beauty is the simplicity with which you can create this coincidence. Talk to your neighbor - who works in a very different field - about a problem that concerns you. Get inspiration from the people with whom you, for example, do sport with.

The drinks together afterwards is a perfect moment to brainstorm about possible cross-links. Organize an event that brings together people from different mindsets and from different sectors. REshape does this, for example, with the TEDx conferences, where more than a thousand people from different backgrounds and different blood groups arrive.

But we also do it with our breakfast every Wednesday, where people from inside and outside Radboudumc can freely join. And we do it with the Dutch Hacking Health hackathons that we regularly organize and where now six other UMCs will be hooked up. This idea is also copied in other sectors of healthcare. Recently, for example, 21 organizations in the care for the mentally disabled organized a similar event.

What matters is that you do not have to wait for unexpected twists, but you can <u>create them yourself</u>.

CHAPTER 36

"We need an innovation atlas"
(vignette)

Maarten Steinbuch is Distinguished University
Professor at the Eindhoven University of
Technology and a part-time entrepreneur. He
has established several companies focused on
(healthcare) robotics.

We need a system reversal in healthcare, according to Maarten
Steinbuch. There is no lack of pilots, but what is missing is an
"atlas for collaboration and innovation", so that you can see - at
a glance - what is happening. "This innovation atlas helps us to
see where the bottlenecks are and where opportunities lie. It
creates a structural way to work together, to jointly design this
healthcare transition."

Lucien: If you look at society and healthcare from your
role, as entrepreneur and professor at the Eindhoven University
of Technology, what should change? What is your vision for
healthcare in 2030?

Maarten: "I hope the patient will really be central in 2030,
because despite all the roaring texts on websites, that is still not the
case today. Everything revolves around the healthcare provider
instead of the patient. I think we will see an 'Uberization' of

care: digital, close to the patient or client, making maximum use of data.

My own domain is robotization, and we are on the brink of some big changes in that area. At the moment, care robots are mostly used as social robots, or as warning systems that are using sensors. But we are working hard on robots that can also perform physical tasks, such as taking a carton of milk from the fridge.

These robots will actually be used in 2030, making it possible to assist elderly people to live at home considerably longer. Apart from these social or task-oriented robots, I also work on high-specialized robots for surgeons, who can assist surgeons with delicate or intensive medical procedures such as eye operations. As a result, less trained surgeons can perform complex operations, and surgeons will be well equipped to operate even at a higher age. This allows us to solve the shortage of trained surgeons in poor countries and improve the quality of operations."

Lucien: Putting the patient first is something that we indeed hear a lot, but don't see often. I use the metaphor of Copernicus: he discovered that the sun does not revolve around the earth, but the other way around. Healthcare professionals must also have such a Copernicus moment, realizing that the system does not revolve around them but around the patient, as the center of their universe.

Maarten: "That's true, and the good thing is: digitization will accelerate this process. If we currently talk about data in healthcare, then care providers still think of a database in which they store all the information about their patients. However, data just sits there: healthcare providers do not do anything with it.

Using this data and gaining new insights are vital for the digital transformation that healthcare institutions are experiencing.

The difficult thing for our branch is that in healthcare - unlike in other branches or companies - many different value models are intertwined. All these value chains and models will have to be unraveled in order to digitize them. That's not a simple task. Sometimes, I would like to put a piece dynamite in the system to blow it up!

I think of it in this way: money always follows the easiest path. It is just like water: it flows to the lowest point and searches the path of the least resistance. So, we need new business models. I like to draw a parallel to electric driving. At first, governments had to help with financial benefits and grants for electric driving. Then, there comes a moment when electric driving becomes cheaper than our fuel based transport. We need to create such a situation in healthcare as well, a stimulus for digitized, new business models."

Lucien: What could that stimulus for care look like?

Maarten: "From Eindhoven University of Technology, we want to do this with the Eindhoven Engine, an initiative that brings together research institution, knowledge centers and companies. In this larger initiative, we can achieve and accelerate system reversal in domains where technology is or becomes dominant. Care is one of those domains. In the Eindhoven Engine we work together with various parties on well-defined, agile projects with an unambiguous goal, clear deadlines and financing, so we show what digitization can bring.

Next step would be to bring all those projects together in an atlas for the whole of the Netherlands, so that knowledge and experiences are easily shared, preventing the "not invented here" syndrome and working on coherence instead of fragmentation."

Lucien: And what happens if we miss this opportunity?

Maarten: "I'm afraid we will be become a marginal player, overthrown by some American technology giant who has a razor sharp focus on their customer and overthrows all the barriers that impede optimal customer service. It is up to caregivers, insurers and the government to choose: are we going to let international companies determine the future of our national healthcare system? Or do I want to help determine the direction of this transition, by taking a proactive approach to current obstacles in the area of financing and legislation?

CHAPTER 37

Future crooks (in medicine)

Why there is no such thing as 100% safety and security

In my lectures, I always talk about the absurdity of making the case that all technology and processes should be a 100% safe, secure and private. 100% safety and security is an illusion. As long as we know, even the 'most secure' systems get hacked, since there will always be someone smarter than the smartest system. These days, you can even buy zero day exploits or DDoS attacks on the dark web. Cyber crime is for sale, and only costs you a few bucks. There is no such thing as a 100% safety and security guarantee. Of course, we should always strive to make products as safe, secure and private as possible!

This notion of '100%', that we hear in political discussion as well, even turns into an ethical or moral question, it seems to me. What happens when politicians, companies and advocate groups argue that products should be 100% safe, or else these products are flawed? They create goals that cannot be reached, thereby running the risk of blocking innovations.

We should do our utmost to prevent anything bad happening with our data, our records and our identity. But in this hyper-connected world, it is an illusion to think that policymakers in other country will 'prevent' or 'block' bad things happening in another country.

I thought it would make sense to share a video of <u>Marc Goodman</u>, <u>colleague faculty</u> at Singularity University's Exponential Medicine, with you. In <u>this talk</u> he gave at vision on crime in the future, at TED Global in 2012. The world is becoming increasingly open, and that has implications both bright and dangerous, as Marc Goodman points out. A good read afterwards is this <u>Wired article</u> from his hand together with (also SU Faculty) Andrew Hessel.

If you are intrigued by Marc Goodman's talk, and his notion that technology's rapid development could allow crime to take a turn for the worse, also make sure to get a copy of his book "Future Crimes". After seeing his talk, or reading his book, you might even be more concerned. But now let's try to re-balance the risks and our normal life a bit more than we are doing right now, since there is no such thing as 100% safety and security.

CHAPTER 38

How one case can set a whole sector back for years

The case of Theranos

LinkedIn Update April 16th, 2016

That's all folks, I have to admit I have lost faith in this going the right way as in being a credible real innovation that could've helped boost innovation in healthcare and solve some of our challenges. With all the recent developments (Fox created a manual how to blow $9B in 6 months) from the side of the FDA and the Wall Street Journal's ongoing investigation into Theranos, the company fails to adequately reply to these facts.

I really did hope Theranos was going to be 'proof' of the real, exponential shift that's going, as you can read in my blog below. But unfortunately, Theranos did exactly the opposite. This case will help the naysayers, the laggards and the critics to point out the flaws in the system, even when other authentic, credible, sincere people try to change healthcare.

That's too bad. No, I will not lose faith in change, nor in all the innovation that is going on. As I state in all of my keynotes: "There were crooks in the Middle Ages, and there will be in the future." And yes, it looks like we will also have some crooks today. Yes, healthcare is a very regulated branch and must remain a regulated market. Because we don't want flawed, unsafe medical technology coming into the market.

Over the course of the past weeks there has been a lot of media coverage about the Silicon Valley company Theranos, founded by <u>Elizabeth Holmes</u>. "With a couple drops of blood, she is able to process up to 200 tests for a couple of dollars, that would normally cost you hundreds of dollars" was my statement during the keynotes and lectures I delivered at numerous occasions.

As a Stanford dropout that started her own diagnostics company at 19, Elizabeth Holmes certainly is the poster child for innovation in healthcare, gracing the cover of magazines like Forbes, Quote and others.

The promise of Theranos - delivering painless tests, with faster results, comparable to the industry standard - appeared to be false. As the Wall Street Journal exposed out in a series of articles, the supposedly transformative diagnostic technology was flawed. Holmes knew (and lied) about it.

I will not dive into all the controversies, you can read that anywhere online. It seems that - mainly due to the expected transparency - Holmes has fell into disgrace, even by the magazines and publications that put her on a pedestal for years. Her biggest competitors - laboratories in de United States - might find some comfort in the current situation as well, now that this 'disruptor' is gone.

What's also not helping is the lack of transparency at Theranos, and the wrong (strategic) choices in communication. <u>Sometimes innovation fails</u> or doesn't work out the way it was thought of, that's all part of the game.

Elizabeth's mission clearly resonated with me in terms of changing healthcare into a more patient oriented sphere, bringing the costs down and user-experience up. Theranos' mission fits clearly into my 4D model (see chapter 4D bird's eye view), where I use 4 global, driving forces. Aim of Theranos was bringing diagnostic services near people (<u>Delocalization</u>), and by providing them with their own data (<u>Digital</u>) they can start to choose who to share it with (<u>Democratization</u>), all the while drilling down costs (Dollars). Also, Theranos technology had the potential to strengthen the power of patients to ignite <u>Patients Owned Research</u>.

One point is frequently missed in the developing Theranos story in the media, in my honest opinion. That is the price point Theranos offers for their services. Even if the technology that Elizabeth Holmes used is not their own proprietary system but build on commercially available lab equipment, she still has been able to drill down the costs up to sometimes even 10-fold of the diagnostics tests. That at least questions the current pricing of the existing laboratories and could be seen as an achievement on its own, don't you think?

Secondly, I think there is an extra burden on the shoulders of Elizabeth, a burden that has a major impact. I still think someone is not 'guilty' unless proven 'guilty', so no changed opinion at this side yet, although cautions following the story for facts, as opposed to opinions. I think this could also touches how we 'run' <u>ethics in healthcare technology</u>. But IF the critics are proven to be right, it will ignite a setback for all of us working in health(care) innovation globally. It will bring strong arguments to the hands of the critics who -with the well know 'I won't say I said you so' - start using "Theranos-Gate" as exemplifier to debunk any innovation that questions, tackles, or changes the current status quo of health(care).

However this may end, it will be in the history books (or Wikipedia ;-) of healthcare as a turning point. Yes, this is part of innovation and that is clearly known by those who are in this field to <u>lead instead of following</u>. The narrow line between truth and reality, between sharing and keeping your knowledge is sometimes like accelerating with the handbrake on, meanwhile trying to catch the next train.

Dear Elizabeth: I really hope that with your strong willpower, confidence in your own mission and perseverance, you will be able to give the data and information needed to debunk the myth on Theranos. Not being able to do the things you committed almost half of your life to must be a terrible state of mind. A lot of people out here are having hope that every now and then a breakthrough in healthcare occurs, like the one you are striving for. Of course you are entitled to keep your proprietary technology knowledge as long as possible, but by now this situation has impacted not only Theranos but many stakeholders and companies around Theranos.

I salute you as well, your vision and persistence are an example for me and many others. We both use a quote of Gandhi, I still trust this to be true in the end. First they ignore you, then they laugh at you, then they fight you, then you win.

LinkedIn Update 29/10: Just for the record, based on some comments, I wanted to make sure what my position in this discussion is. I am not choosing a side as in whether it (if Theranos is capable and compliant) is true or not true (like the title suggests). I think this blog (and also the comments) reflect my opinion on that. As I wrote above, the mission Elisabeth is on is still also mine "...of changing healthcare into a more patient oriented sphere, bringing the costs down and user-experience up...." Whether or not Theranos is living up to that and complies to the rules, or if journalism has taken an incorrect path, is not up to me, nor to a lot of the people who start blaming others already.This should be a proper regulatory or even legal trajectory (as I think this will become, as I read the <u>latest Wired article</u> on this.)

CHAPTER 39

Digital transformation and leadership (vignette)

"The care will have to change first "

Maarten van Rixtel is chairman of the board of directors at Sensire, member of the board of Omaha, and the Dutch Neighborhood Nursing Association (Nederlands Wijkverpleegkundig genootschap).

Professionals in the long-term care, home care and elderly care have long believed that their sector would not be digitized. Apart from some useful apps and sensors, home and long-term care could not be digitized, according to many. Slowly, care organizations are beginning to realize that they too cannot escape a real transformation. Sensire is one of the leaders in this transformation in the Netherlands. We spoke with Sensire board member Maarten van Rixtel about the transformation in his sector.

Lucien: What do you think care will look like in 2030? What do professionals at Sensire do, by then? And do your employees share the image you have of the future as well?

Maarten: "That is an exciting question, because in the long-term care sector we have only began thinking about this issue fairly recently. In the care - long-term care, home care and elderly care - we have long thought: this sector is all about contact. Digitalization mainly takes place in hospitals, in diagnostics and other sectors.

Only in the last three or four years has it dawned on us that we also have to digitize. Most healthcare professionals see it as a shift from physical work to 'doing some things digitally'. It is still a very instrumental approach. That is not surprising, because care providers are fairly conservative in nature. They work with the health of others, you do not want to experiment with that. So yes, a conservative attitude is good, but that conservatism should not be translated to: we will continue to work exactly the same way we are used to."

Lucien: Society is changing, clients are also changing. The health care sector does not take that much into account. Most classic business models are organization-centric, not client-centric. Our care is shaped around the professional. This naturally leads professionals to thinking that they can also determine how they work, I think. How should care organizations tackle the change?

Maarten: "The most important task of directors and board members in healthcare is facilitating, realizing it is not about them but about clients and healthcare providers. If you do not realize that digitization is not something you can do on top off your existing processes, but requires a change in your current model, you need to stop doing what you're doing. With that mindset, in ten years' time healthcare will no longer be affordable."

Lucien: That raises the question: who will make the first move? Because all stakeholders - the politicians, insurers, healthcare organizations - have locked each other in.

Maarten: "In the future, we will see parties that do put the patient or client first, who facilitate people with their demand for care from the beginning to the end, and who can predict exactly what these people need at the time on the basis of data.

This will happen in all sub-sectors of health care, but perhaps first in the care, because the urgency is greatest there. In the care, the largest personal financial contribution of people is asked. That makes clients susceptible to alternatives.

Moreover, the elderly of these days are digitally skilled. They want to keep the control themselves, as long as possible, and want to live in their own homes for as long as possible. You can already see all sorts of commercial services that focus on that development. Through digitalization, the supply of these services only gets bigger. Coming from that service and home care sector, these developments will also slowly penetrate the nursing care. "

Lucien: What about American tech giants, such as Apple and Amazon, who are even starting their own healthcare clinics, choosing the route of well-being and prevention. What role do these parties play in long-term and even home care?

Maarten: "I think people have more and more money to buy comfort. I do not mean comfort in the sense of luxury, but comfort in the sense of: I want to make my world predictable and to anticipate a physical or mental decline. I want to arrange things now in order to be able to keep control at a later phase in my life. People already think about the follow-up in the initial phase of their illness. For example: how do I prevent my social circle from shrinking if I am less able to move? That is why Sensire has established a venture capital company that focuses on the early stages of chronic diseases. In that phase you can really make the difference."

"Traditionally, the healthcare sector is characterized by risk avoidance. That leads to a fear of investing, but we desperately need investments, especially across the entire chain: in hospital, GP's office, home-care and elderly care, etc. We have to share the costs, but also the proceeds.

As a healthcare provider, I especially need room to invest. If I see how much I have invested in the past few years, and look at the return on those investments and the lack of extra turnover or additional sales, I find that difficult. Colleagues or companies that do not invest, have a higher margin. That situation should be fixed. Ultimately, insurers and healthcare providers must become partners in innovation."

Lucien: What you are actually saying is that insurers have to let go of their short term horizon, focused on return on their investments, and look more towards the long term?

Maarten: "That is exactly why I stepped down of the board of ActiZ. We talked about initiatives to achieve outcome and population based financing, but there was no agenda for 2030. In the end, it become just another classic project.

We can not change the world with projects like these, we need radical innovation. You do not want to change something on the edge of the system, you want to change the system at its core. You can only do that if you take a long term horizon, the agenda for 2030, as a starting point and use that to extrapolate your next steps in the coming years."

Lucien: The famous Dutch soccer player Johan Cruyff always said: football is simple. You don't have to be where the ball is, but where the ball is going.

Maarten: "Yes, and that is why I get agitated that so little is happening, because everyone can see where the ball is going. There is hardly any discussion about it: we all see that the demand for care increases, the budget stays the same and that we have to arrange care differently. But what do we do? We keep our basic healthcare system the same, put some additional digital technology on top off it. Doing digital instead of being digital, I would call it.

Real change requires leadership. A few leaders are really sharpening and executing their vision, but they are seen by the majority of their colleagues as outliers. They pose a threat to the status quo. The hardest part for board members and directors is to keep going. Change is necessary."

CHAPTER 40

"There isn't a problem with medicine, there is a problem with leadership in healthcare" (vignette)

Interview with Simon Sinek, by Lucien Engelen and Yvonne Keyzer, printed in ICT & Health magazine 2017

In 2011 Simon Sinek spoke at the Radboudumc organized TEDx Maastricht, where he baffled the audience with his view on leadership. Sinek is best known for his concept of the Golden Circle (2009). Today Simon Sinek teaches leaders and organizations how to inspire people. So we couldn't wait to speak to him about the changes and future of healthcare. And again, he surprises us with his insights on leadership and human relationships. "Technology is making us better. But we must remember that we are in inter-personate relationships."

The changes we are seeing in healthcare, not only technology, but also leadership are more and more embedded in every curriculum in healthcare. Do you see leadership has changed since your speech at TEDx in Maastricht in 2011?

"Well, to start with: it's almost embarrassing that I have a career on this. It's obvious that people are not yet pleased and satisfied with their leaders. There seems to be momentum for this. So yes, I see change. But we still have a lot of work to do. The vast majority of organisations is still working as usual."

How does this apply for healthcare?

"I fear hospitals are some of the worst examples of leadership. It may sound strange, but too many administrators and board members think of their patients. And that's wrong. They have to think about their employees: the doctors and nurses. They have to think of it as a job. They must manage. And of course; in their turn, doctors and nurses; they must think of their patients."

"The workload in hospitals is massive. Of course I am talking about the United States, but I imagine this is the same in the Netherlands. There are too many accidental accidents, some by little, simple mistakes like a chart that's in the wrong place. These things happen too often. In the USA alone, there are about 250.000 accidents like these each year."

"I myself have a trauma of a recent experience. A very, very good friend of mine had a miscarriage. We rushed to the hospital, but she didn't receive any help until, after a lot of time, she signed oa form. She couldn't even go to the bathroom to wash her hands, which were covered in blood, prior to having signed this form. On top of that, she was tested five times. And worse: somebody even congratulated her with her pregnancy. Mistake on mistake on mistake. And this ought to be just a routine process. Nothing extraordinary or fancy. All and all, she was 13 hours in hospital. It was awful."

"So no, there is no problem with medicine, clearly the evidence for interventions is there, but there is a problem with leadership. The leaders must see the hospital as a business and manage it like that and facilitate doctors and nurses to treat their patients properly and in a humane manner."

The interesting thing is that we in hospitals in The Netherlands treat patients more and more as partners. We give patients choices and meaning. What do you think about that?

"You have to take patients out of the equation. That is not the issue. The point is: do staff members feel that their leaders care about them? It seems scary but that is the right question to ask. But this is the discussion that is missing. We never discuss this topic in hospitals. I don't care about the quality of this industry. It is generic of this industry, it's like expecting the plumber to plumb, right ? We have to take care of the people that work in this field. And then they can take care of patients."

People in healthcare are also aging. We are getting a younger generation on board. What about millennials?

"There are a few things happening to this generation that we tend to neglect with millennials. First, they are subject to another parenthood than we have experienced. They were all little princes and princesses. When they failed at school, their parents were complaining. But, as soon as they get a job, this changes. They have to take care of themselves. And they are not used to this. So they get stressed out."

"Secondly, there is a huge amount of technology in their lives like cell phones and social media. And every time they receive a notification or a 'Like', a little bit of dopamine gets released in their brain. As you know: dopamine is addictive. And remember, we are talking about kids here. There is no age restriction on using a phone."

"So this is a highly stressful time for young adults. It's like an addiction to alcohol, when every time you drink, you feel better. The same is happening with phones and social media.

The kids look great when they go online, but their self-esteem is low. They are like ducks, they look happy, but nobody knows they are kicking as hell with their duck legs."

"This addiction to technology is destroying their relationship with other people. So, we do see a rising rate of young adults with depression. But we are only treating the symptoms. It's like we see an epidemic level of drug overdose, but we don't do anything about the cause."

"This is going to be a big healthcare problem. And the healthcare system has to deal with that. In fact it is a twofold problem: healthcare has to deal with this addiction causing mental health problems and we have to take socializing skills in the curriculum of these future doctors and nurses. They have to incorporate coping mechanisms to deal with real live relationships."

There is already a big problem of burned out physicians. What do you think about this?

"More and more people will drop out of jobs. It has everything to do with the quality of healthcare. So there should be an emphasize in the curriculum on how to manage real-time conversations and relations in healthcare. They need support and they need real communities."

"How can healthcare help them? Firstly you must publish about technology addiction. It must be put on the agenda. And secondly doctors and nurses must learn social skills. We must emphasize the need for a reduction of use of cell phones. You see, it's happening, They ask for help. The younger generation needs this."

"So I want doctors and nurses to talk to each other, instead of just e-mailing a note. Because in interpersonal relationships magical things happen. It's not only about non-verbal communication. It's about the fact that ideas arise when you are talking with somebody. Just talking about a problem can bring new ideas to the table. And that's not happening when you are only available through email."

"Young adults must learn and be aware of this kind of communication. I can't emphasize enough how important this is."

Great points, Simon. Do you think mindfulness techniques will help?

"Yes, the technique is great, but the marketing of mindfulness is all wrong. It's great for creating awareness, of being present and provide focus. But we will have to find a way to better communicate this. People don't want mindfulness because of the looks of it."

"We will have to communicate it by its USP's. It's like the 'People don't want to buy a quarter-inch drill, they want a quarter-inch hole'-thing (quote from Theodore Levitt, red). We need to focus on social, teamwork, feeling. And talk about this with these young adults."

Back to your books and the StartwithWhy. I have a question from Raymon Klein, one of the founders of Layar. The golden circle starts with why. But shouldn't it start with who?

"No, who is so obvious. The golden circle is based on human decision making. The who is incorporated, it's already there. Why we do things, what we do and how we do things all relate to who. Without who there is nothing."

So, if you start with 'why', is it possible for an organisation to change this why over the course of time?

"I don't think so, once you've established the why, you can't change it. But you can change the way to come to your why. Let me give an example. There is healthcare, and there is care for your health. It sounds like a little change, but it isn't. The way to get to healthier people is very different. Care for health is a broader and expending way to come to the why."

"This is a major insight, because it is just what we are experiencing right now in healthcare."

What's your vision on technology in healthcare?

"Technology is making us better. That is really remarkable. But we must remember that we are in inter-personate relationships. We must not forget how big this impact is. For instant, when a doctor sees a patient who just comes out of a crash and is heavily injured, he will probably say: 'he is a fighter, he won't give up.' That sentence alone can really help this patient. We often take these interpersonal and social components for granted, but we must not. A doctor of nurse with good bedside manners, delivers better care. I am convinced of that."

"Working in healthcare is still an inter-personate job. And most healthcare workers are doing this because they want to help each other. We sometimes tend to forget this. But feedback, listening; these are qualities we don't want to throw away."

About Simon:

Simon Sinek (1973) earned a Bachelor's degree (BA) in cultural anthropology from Brandeis University. Currently he is professor at Columbia University, founder of Sinek Partners (Corporate Refocusing) and author. He is best known for popularizing the concept of "the golden circle" and to "Start With Why". Simon Sinek is also an adjunct staff member of the RAND Corporation. He is renowned for many quotes. Our favourites are "If we were good at everything we would have no need for each other" and "The trick to balance is to not make sacrificing important things become the norm".

Publications and books by Simon Sinek et al.

- 2014. Leaders Eat Last: Why Some Teams Pull Together and Others Don't. Portfolio Hardcover; 1ST edition (January 7, 2014), ISBN-10: 1591845327, ISBN-13: 978-1591845324.

- 2011. Why Entrepreneurs Love Steve Jobs. Entrepreneur.com, retrieved from http://www.entrepreneur.com/article/220491.

- 2009. Start with why. Retrieved December, 5, 2012.

- 2009. How great leaders inspire action.

- 2009. Start with why: How great leaders inspire everyone to take action. Penguin.

CHAPTER 41

The digital patient: a double-edged sword?

In November 2016 the (independent) health charity Nuffield Trust published a report on the digitalization of primary care by the 'Digital patient''. The report reviews the evidence that exists on digital technology and its impact on patients in primary care. Although the focus of the publication is the on the British National Health Services (NHS), nonetheless there are useful insights on the emergence of the 'digital patient'.

According to Nuffield Trust, patient-facing technology has shown promising results for improving care for patients, reducing the burden on the healthcare service. Digital services offered by the NHS such as monitoring technology, online triage and booking tools, online access to records and care plans and remote consultations hold great promise for patients, particularly for people with long-term conditions such as diabetes or COPD.

However, this rapidly evolving market comes with risks. Many apps, tools and devices have not been officially evaluated, meaning that their effectiveness is unknown. In some cases, technology can increase demand for services, disengage staff and have the potential to disrupt the way that patients access care.

Moreover, the report warns that policy-makers and politicians should avoid assuming that self-care-enabling technology will produce significant savings, at least in the short term.

The report also presents a series of lessons and recommendations to NHS professionals, leaders and policy-makers about how best to harness the potential of technology and avoid the pitfalls. The lead author of the report, Sophie Castle-Clark states: "This technology could be a double-edged sword, and there's still a lot we don't know. Without regulation and a careful look at the evidence - not all of which is compelling - these digital tools could compromise the quality of care and disrupt the way care is provided."

The NHS has launched numerous pilots and projects to experiment, explore and validate new technology. One of the earliest projects was the NHS App store, a growing library of tested and validated health apps by NHS professionals, launched in 2013.

The NHS itself did not develop apps,but provided existing health apps with an NHS quality mark in their Health Apps Library. Two years later, the project came to an end, after the App store became scrutinized when researchers showed that a large part of the apps recommended by NHS generated serious privacy threats and were not proven effective.

Meanwhile, the app project of the British National Health Service has been pivoted and launched again. The current App store is still in beta version, and the exploding amount of mobile health apps makes it difficult to develop a research framework and locate time, money and people for the review process.

The work of the NHS and this report of the Nuffield Trust

point in the same direction: both maintain a techno-optimistic approach, with a skeptical view on the scientific validation of new digital tools. And that is exactly the attitude and approach we maintain as Radboud University Medical center through our REshape Center. We are cautiously optimistic about new digital services and tools, while we gather more and more scientific validation and evidence. So that might make us techno-realists ;-)

THEME 4:

Where to start?

CHAPTER 42

9 shifts of Digital DNA framework in translation

A bit of guidance to the "current' world and the "next" world in this digital transformation of health(care).

I often talk about these two worlds that exist within I think every organization, at present often referred to as the "old world" and the "new world". Although some like to think that there's only one world, from my experience in the past seven years and also from the research literature out there, I do think there are indeed two worlds, with a difference in governance, culture, finance model, legislation, and also mindset. While the "old" world is optimizing within the boundaries of existing paradigms, the "new" world tends to try to translate a current paradigm into a new one.

As described in this book, I really do think that new players use business models with new user interfaces that are going to change (the face) healthcare as we know it.

There is no good or bad in this equation, the old world and the new world do exist and have to coexist, as a matter of fact they have to blend in the end of the day.

So as "old' and "new" have this negative connotation I rather speak about the "current" world and the "next" world from now on. Keeping the things that are good in the current world, using the things that can improve from the next world, should be the mission for the era we live in.

I often use the metaphor of highways where the current world is a lane and the next world is one as well, together they will merge at the end of the road in a gradual way. Sometimes the turns will be sharp, sometimes more gradual. A thorough approach has never been more needed, as some international (tech) companies are eyeing in the healthcare sector.

In the research for this book, I also wanted to give some guidance in how to possibly approach the challenges I had, coming out of this digital transformation. During the process, time and time again I reached out to the work that Deloitte has done in this realm. It appeared they really had picked up the signals of the things leading to this transformation early, and tried to make sense out of it in terms of an approach for organizations.

The interviews I had with them about getting to know more about their work, gradually turned into a partnership to co-create this chapter of my book.

Again, it is not a handbook, nor a blueprint or a generic approach. It's more a framework for the different steps one could set to see whether or not they're ready for the challenges lying ahead, and to offer some assistance.

To cover all of the aspects touching this transformation processes, Deloitte has identified nine shifts that are specific for this digital transformation, that I translated it into a healthcare setting with its specialties and its culture. So below you will find a blend of the work done by Deloitte Digital and mine over the last year. At present we are blending these strains as I was recently appointed, next to my roles at Radboudumc, as an Edge fellow for the Deloitte Center for the Edge, taking on the role as Global Strategist Digital Health.

A first step in translating Digital DNA framework into a health(care) setting, in close collaboration with Deloitte Andries van Dijk , Hans van Grieken and Mathieu van Bergen.

Introducing the nine big shifts

The digital evolution is impacting the way we work, the resources we use, and the nature of technology itself. If organizations hope to respond swiftly to change, reap the business benefits of new digital innovation, and attract top-tier talent in the future, their TOMs (Technology Operating Model) must evolve accordingly.

For a lot of organizations however, the digital strategy that they have identified does not fit their current (traditional) Technology Operating Model (TOM): it's like trying to fit a UK plug into a US Power socket or to fit a square peg into a round hole as they say. In the scheme below, created for financial services, one could easily see the almost 1:1 resemblances for healthcare.

To help address these challenges, Deloitte has identified nine big shifts that will influence the model of the future and that need to be addressed in conjunction with each other, since they are highly interdependent.

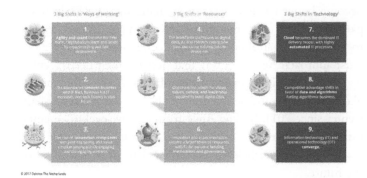

© 2017 Deloitte The Netherlands

Big shifts in the way we work

1. Agility and speed

The new paradigm of the digital economy is 'speed over perfection'. As disruption becomes more pervasive, organizations need a new strategic approach - one that positions them to change course in real time based on current realities. The centuries old model where doctors and boards control how health(care) is being delivered, no longer is valid enough. New players use different 'game-play', don't have the legacy we carry around and certainly have a different mindset and ambition. That means institutions must hone the ability to test multiple IT innovations and process models, rapidly measure their effectiveness, and learn from their successes and failures in real time. Two approaches that offer the greatest potential to provide this speed of delivery are Agile and DevOps.

Agile : Agile is based on realizing new features in short sprints of 2-3 weeks by multi-disciplinary teams. It eliminates the boundaries between operations and IT, allowing the two functions to become better aligned - essentially replacing one IT business partner with a cross-functional development team - leading to increased organizational agility. To be effective, institutions must approach Agile in a way that best fits their needs - either by taking a hybrid approach, or combining Agile with concepts like Lean startup and design thinking like we did in our REshape Center since 2011. Scaling Agile from a team level to an enterprise level is incredibly challenging - often taking years of hard work - but is nevertheless an essential element of the TOM of the future.

DevOps : End-to-end Agile extends beyond the development phase to include deployment and operations as well. This is called DevOps, a culture that promotes close collaboration between development and operations. The objective of DevOps is to release software and new process schemes more rapidly, more frequently, and more reliably. DevOps teams work according to the adage 'you build it, you run it'. For DevOps to work, organizations must employ people who value change, risk reduction, and stability; adopt automated processes for building, testing, and deploying; and componentize applications to allow scalability.

2. Business/IT boundaries blur

As digital technology redefines the way work is done in virtually every job, the distinction between 'business jobs' and 'IT jobs' is fading - and new roles are emerging which include elements of both.

As such, the days when enterprise technology could be viewed as someone else's concern are coming rapidly to an end. As an example, business leaders - executives and strategists in particular - must now understand both top-level technology trends and how those trends affect the operation. The board members responsible for innovation and IT for example, who have the final say on whether a new technology-driven initiative gets funded, should be fluent in that technology's capabilities and risks before the project proposal is even written. The Control board or other bodies that appoint board members should - given the current digital transformation - consider emphasizing on this highly strategic topic for the next decades, not only from an IT standpoint of view, but also embedd experiende and knowledge on the entrepreneural world, as the outside world has the inside health(care) world on it's menu. There should be a strong connection between those accountable for the institutions strategy, innovation and IT. I think there is a strong case to be made to have all of those three aspects in an optimal scenario in one and the same hand.

In the design of a future Technology Operating Model, we see a trend towards IT capabilities being organized closer to - or even embedded in - the operations, fueled by other prevailing trends such as Agile and cloud. These trends "disrupt" the IT department's traditional monopoly on access to, knowledge about, and funding for information technology.

Specific in health(care), I think there are two important distinctions to be made: the current world where the healthcare TOM is mainly internally focused and aimed at the professional (see chapter about EOL of EHR, apps and portals) and the next world where data from outside, stored outside and created outside will start to blend with the internal data on a "loan" base, as healthcare institutions will start to take a subscription to patients' data.

Next to the other shift that is currently happening - whereas "privacy by design" is becoming the de facto standard - we also should make sure we aim for "connected by design" devices and processes, hence two approaches that at times even will collide as they have different objectives and tasks. At Radboudumc, we coined these "eGo" and "eCo" models, whereas the "eGo"-perspective is the internal view on generated data generated and the focus is mainly on the internal processes, with a (growing) ambition to also have an outside "window". The "eGo"-view has a de facto outside view where the patient lives his un-siloed life, gathering data to be shared whenever needed. The average patient nowadays has to use multiple portals, logins, passwords to enter the different eGo-systems. So those responsible for IT and innovation should make sure both perspectives will be addressed equally, otherwise the strategic position of the institution could also come at stake.

In addition, we see more companies - lead by their Chief Information Officers or CIOs - offering tech education programs to help their people understand the major systems that form the technological endoskeleton of enterprise IT, the technology forces that are changing the world in which we live and work, and the way technology is used in the market to enable competitive advantage. There is a tendency to invest in IT or - if it concerns real estate operations - into buildings without really addressing the real change that is needed to make the strategic choices stick in practice. Human centered design should be and is more and more becoming part of the digital transformation, but is often still embedded in the budgeting under "generic". A lot of these choices assume or actually need change management as it directly influences the culture of the organization. It would be a great addition to IT- or real estate programs to have either such a program or from the organizational toplevel embedded as part of the organizational fabric.

The combined impact of these changes will create a host of challenges for the board, forcing the revision of talent attraction and management approaches, the strengthening of brand images, and the adjustment of digital talent value propositions. But also the (internal) training facilities, and the curricula of professionals need to be revamped. At Radboud, we changed the curriculum for medical students and Biomedical engineers in 2015, but it will take until 2021 before the first medical professionals trained in that paradigm will graduate. We created our own venture to start training the healthcare leaders of the future in new ways, to innovate and to be aware of the every increasing speed of the digital transformation: we started the Health Innovation School.

Building a new hospital with addressing the change management that supports the employees in getting acquainted, used to and interested in the new technology, processes, a new TOM and ways of work, is needed. In classical IT processes, one automates processes (or digitizes them), while in digital innovation, these processes or even the paradigm shift.

3. Innovation ecosystems

Today's leading digital innovators don't limit their innovative power by restricting themselves to internal resources. Rather, an increasing number are starting to turn their attention outward - to non-traditional partners and completely different industries - to enlarge their sensing capabilities, gain access to talent, establish an environment of experimentation, and develop new business models and collaborate with new players and partners. Although healthcare is a highly regulated sector, it is impossible to innovate on an island. So when we started the REshape Center in 2010, this was one of the core values to deliver: to (re)connect the organization to the outside world and to bring as much of the players to the table from the get-go.

The new business ecosystems are based on open innovation, solving a complex problem collaboratively, creating an innovative new service that no organization could have created by themselves. This requires an ecosystem of actors with complementary capabilities, that collaborate in joint risk taking and value creation. By joining resources, facilitating cross-overs and actively reaching out, the business ecosystem is able to create new business models, services, and customer experiences that would have been out of reach of the individual actors. A closed and - for obvious reasons - risk averse sector as healthcare has to get used to such an approach however. Missed opportunities in the past, as in fraudulent or IP-stealing examples, resonate in the organizations for decades. It is all about scale, no more thinking about the impact of solving the issue for (just) one hospital, but for the whole eCo-system.

In this environment, data is the most valuable asset an organization can share. Although each institution has only a small portion of patient data, the collective - consented data - of the patient can really boost developments and innovation. As such, organizations must rethink their approach to intellectual property. For instance, they must determine which data and algorithms they are willing to share as part of their value contribution to the network, and which represent the core of their strategy and must be protected at any cost. This is true for both private sector networks (e.g. supply chains, business webs, ecosystems), and also public sector networks other than healthcare (e.g. in traffic control, security services, and military operations).

Traveling the world, meeting others in innovation that were running an innovation center/shop, the notion dawned on me that we all face many of the same challenges. To deal with those more effectively, we initiated the creation of GNHIC, the Global Network of Health(care) Innovation Centers. GNHIC was launched in 2016 to bring together innovation movers from 15 forward-thinking health systems on 3 continents. The group recognized the collective need for a community of practice to explore exponentials in health and streamline the path to creating new value for patients from these technologies. After all, we can spend our money only once, and it would make sense to at least explore the options to do some of the exploration and developments together.

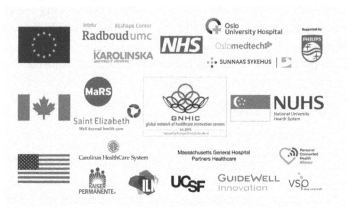

The Global Network of Health(care) Innovation Centers has 3 pillars of activity:

I. EXPLORE– what are these exponential technologies, how do they work, what are real world use cases

II. LEARN– develop and deploy playbooks for adoption into complex health systems

III. DO– jointly work on adoption and leverage the learnings across the network

It is a network in its first phase, the building blocks still are rough, but as the digital transformation is spreading into healthcare, we see a growing demand and ambition to collaborate on an international level.

Modernizing the core technology platform to meet these new needs will also involve redefining sourcing strategies, some of which easily could be a joint effort as boundaries blur in this digital world. But also within your own organization, explore of it is an option to establish a revolving innovation fund from savings on the "run" part, to fund innovations, social recalibration and exploratory IT. My colleague Ronald Lolkema, director of Strategy at Radboudumc and I often dreamed of a ten percent of the annual revenue contribution available for structural business process redesign.

<u>Big shifts in resources</u>

4. Workforce transition

Each of the nine big shifts will have an impact on the IT workforce. Whether you're introducing agile, enterprise-wide tech education programs, cloud, or IT/OT convergence, each move will inevitably cause existing roles to disappear, remaining roles to change in nature, training needs to increase, or new roles to be created. Not just from an IT workforce perspective, also for health(care) professionals specifically, this digital transformation could mean a shift in their daily work, for instance when more e-visits will come into practice. Next to changing the TOM from an IT perspective, we need to look further than traditional training for physicians or nurses, since we will face a growing demand of professionals trained in remote monitoring. A workforce that is equipped for the future needs training and experience in e-visits, working at a distance, tech-savviness etc. Already Kaiser-Permanente had over 52% of their members doing e-visits in 2015..

In Southern-China, Longmaster supports over 3000 patients a day remotely from its 'internet-hospital" in Guiyang. Via online services like Hao Yisheng or Chunyu Yisheng, both part a recent IPO valued over $7B, people can select their own physician. The Dutch Financieele Dagblad in the Netherlands referred to a study of Peking University Medical College, that counted over 40 'internet-hospitals' in China that are operational today. The medical features within WeChat (China's Facebook equivalent) have been used by over 110 Million people already, combining functions of Whatsapp, Facebook and payment services in one.

Next to the transformation of the doctors' role, the importance of nurses will be also affected by this change. With new technology, they will be able to perform tasks that up until now were applicable only for physicians, but the hardware combined with the software reshuffles the tasks between these two groups profoundly as well.

To adapt to this successfully, organizations must calculate these workforce changes into their TOMs - and take a greenfield approach to predicting how these shifts will impact demand for specific roles, competencies, and skills in the years ahead.

5. Digital DNA

The digital era does not only impact highly visible aspects of the Technology Operating Model (TOM), like workforce, systems, and infrastructure. It impacts less tangible - but equally important - aspects like vision, values, culture, and leadership as well. To achieve digital maturity, organizations must invest in both, equally.

This involves developing a digital DNA - a unique set of traits that allows the entire enterprise to view the world subconsciously through a digital lens. For instance, a company that is digital at its core goes beyond the mere digitization of customer touch points, and instead reimagines new methods of customer engagement.

Digital DNA doesn't develop accidentally. It takes time, commitment, and leadership to establish. Instead of trying to make quick fixes, digital leaders play the long game - they imagine what kind of organization they want to become over a 10-year horizon. Many (just) see the part above the surface, like apps being created and gadgets coming along. The reality is those all are parts of the three phases of innovation (awareness, groundswork and scaling, as described in The digital (r)evolution). Then, they commit to developing the digital traits needed to achieve that goal, put their money where their mouth is, and deliver.

The effort is worth it. Strong digital capabilities combined with strong leadership capabilities result in high profitability. In fact, "conservatives" - or those with few advanced digital features but strong leadership capabilities - significantly outperform "fashionistas" (companies with many advanced digital features but no overarching digital vision or coordination). So you need either one of those, ideally of course both, depending on the phase of maturity on the digital horizon you want to be. Next to having the vision, and this is again where the leadership capabilities come in, the execution on the vision is key. In this perspective the assignment of a CINO might be an interesting consideration.

In their book "Innovation Intelligence" (2015), Albert Meige and Jacques Smitt wrote after interviewing dozens of Chief Innovation Officers (CINO's) and other C-level functions of large companies like Airbus Group, Danone, Total, and Faurecia and others about this fairly new role.

An analysis with Google Trends on "Chief Innovation Officer" shows an increasing interest starting in 2010. The term was actually coined and described by Miller and Morris in 1998, but it seems to have only received interest in the past 4-5 years or so. While the Chief Innovation Officer's function is becoming increasingly strategic, its description is still in its infancy and varies among companies. In the following era will see why the perimeter of the Chief Innovation Officer should be new territories. Not more, not less, although it is a role in its infancy.

And yet many institutions 'kill' their innovation budget when things get rough in terms of financial health of the organization, while it might be the innovation that could save the life of the organization in the long run.

6. Funding and governance

Although digital technologies deliver cost efficiencies, they do not do so by replacing existing technologies. Instead, technologies like the Internet of Things (IoT), artificial intelligence (AI), and robotics augment the technology footprint and extend the technology stack, hence Augmented Health(care) ™.

As a result, the role of technology in the enterprise is set to only expand, permeating the very heart of the company's business processes.

This expansion will inevitably lead to an increase in costs - particularly in the areas of design, implementation, and operation - which creates a challenge for cost-conscious boards. To alleviate these challenges, the TOM should make room for three fundamental shifts in IT financial strategy:

- A larger share of the budget must be allocated to innovation, at the cost of traditional technology expenses (i.e. save to invest).

- The total technology spend must increase, since new digital technology cannot be funded from cost savings alone.

- Digital innovation must be funded from outside the traditional IT (budget).

In addition, because digital technology innovation is exploratory in nature, it requires a unique financial management approach - one that's iterative, with shorter cycles, and that allocates budgets to the most promising initiatives. Despite the hype surrounding the term, I still think that "moonshot thinking" is a very good way to make sure the distinction between process-improvement and real (radical) innovation is being safeguarded.

For instance, organizations may consider managing tech innovation as a portfolio of initiatives, where each initiative is based on hypotheses that are tested during each phase of exploration. So, rather than subjecting every new initiative to a formal approval process (which would, in all likelihood, kill it), companies could set aside innovation funds to start small, under-the-radar projects capable of delivering the learnings and tangible results required to submit a formal budget request.

This will lead to a more prominent shift from project-portfolio management to product-portfolio management, with product-funding replacing project-funding. Agile teams will be responsible for digital products - with "run" and "change" functions combined in one single product backlog - leaving the detailed allocation of product budgets to the relevant product owner and Agile team.

Due to the siloed structure of healthcare, the benefit of an innovation could easily fall in a different pocket. For that you need to be able to change the model, structure or even payment models. That is not an easy process, as governments, insurers and policymakers have to be willing to collaborate on this and/ or be willing to offer comfort for a certain transition period.

<u>Big shifts in technology</u>

7. Cloud and automation

While cloud computing is not far from becoming the dominant delivery model for IT, organizations must do much more than simply "lift and shift" their existing on-premise application portfolio to successfully leverage this technology. For a cloud transformation to work, it requires a cloud strategy that fits into a modernized TOM. At the moment (Spring 2018), we see a tendency from the debate around the GDPR to move away from the cloud and back to premise. Just like the eGo vs eCo challenge, this is one we have to face. As with many innovations, this is an iterative process. At a high level, such a strategy would include a combination of four different strategies:

- Replace: On-premise application is replaced by a software as a service (SaaS) application.

- Refactor: On-premise application (or parts of it) is rebuilt in a Platform as a service (PaaS) environment, making the PaaS provider responsible for anything other than the application and data.

- Rehost: Existing application workload is moved from an on-premise server to a cloud server to an Infrastructure as a Service (IaaS), either with as little effort as possible (i.e. lift and shift) or by deploying the native capabilities of the IaaS environment. The latter allows companies to reap more IaaS benefits but limits portability.

- Remain: Applications are kept on-premise. (e.g. because it will become obsolete in the short term, preventing a company from recovering the cost of migration to the cloud.)

A strong cloud strategy should serve as a guide, allowing organizations to better assess their current IT landscape and define the cloud services, vendors, and preferences they require moving forward. The common trunk of all of these migrations is they move towards Xaas (X as a service) interestingly just like health(care) is moving to HaaS (Health as a Service, as I coined it lately).

8. Data and algorithms

The digital data we create is rapidly expanding to the point where, over the next few years, the total volume of data stored will quadruple, while high-value data (i.e. that worth analyzing) is expected to double. Specifically for health(care) we'll see an shift from spot measurement to continuously monitoring and remote monitoring.

Analytics will expand to include non-traditional data formats and use new techniques like computer vision, advanced pattern recognition, and deep learning. This will create a better understanding of patients, employees, systems, environment, operations, and markets - and, as a result, these algorithms and data will increasingly become a strategic asset in the digital era TOM.

While this shift will undoubtedly bring opportunities, the concept of algorithmic business raises new issues surrounding privacy and ethics. In many ways, algorithmic business is just as much a new frontier for ethics and risk assessment as it is for emerging technology. To me, the question still is where the ethical assessment should be safeguarded, as this is not an IT responsibility nor is it the one from the department 'ethics'. We have to be aware of another siloed approach. This new digital world will invoke whole new challenges to resolve.

9. IT and OT converge

Information technology (IT) and Medical technology, in other sectors often referred to as Operational Technology (OT) have long been separated and under the control of entirely different groups - with entirely different cultures. The same goes for the internal and external innovation approaches. Though long separated from each other, IT and OT followed similar journeys and now exchange technologies (e.g. networks, operating systems, databases) at the edges of their worlds. This is, however, changing.

Thanks to Internet of Things (IoT) - and in health(care) the IoMT (Internet of Medical Things) - physical OT assets are increasingly equipped with sensors and connectivity, which has led to the streaming of data and intelligent IT systems that provide real-time insight and control. This, in turn, is generating a drive towards a full convergence of OT and IT. That said, a seamless integration of OT and IT remains a challenging and audacious goal for most organizations.

Although there are strong arguments in favor of bundling IT and OT capabilities in some industries, the current reality is that this is only partly the case.

To help fuel a successful OT/IT convergence, the TOM of the future must address four key factors:

- Cybersecurity. As IT technology becomes prevalent in OT, so does the vulnerability for cyber attacks. A TOM should outline new methods of protecting OT, particularly if the physical equipment is life or mission critical.

- Management. The use of standard operating systems, databases, and middleware in OT systems creates the need for new processes like upgrade cycles, release management, and patches— practices that were traditionally reserved only for IT.

- A broader view. As OT and IT blend into each other, their capabilities, processes, and best practices need to blend as well.

- Being adaptive to the outside change of health(care) being brought by new players, new technology that is able to (re)connect institutions to their targeted group including "social recalibration"(quoting Dr. George Post during Cambridge GAP Summit 2018, which I was part of).

THEME 5:

This revolution will not stop

CHAPTER 43

Augmented health(care)™ explained

What does 'the day after tomorrow' look like for health(care)? Of course there are various scenarios, for me they come together in the bundling of different strains of developments that are going on right now in healthcare. I coined it : Augmented Health(care) ™. What is it? And what parts of health(care) will be affected by this development?

Most people have heard of the concept augmented reality. It is sometimes confused with virtual reality. So a small piece of theory, that the experts can skip.

Virtual reality is a virtual actuality that can be completely separate from the real reality. You put on large (diving) glasses with a screen in it. Or you slide your smartphone in a VR-set. And suddenly you imagine yourself on a pearly white beach in the South Pacific, while you are sitting at your kitchen table at home. Virtual reality makes it possible to have physical sensations and feelings that can seem lifelike, while we are in a virtual world.

A further developed form of virtual reality is mixed reality, a mix of the physical world around us and virtual reality. Mixed reality combines a physical place with a virtual layer. For example, you see the image of the kitchen that you want to order projected over reality. In addition to a screen on the inside, these glasses also have a front camera that shows what you are looking at. Thus the two worlds are combined, blended. In this way you get a very real picture of what a kitchen looks like in the setup you have chosen, in the selected space of your house and with the light in that room. That is a mixed reality.

Finally, augmented reality is a layer that is situated over reality, projected over it, as it were. Google Enterprise Edition, the successor of Google Glass, and the Hololens from Microsoft and Metaglass are examples of this. You put these glasses on and they project the information you need to perform a task in the corner of your eye, against the inside of a mirror surface or your glasses. This way you have your hands free to do that task and you can still access information at the same time.

Although some might think the Google Glass project failed, the glasses are actually widely used by mechanics and order-runners who receive instructions through them. And there are many possible applications in healthcare as well. Within our 3D-lab at Radboudumc, we've frequently experimented with virtual reality and put this technology in practice during operations.

To me, Augmented Health(care)™ is about a layer of smart technology and data that is surrounding and that helps us make better decisions. With us, I mean everyone who is involved in care: care providers, patients, their family and informal caregivers. Whether that layer is projected via glasses or on your phone, refrigerator or smartwatch: what matters is that in the future everyone will have exactly the information they need to do their work properly or to follow therapy correctly. The right information at the right time.

After the digitization of the X-rays (from film to screen), a new digital transition process follows. Besides the conversion of analogue images to digital images, extra information can be displayed, such as counts and patterns that are recognized. Because of this digital transition process and the accumulation of data, computers are getting better at pattern recognition and eventually even predictions can be made. Based on data from 33,000 patients, a company developed an algorithm that can predict whether a patient with breathing difficulties will die within three days or not.

With Augmented Health(care)™, professionals and patients get digital tools to process and analyze the ever-expanding ocean of data and present this information in a suitable way, in a specific context. A model based on artificial intelligence is more likely to detect that a patient is deteriorating or in need of extra oxygen than the doctor. This information can be used by the care provider: a doctor ultimately decides whether or not to give oxygen to this patient.

But new applications can also be found with Augmented Health(care)™, as support for the daily, social tasks of health-care professionals. Take an informal carer as an example, who pours coffee for all residents of the nursing home in which his or her relative resides. It is difficult to remember who likes to drink their coffee in which way. And it is dangerous to rely on what people say, because the diabetic patient might asks for a scoop of sugar in the coffee, which is not allowed. Envision the convenience of accessing this information about each resident - any diets or sugar restriction - without you having to look for it yourself. Your glasses (or smart contact lens) recognize the resident's face, and all necessary information appears.

Recently, a company received FDA-approval for a piece of software that can detect whether someone has diabetes based on a digital photo of an eye. This so called 'IDx-DR-'system uses artificial intelligence, based on thousands of medical images of eyes. The AI system recognizes diabetic retinopathy, damage to the retina, which is one of diabetes' most common complications. In a clinical trial, IDx-DR was able to correctly identify the presence of diabetic retinopathy 87.4 percent of the time and identify those who did not have the disease 89.5 percent of the time.

A final example that I want to mention here is a radiologist who sees what deviations an AI algorithm has found in a scan. Currently, medical images are usually only assessed and compared with the human eye, usually by a radiologist, or by two radiologists. But thanks to image analysis software, doctors and researchers can diagnose faster and better and have an extra analysis done by software. Artificial intelligent software helps them to compare one image to thousands of previous medical images or scans. He can therefore focus on the specific part where tumor cells are found. Augmented Health(care)™ also means that healthcare professionals receive very targeted notifications when they are required to take action.

This layer of medical reality will change everyone's role. There is resistance to this change in certain professions, based on the fear of their profession disappearing. That is completely unjustified in my honest opinion. The fact that a radiologist receives support from AI when assessing images does not mean that the radiologist becomes superfluous. It means that she or he no longer has to spend time on routine work and can focus on that part of the work for which she or he has followed six years of medical education. Also a radiologist can make more diagnoses of higher quality in less time. And with the growth of the demand for care that is approaching us, that is badly needed.

This also could give room for more explanation and interaction with the patiënt.

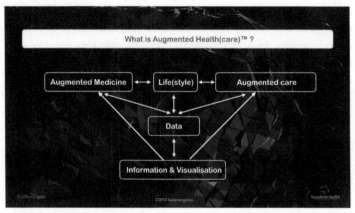

At the top left you see the field of the medical professional: Augmented Medicine, medicine therefore. This is the layer in which all data about the patient come together and where smart algorithms try to make sense out of all of that. Being supported by informatics, translated into graphical framework able to see in an instant where their attention is needed.

Take cardiology, a field that uses a variety of diagnostic tools - from an ultrasound, ECG and CT scan to the images of a catheterization or the data from a Holter examination. Add some data from a blood test, the analysis of a food diary and the observed movement and it is clear that this amount of information can't hardly be processed by a human brain anymore.

Computers are much better at combining and analyzing this enormous amount of information. Us humans can quickly recognize a pattern in outline, but we are far less likely to recognize marginal deviations from that pattern that may indicate a different diagnosis than the most obvious one, and we might not always be on top of our energy and attention level. Also minimal changes that make it difficult for the naked eye to notice: features that help the radiologist and neurologist diagnose a disease and monitor its progression. That is precisely a task that algorithms are much better at.

But algorithms alone cannot handle the work, because you can only train them to recognize common patterns. Algorithms will overlook a rare condition. It is therefore the combination of man and machine that makes it so strong. Smart algorithms can point the cardiologist to particular deviations. The cardiologist no longer has to spend time analyzing patterns that he already expects, but can focus on everything that is special or deserves extra attention.

At the top right the Augmented Care is located. This is the world of the patient or client, his or her family and caregivers like nurses and others in the support team. In Augmented Care, it is not (or should I say no longer) the disease which is central, but it is life, caring. With measurements that are transmitted remotely to the hospital or to the medical service center and that form the basis for decisions to further optimize the care.

In the middle you find lifestyle. Augmented Medicine and Augmented Care helps patients and their families to organize their lives in a way that their condition is no longer the center of attention, but at most is sometimes more 'present' than at other times. Take, for example, a type 1 diabetes patient, who is counting the day in his mind all day long: how much exercise did I have today? How high is my glucose level now? How much should I eat now if I want to exercise later? How much insulin should I take if I just want to enjoy this dinner and still take that dessert? In an Augmented Health(care)™ world, all that information is immediately available and actionable, without having to count. In fact, the pump automatically gives you the right amount of insulin, tailored to your day. The day of the dinner party that evening a little more, the day of intensive training a little less. Technology that fits seamlessly into our lives, supports us and offers context, without having to look for it.

The beauty of this augmented world is that the amount of data available for analysis increases quadratically. That data has a different meaning for each stakeholder, and that translation is also made. Data is made into information and is usually translated via visualizations into possible actions that only arise when they are needed, based on the context, maybe even the location or future agenda-items of the person living with a condition. That is the bottom block from the figure. The dietician will receive exactly the information he or she needs to put together a diet for this individual patient. The regular training buddy sees if his sports partner is completely fit and can therefore train full action, or that it is wise to take this training down a notch. The GP proactively receives a signal if abnormal blood glucose values or an irregular heartbeat are detected and action must be taken.

This new world requires a major adjustment in the way we view healthcare. Care providers have to change. They have to be trained in a different way, focusing on shared decision making - based on data - with the patient, the family and informal caregivers.

Some still think that this development won't go so fast, but you already see it in the world around us. For example, I see it at one of my hobbies: golfing. I always thought it was 'playing with marbles for adults', but during my sabbatical I started learning to play Golf to clear my mind a bit. Out of habit, I looked for possible technology applications in this field as well. Jordan Spieth is one of the best golfers in the world and he pays a caddy (assistant) to support him. Not only with carrying his golf bag, but also with strategic advice. The caddy knows exactly where the golf course goes to the right or goes down, he keeps track of where the wind comes from and scours the track for obstacles. The caddy also advises which club Jordan can best use.

Of course I cannot pay for a caddy (waiting for the sponsors to come ;-)), but I can purchase a golf app. The app collects the data from the sensors that come with the kit. The sensors are screwed on top of my clubs, and keep track of where I am and how often I have used a club. Based on my GPS location, the app calculates how far I have hit the last time and keeps all sorts of lists and statistics. This data tells me I have a slight deviation to the right, generally take a swing too soft but as the course goes on, often just too hard. I now get advice about which club I should take, how I should take the wind into account in a certain spot on the course and how hard I should hit. I still see myself as a golfer: technology has not reduced or changed my experience and the pleasure in golf, but is improving my scores and progression.

This is augmented golf, which makes me an ever better player, supported by technology and (especially) data that is translated into information and visualizations. Translate that example again back into Augmented health(care)™, where healthcare professionals, patients, informal carers and family members are supported by technology and data. We will see this in medicine, in long-term care, in the field of lifestyle and certainly in research.

Finally: I often get a lot of questions about 'what exactly does this deliver in terms of better care or lower costs?' I cannot give you the answer for the simple reason that many of the developments in this Augmented Health(care) ™ concept do not yet exist in this form for long enough, let alone that we can already thoroughly study it. It is still in the phase of awareness and the very first groundswork, as I also outline in theme 2 - the digital (r)evolution.

Much of the research on digital care has a limited focus. It concerns a (very) limited group of users or patients under very defined circumstances. In addition, there is usually only the costs for that specific professional or even just for a specific sector - such as GP care or hospital - while the 'profit' or effectiveness often lies elsewhere. We need to do research more on a macro-economic level and more on the full width of the patient's life, it is currently too fragmented so that the overall picture is lacking. Although I understand that they often have a specific task around a certain condition and assignment, the funds might be able to initiate this process and encourage it by collaborating.

Space for the right hemisphere

We cannot yet calculate exactly what augmented health (care) provides, but we can conclude that it provides a relief of the left hemisphere of health care providers. Especially now that healthcare is under pressure, health care providers easily get into behavior that fits the left hemisphere. That is the part of the brain where facts, logic, science, strategy and a practical approach are central. The part of the brain in we use o make diagnoses based on lab results and MRIs, with which we make and execute treatment plans.

If you address your left brain too unilaterally, which happens easily under time pressure, then there is not enough energy to spend on tasks that we perform with our right brain: showing compassion and empathy, reason from meaning and appreciation, search for possibilities. A hand on the shoulder and the corresponding space to really listen to what a patient says and to observe things that you do not see on a scan or in a blood test. Abraham Verghese of Stanford University called it the power of the human touch in a TedTalk. Patients often give a lot of implicit and explicit signals that are totally overlooked because the left hemisphere at times is too dominant. If we want humanity to return to health care, then we need to do something to support that left hemisphere, so that more energy is released to use the right hemisphere. Augmented health could offer a partial solution for this.

Every doctor and nurse ever chose health care because they want to work with people, want to have an impact in some-one else's life. But during the training and then in practice that human-factor gradually dissolves into the background and the focus is on tasks, like the many registrations. Augmented health offers the opportunity to automate that part of the work to a large extent, so that time and space is naturally created for that which really determines the quality of care: the relationship between care provider and patient.

Functions of the left hemisphere:	Functions of the right hemisphere:
• logic	• the big picture
• detail	• impulsive
• reality	• imagination
• practical	• symbols and pictures
• names of things	• time awareness
• facts	• philosophy
• words and language	• religion
• present and past	• meaning
• math and science	• conviction
• understand	• valuation
• know	• spatial insight
• recognize	• fantasy
• patterns / order	• functional insight
• strategy	• see possibilities
• safety	• taking risks

CHAPTER 44

The Future Physician: Augmented, Connected, Proactive

Daniel Kraft

Today's Physician: The doctor of today has clinical experience and expertise generally limited to where and who they trained with and which patients and conditions they have seen. Skills can deteriorate, and knowledge bases can rapidly become out of date. Options for interacting with patients are primarily based on in-person interactions and occasional phone calls. Patient data is limited to collection at clinical sites, is rarely synthesized, and often silo'd in EMRs with limited and time-consuming user interfaces, and burdensome documentation and billing requirements. Incentives are often mis-aligned... especially with Fee-For-Service... not 'Fee-For-Health' or Outcomes, which drive 'Sick Care' rather than a 'HealthCare' model.

The 2030 Physician... Will have at their disposal a vastly expanded globally crowd-sourced and Intelligence Augmented (IA)experience information sets to draw from. The ability to have just in time individualized and contextual patient relevant information synthesized at the point of care to guide clinical across the healthcare continuum.

From Knowledge Based Medicine to Intelligent and Crowd Sourced:Physicians will be able to pull up a "Digital Twin" of their patient... and leverage multi-variable "predictalytics' fueled by a continually updated informatics that will apply forward looking algorithms to predict and identify problems early, and define optimal care paths and outcomes from the increasing set of therapeutic options.

From Quantified Self to Quantified Health: 20 years after the launch of the first FitBit, the ability to quantify has moved far beyond steps and sleep data living on a smartphone ... to an era of IoHT (internet of health things) which will have blossomed and be riding 7G networks (1000x the speed/bandwidth of 4G today) connecting the dots from disparate data sets of PHR to EHR. With multi-dimensional measurement from analyzing speech, gait, sleep patterns, and expanding array of digital exhaust, from wearables and to home WiFi that can detect behaviors and vitals, to 'invisible's and 'insideables[1]' that share and stream data, 'quantified health' data will fuel prevention diagnosis and therapy. No clinician will be able to track these expanding data streams in real-time, so continuous monitoring algorithms will serve as a 'check engine light' for the healthy, and alert care teams for early intervention across disease states.

Knowledge gleaned from massive multi year studies including Verily's Baseline, the AllofUS crowdsourced research platform, and the UK's 100K Genome projects have by 2030 provided growing context and useful knowledge from the digital exhaust, phenotype and genotypes from millions of individuals across disparate locations, racial and socioeconomic backgrounds.

From Reactive to Proactive: With an aging population in most of the Western world, complex chronic disease will remain a challenge, but as dollars and incentives shift to prevention and even optimization. The Physician's role can increasingly include health maximization. Beyond standard vaccinations based on broad population sets, each patient can be seen with the lens of a dynamic healthcare journey and map. Transformative Technologies can be prescribed... ranging from video games for sharpen and improve cognitive abilities or treat ADHD to Autism.

Beyond the one-size fits all pill

The 'let's try this and see how you do' era of prescribing has entered one where medications, 'digiceuticals' and even medical devices are dynamic and adaptive. Hypertension for example and which in 2018 often required months of trial and error combinations with 3 drug classes and combinations, instead the physician 2030 prescribes the HTN protocol: The patient starts on 1 or 2 medications matched by dose and combination to their pharmacogenomics and other metrics. Voice based interfaces can help the patient stay on top of adherence, and manage potential side effects.

Virtualization: The clinical visit will increasingly blend in-person with virtual consultations augmented with IoT integrated data and when indicated, patient generated labs and physiologic data. The friction points of documentation have been eased with virtual scribes leveraging NLP voice recognition and video. Increasingly clinicians will be paid to enhance health outcomes and utilize a more holistic systems medicine approach for 'precision wellness' and for optimally managing disease. Incentives will better align with integrated technologies that provide a continual and adaptive digital wrapper around prevention, diagnosis, therapy and clinical trials.

Clinician as Coach: Behavior change is hard. Disease management is hard. The broken or non-existent feedback loops of the early 2000s have been replaced with a personalized digital wrapper, that learns, adjusts and with virtualized extenders/coaches. Instead of handing a patient a brochure on diet, or weight loss, the physician will have at their disposal a set of highly intuitive and individualized 'behaviorome' based interventions for the patient (and their family/ caregivers) based on an integrated map of the individual's base genome, dynamic microbiome, metabolomic response to glucose and protein challenges.

CME becomes engaging, real-world and actually educational.... Recognizing that knowledge is increasingly dynamic and less dependent on rote memorization but the integration of systems medicine, physiology the clinician will be able to enter on demand a virtual clinical environment interacting with 'practice patient avatars' for everything from discussion of end-of-of life wishes to full on surgical/procedural simulations where just like an airline pilot practices emergencies and rare events, so can the practitioner. From the 'See One, Do One, Teach One' era to 'See One...Simulate One... Sim One... and then Do One.

By 2030 Medical School curriculums will have further adapted selecting medical students with more of a focus on EQ than pure IQ, memorization talent and test scores.

Augmenting Surgical Procedures while not yet fully autonomous, are increasingly guided by AI and machine learning. A virtual or real coach/mentor can follow along a procedure remotely, or even lend a hapticly sensored hand to take over a robotic surgical intervention, or to point out a problem or new approach in real time. In this way a general surgeon, in a remote region without depth of experience or for a rare case can be helped as needed. In laparoscopy for example, the screen (or AR/VR version) will label anatomy as needed, remind the surgeon during a challenging area (don't cut that bile duct!), and point out with augmented reality hidden anatomy beyond the field of normal view.

Care Continuum: From 'Take Two Aspirins and Call me in the morning...' era to one where the physician will have continual tracking and feedback (when indicated) to enable knowledge of how a patient is doing. Is the fever curve responding as expected, are early symptoms indicative of a surgical related complication arising, is the change in tumor biomarkers shifting after therapy in a way that suggests long-term remission or early relapse?

When things are 'nominal' green lights on the patient dashboard, yellow to red enables a busy clinician to screen a large panel of patients, respond proactively to 'yellow' and super engage on the red.

The Doctor will be 'Avatarized ' and can do true 'virtual consults' in a social VR environment. The interactions will feel like patient-doctor are in the same room.

Prescribing Solutions not drugs, apps or devices: The pharmacopoeia of 2030 looks quite different than today. The clinician when faced with an issue from HTN, to Diabetes, to managing chemotherapy, or mental health challenges, can prescribe an integrated set the HTN regimen includes the seamless real time noninvasive blood pressure monitor, the set of medication or printable cartridge.

For the infirm patient, a home care robot can provide virtual companionship and enhance safety and memory. Electroceuticals will help manage conditions treated by drugs or surgery today, like Sleep Apnea and even Obesity. Microbiome manipulations will become common especially in cases of autoimmune diseases from IBD to Lupus.

The remote clinician: The world faces a shortage of primary care and specialists in many parts of the world. The augmented clinician and augmented physical and virtual clinic will increasingly have the capabilities of tertiary care centers. Drones will regularly deliver within minutes blood products, drugs, and laboratory samples. Clinical grade 3D printers will be able to produce everything from individualized orthopedic devices to prosthetics.

CHAPTER 45

Dreaming of a world with circular pharmaceutical care (vignette)

Pharmacist Claudia Rijcken is Regio Europa Digital Innovation and Performance Director at Novartis.

What keeps you awake at night? It's a question all of us sometimes get. Apart from the fact I hate to be awake unnecessary, a couple of things can puzzle me for hours during these darkest moments of the night. Amongst the most recurring ones are the global food waste as well as the medication waste challenges that hit our world every day and every year. Annually, still about 3.1 million babies die because of hunger, whereas the western world throws away 1500 kCal worth of food per day per capita. These numbers never cease to amaze me: we live in a strange world sometimes.

The same ambivalence goes for medication. Recent reports underline that some 1.5 billion people in the world do not have access to essential medication, while in the developed countries costs due to inadequate drug use (like avoidable mistakes and/or medication non-adherence) are estimated as high as above 300 billion US dollars. An amount that is equivalent to the sum of the total health expenditures of approximately the poorest 95 countries in the world.

As a pharmacist, it makes me obnoxious. For sure, the pharmaceutical industry has made many positive dreams come true. Brilliant things came and come out of the industry, where drug development has – amongst other things - changed the complete outlook of many oncologic disorders, of hepatitis and of HIV. In hospitals and in community practices, pharmaceutical care teams are collaborating successfully in disease management teams and supporting the individual patient to get the highest impact of drug intervention.

But still, the figures of more than 300 billion US dollar costs related to medication non-adherence and avoidable harm, remain.

What can we do? Concepts and principles like value-based healthcare, outcome-based financing and patient-centricity are driving strong paradigm changes, but velocity of change is not always Formula-1like. Desilo-ing, integrating and aligning of healthcare systems takes time, although big promises for patients are in front of us and definitely in some areas Elon Musk-like achievements already have been made.

Digitalization will speed up many of the processes we are working on, as this book addresses nicely. Data-insight excellence, continuous monitoring and breath-taking technology is supporting mankind to become more sophisticated than ever and we are only witnessing the end of the beginning.

In pharmaceutical care it means that we will finally have the chance to move to something I would call circular pharmaceutical care. A concept derived from economics, where it is related to reducing the waste in cycles by closing the loop of the production, use and demolition of products.

Knowledge and service models can get circular as well. Here lies a huge opportunity for the pharmacist of the future. In order to get fully circular, broad adoption of digital health tools may give significant changes to continuously monitor drug impact. However, today these tools are only used sparsely.

Pharmacists may for instance, consider asking for better 24/7 direct insights in parameters that predict adverse events, that identify non-adherence or that flag overdosing. By having access to these – often patient generated - health data, they would be able to take on a Tesla-like role, meaning they could call the patient proactively before exacerbation of disease or worsening - due to adverse events - even has the chance to take place. Compare it with how electric car manufacturer Tesla operates: Tesla pro-actively calls the driver to start repairing software issues, that are remotely signaled to Tesla headquarters, even before the driver gets stuck in a broken car.

This future scenario would lead to pharmacists of the future acting as pharmaceutical intelligence experts, doing risk stratification on holistic patient data sets and advising (health) care providers on the optimal, personalized medication profile for every patient in need. They would consult patients not only on the best drug and how to use this medication, but also how the drug relates to the individual pharmacogenomics and metabolomics profile. The pharmacists of the future can measure outcomes with personalized digital health tools. Data derived from these tools can in turn be fed into the individual circular pharmaceutical pathway. In many countries in the world, this is yet a rather uncultivated area that is going to deviate the pharmacists' role further from logistics and distribution but brings it back to the core: the medication expert and highly-educated professional that is responsible for assuring optimal impact of the drug provided.

This scenario will require changes of course. Changes in educational patterns, in defining daily responsibilities and in acquiring deeper insights in which technology can best measure optimal drug outcomes (which may be called Technology Enhanced Drug Impact, e.g. TEDI). Insights that will incrementally grow as the end of the beginning of the digital health revolution will bring us new lakes, or even oceans of even better data and the accompanying analytics.

It will also involve a change in the ethical role of pharmacists and how their professional, human factor can discriminate from the services which future pharmaceutical support robots, chatbots and voice-interfaces will offer.

In this respect, I would say it is the patient that has the final say in choosing who is the best candidate in offering circular pharmaceutical care. Circular pharmaceutical care starts with the patient, it ends with the patient and in between the loop is closed by the pharmacist, fully supported by the digital epoch we are in.

Meanwhile, I got into a dream of a promising future and wake up happy.

CHAPTER 46

Quantified Self; personal discovery through everyday science (vignette)

Martijn de Groot (Ph.D.), co-founder Quantified Self Institute, Hanze University of Applied Science, Groningen, the Netherlands.

We all have our questions in our lives. Especially once we are confronted with a disability or a (chronic) illness. We turn to a healthcare system that is based on group research and a complex system of values, different stakeholders and incentives. The off-the-shelf solutions offered by this system work for many people, but not for all. In addition, with an increasing collective awareness about our health, more and more people raise questions about their lives, health, and wellness.

Exploring your own life is not new, but actually as old as human culture itself. Self-observation and self-experimentation predate professional science by thousands of years. What is new is the fast-growing number of people that have become involved in self-exploration in the last decade. This movement has gained attention especially thanks to the Quantified Self community.

This community of practitioners and creators of tools and methods aim to make a personal discovery through everyday science. Quantified Self (QS) has grown as a movement by affordable sensors, the Internet and a social economy that is built upon digital technologies, enabling a single person to track a wide range of phenomena, such as physical activity, sleep, food, mood, stress, breathing, blood glucose, heart rate and its variability, blood pressure, menstrual cycle, temperature, weight, concentration, strength, endurance, mobility, and so forth. There is a long list of health aspects that people have tracked themselves and the list is getting longer. Tools that until recently were only available for professionals in healthcare and science have become ubiquitous. Or, to put it in the late Seth Roberts' words, we witness the 'rise of the personal science'. Technology allows each and every individual to become the principal investigator of their own life.

This development could support the transformation of the current healthcare system. Ten years ago, patients started to run an internet search to find information about their condition. This changed the relationship between the healthcare provider and their patients. Nowadays, more and more patients bring their own data to their physician. Again, this changes the relationship. In ten years from now, the clinical observations can be seen as an enrichment of self-collected data and personal observations, allowing patients to make better informed decisions and to be supported by health care professionals rather than to be dependent on them.

The key activity within the QS community is self-tracking, which is a method of inquiry that starts with a personal question. It is a self-directed process that includes designing and planning a personal project. What follows is a process of making accurate observations with the subsequent data analysis and a visualization that allows you to interpret the results. Self-tracking can be seen as the deliberate and purposeful act of collecting information about yourself by making accurate observations.

Self-tracking is NOT about collecting data for somebody else or any other form of covert surveillance. One element that typically enhances the learning experience of a QS project is to share what you've learned. In the QS community this is done in show-and-tell talks during meetups that allow each and every member to share their project by answering three questions: 'What did you do? How did you do it? What did you learn?' By answering these questions, you not only share your own approach, results and lessons learned, but you also allow others to learn from your personal experience.

There are many similarities between the tools and methods for self-tracking and methodologies for scientific research. While there are ample books that explain the scientific research process, self-tracking data comes with its own difficulties that are well-known under the overarching term 'single-subject-research-design', or N-of-1 research. N-of-1 research has been in applied in the fields of psychology, education, and human behavior, where it has benefitted from extensive methodical research and practical guidance for practitioners. However, over a half-century of study and advocacy, including pioneering publications in well-established medical science have failed to establish single subject science as central to research and practice in medicine. The combination of increased public interest and reliable instrumentation broadly available however may reduce the barriers to application of N-of-1 methodology.

For this perspective to become a practice, we need to overcome existing barriers. The QS community advocates discussions about ethics, privacy, incentives, data ownership, the personal benefits, but also the costs and strains of self-tracking.

Self-tracking in general and an N-of-1 study in particular is not an easy task. It can also lead to stress, confront you with a disease you'd rather not have, or inhibit the flow we experience when we do things almost unconsciously, without thinking.

With many of the apps and wearables that have become commercially available during the last years, there are concerns about data access, control, privacy, and security. Participants of the QS community stress that these concerns need to be addressed. While in popular perception Quantified Self has been identified with these tools, QS is NOT synonymous to apps and wearables. Quantified Self is better understood in the context of the fundamental right to freely participate in the cultural life of the community, to share in scientific advancement and its benefits, as stated in article 27 of the Universal Declaration of Human Rights.

CHAPTER 47

The GP in 2030 (vignette)

Bart Timmers is a general practitioner (GP) in 's-Heerenberg and an educator for future general practitioners. He takes a look back from the future: from how GP care looks like in 2030?

The GP in 2030

Looking back from the future to 2018, it strikes me how long the family doctor has sustained. Specialisms have fallen, for large parts replaced by artificial intelligence (AI for short). Do-it-yourself-care has become much easier with modern techniques. But people's need for a recognizable person or a group of persons proved to be a constant factor that made the GP maintain a part of his/her position.

The profession is now barely recognizable, and that do-it-yourself-care has also made it possible for patients with very different questions to connect. Where you used to have consultation hours, that has now largely been replaced by holo-consults. Only where the old-fashioned manual research is still needed is the virtual reality exchanged for a physical and the patient still visits the practice.

A substantial part of it turned out to continue for a long time, even when the holo-projections were a widespread part of the daily reality. It is always striking how people, despite the progress, turn out to reach back to nostalgic wishes. Just as a part of us humans also preferred animal grown meat for a long time out of nostalgic considerations over the much better tasting cultured meat. Or music on vinyl over the much easier streams from the airpods.

Speaking of airpods, the development of sensors went so fast that the data from these airpods formed a substantial part of the continuous flow of body measurements. That was also a breakthrough afterwards. The initial anxiety of many doctors for that tsunami of data turned out to be unjustified. The personal AI of the people wearing it already interpreted much more than was previously thought possible. After the initial hesitation, patients soon relied more on the personal assistant, who also gave preventive advice. And sometimes that artificial intelligent assistant gave the advice to reach out to the doctor directly. He then received an invitation to connect to the patient's personal health environment (PGO), well in advance, so that he could prepare.

Sure, it took some time to get used to abandoning the GP or hospital information system (HIS, ZIS, KIS in Dutch) or whatever care-giver-centered system. Fortunately, the developers did have capacity to make a nice, smoothly working user's interface for the care provider to connect to the patient's file. Around the year 2018, we had some societal discussions about whether that data was or was not partly the property of the care provider, once data was put into the personal health environment or record of the patient. But that became clear pretty soon: data was donated to the patient. The blockchain provided the much-needed security, which was really necessary, because after the first wave of internet crime, around the beginning of the (20)20s, all digital developments had really slowed down for a while, suffering from the backlash of it.

Internet crime was not the only problem that played a role in society, and therefore also in the healthcare sector. As a society, we were wrestling with the disease model. The whole concept of illness was actually abandoned in the end. The new paradigm was thinking in dimensions, complaints, limitations and most of all possibilities. The complaints about information overload, for example, did not appear to fit into a disease model at all, but were incapacitating and increasingly present in society.

The doctors themselves also suffered from this information overload. Only when real support actually started for professionals, and these topics were structurally embedded in education, did this 21th century "disease" become more bearable. Here too, the AI proved to play an important role in streamlining the ever-increasing amount of information and data. But certainly also the "softer" methods such as mindfulness and a digital detox once every while are helpful.

Looking back from 2030 to 2018, I see that the profession has changed for the GP. The nature of my job it is surprisingly different than in 2018, when I wrote about in the book "Augmented Health(care)™". In the end, it will turn out I was both right and wrong. What I was right about, is this: being a GP is still a great job.

CHAPTER 48

Digital Humans in Health(care) (vignette)

Marie Johnson

Marie Johnson is Managing Director & Chief Digital Officer at the Centre for Digital Business. Marie is a leading global commentator on digital disruption and transformation, including AI. She conceived and led the global co-design and co-creation effort with people with disability to deliver Nadia, the first AI enabled digital human for service delivery.

Digital Humans in Health(care)

For most people, healthcare can be frightening and isolating. Regardless of social status, education or ability – when vulnerable, our humanity yearns for empathy and conversation.

Yet health sector organizations and governments alike have told us that we can no longer afford conversations. Driven by budget and rationing philosophies, the first two decades of the 'online century' simply pasted an electronic veneer over the existing byzantine structures. This forced health consumers to interact through a maze of complex websites, portals, understaffed call centers and thousands of online forms, none accessible. Only the supremely wealthy had the means to avoid these barriers.

This centralist eHealth approach assumes a model of event driven patient interaction with the health system. Such a staccato model relies on and generates data that is fragmented. Absent from this model of eHealth is the data generated between events that is far more expansive and contextual than any point in time data from infrequent doctor conversations.

As an example, take heart patients. Three major events – heart attack, surgery and (maybe) rehab. There is no-one they regularly converse with day to day. There is no 'cardiac coach' to help them navigate the complex and ever-changing rules of secondary prevention or to comfort them when they feel alone and afraid. The end result: repeat surgeries, infirmity or death at a huge human and financial cost.

The past 20 years has been about avoiding the 'unaffordable' conversation. The next 20 years will be exactly the opposite. The rapidly advancing ecosystem of artificial intelligence, neural networks, adaptive interfaces and natural language will forever change the way people and the systems of society interact. Through co-design, the embodiment of this ecosystem as digital humans achieves naturally empathetic and contextually rich conversations.

This is not about chat-bots. Our heart patient can have a digital human on their mobile device that will become their trusted cardiac coach through conversations over time. If connected to the patient's ecosystem of apps, biosensors and services, the digital human cardiac coach can build up a rich contextual knowledge of this heart patient to enable predictive and ongoing precision healthcare.

Think about our heart patient's anxiety in understanding his medication regime, and all the questions that he and every heart patient around the world has. We know that lack of under-standing leads to non-adherence. In the old world, traumatized patients are told to go to a website and look up information. They can't or don't.

In the new world, our heart patient's digital human is an invaluable companion and an integral part of his recovery. Ongoing conversations enable the digital human cardiac coach to monitor for early signs of depression following surgery. Simcoach already does this in a limited way, looking for signs of PTSD in service veterans. Digital humans will also be used by pharmacies to have conversations with consumers to answer a broad range of questions about their medications.

A digital human can converse in any language, including signing, and display additional information as videos, pictures and text. Soon, haptics will enable communication with people who are deaf and blind. The digital human pharmacy assistant will be able to electronically read scripts and be connected to an AI engine containing all knowledge of pharmaceuticals.

Digital humans will be integral to healthcare. They will be companions and coaches for health consumers. On the delivery side, they will augment the human workforce enabling new business and servicing models. There will be new jobs such as trainers of digital humans and designers of conversations.

Visionaries such as Lucien Engelen are bringing about an exponential change, the new and rapidly changing dynamics and economics of relationships driven by digital technologies touching every individual consumer, community and industry across the globe. This is digital disruption in its truest form, where newly empowered consumers have conversations when and where they want. For the first time in history, the democratization of health information empowers and liberates the chronically ill, the disabled, and the disadvantaged.

Nadia, the first digital human, was co-designed by people with disability and has already led to digital humans being implemented in multiple sectors. This is no longer science fiction. This triumph of imagination made real, has triggered the start of an exponential change – digital humans in health(care) delivering massively scalable yet uniquely empathetic conversations to anyone anywhere anytime on the planet.

CHAPTER 49

Space Health (vignette)

Biomedical engineer Jules Lancee (Radboudumc REshape Center) focuses on emerging technologies, their role in changing healthcare and the way they contribute to human spaceflight.

Medical autonomy - a condition for 'deep space' travel

In the near future, space travel will bring us further into the solar system. We will be away from earth longer than our current expeditions to the International Space Station. When it comes to the health of astronauts, the relationship between mission control on Earth and the astronauts will have to <u>undergo a change</u> that resembles the changing relationship between patients and doctors we see in the health care system on Earth.

In space, delays in communication (up to 40 minutes from Mars) and the absence of specific medical devices pose a risk to the health of astronauts. Future missions will also take doctors on board, but the doctor can also get sick and get in need of a medical treatment. Emergency evacuation is no longer an option in these situations. Medical autonomy is therefore necessary for such deep space exploration missions, but also on Earth in remote locations, such as Antarctica and the far north of Canada.

We can learn a lot from initiatives in the field of continuous remote monitoring. At the same time, we can think about how these initiatives can contribute to more advanced techniques for supporting people traveling through the universe without remote assistance.

I see parallels between the challenges that the aerospace community is facing and the challenges we see in the domain of care and innovation.

In this vignette, I guide you along the parallels that I see. We see that healthcare is undergoing a digital transformation. This change is fundamentally different from other leaps in the history of medicine: this fourth industrial revolution offers us solutions that are drastically smaller, cheaper and smarter. With the right technology and design digital solutions can give us a more complete picture of a person's health, in space and on Earth.

Smaller

Progress in sensor technology has led to sensors that are so small that they can be processed in sophisticated devices, or even in patches, which allow continuous monitoring of vital parameters. This allows us to keep an eye on patients more and more, while they are not hindered by wires and electrodes, have no limited freedom of movement, or suffer from them in other ways in daily life (such as while swimming!).

Astronauts will not wear measuring equipment every day of their mission, but these technologies offer opportunities to monitor them more often and more effectively without their activities being compromised. A new smart shirt, called Astroskin, will be supplied to the International Space Station in mid-2018 to do exactly that. The shirt sends measurements back to Earth, where doctors can monitor the health of the astronauts.

Smarter

With the arrival of 'Digital humans', new ways of interacting with computers are being introduced. The past few years have seen an enormous development of human avatars to a point where it becomes difficult to see the differences with real human faces. These realistic avatars provide a natural way of dealing with artificial intelligent computer systems (Artificial Intelligence or AI for short).

A good example is Nadia, developed in co-creation with people with disabilities Australian National Disability Insurance Scheme. Nadia has a human face, human features and the voice of Cate Blanchett. It is intended to eliminate the completion of forms on websites. It provides new forms of interaction on the internet. How could a readily accessible, personal, humanoid assistant offer benefits to astronauts on their way to Mars? Or to patients in remote areas, without access to regular care?

Cheaper

The costs for technology that provide more insight into the deepest layers of ourselves, our genomes (and other ~omes, or omics), have been decreasing exponentially for years. Sequencing your genome, determining the order of your DNA, is getting cheaper. This has led to consumer kits that make it accessible to everyone to test your susceptibility to certain disorders or to suggest lifestyle changes based on your body's response to diet, exercise and stress.

In space, since 2016, genomic sequencing has been taking place with a handheld sequencer called MinION. As far as I know, it has not yet been tested on samples from astronauts themselves, to make similar suggestions aimed at their lifestyle and health.

From data to health

With the digitalization of healthcare, valuable information is stored that is collected by new technologies as described above. In order to be able to analyze the data, algorithms are developed that can find patterns that people cannot find themselves (anymore), due to the size of these datasets. With the digitalization of health information, care can be delivered anywhere (on earth and in space): <u>more and more companies</u> take over parts of the work that is traditionally done in hospitals, universities and research centers and try to improve that work with the help of artificial intelligence.

Next to analyzing data, clinical decision-support systems can help us as well with tasks that humans are not well equipped for. Comparing a certain case or medical image with hundreds of thousands of comparable cases or images is something a computer does better than a doctor, even if that doctor brings a lifetime of experience. But not only doctors can benefit from these improvements in AI. Symptom-checking and triage of patients can also benefit from AI: in the future, this makes <u>'on-demand' and safe medical advice</u> available to everyone with a smartphone - even for minor cases. Decision aids can provide assistance for doctors and patients on Earth, but will be essential for deep space travel, if you can't call the doctor.

Coaching with artificial intelligence

If we fly further into the solar system, one of the difficulties for astronauts will come from the isolation of the crew: the challenge of being far away from friends and family (read: the rest of humanity). Other psychological stress can come from working in an extreme environment, while you are locked up in a small space. New technologies such as artificial intelligence are making enormous progress and could contribute to human-like companionship.

AI services that you can chat with are now being set up and tested worldwide to play a role in psychological coaching, based on "traditional" cognitive behavioral therapy. You can use such an AI chatbot to talk about fears, dealing with stress, or dealing with living with a disease (or it can successfully help to prevent a disease!)

To cope with the 40-minute communication delay between Mars and Earth, artificial intelligence could offer a solution as an on-demand psychological facilitator for astronauts on Mars. Combined with the avatar of a virtual human, this ensures that a conversation is an even more realistic experience.

Real-time medical support

Astronauts are trained for some medical procedures that may prove to be necessary when they are in space. At present, doctors on earth are monitoring the work of astronauts and can offer help via video links. The actual execution comes down to the crew itself. They have to learn, for example, how to draw their own blood (with tools that constantly float away in space...). Knowing that there are robots that already can do that for us, the question is: what kind of tasks could we automate in the future?

We do not yet have virtual doctors floating through the International Space Station. But with the arrival of digital humans, who knows how long it will take before there will be a hologram doctor, such as the virtual physician who provided medical assistance on board the fictional ship <u>USS Voyager</u>. Nevertheless, taking the right decision about an action will be supported in the future by similar decision methods as the algorithms that are being developed for assistance on earth.

Reality check: VR, AR, MR?

Astronauts can rely on medical training for many procedures. These trainings greatly benefit from new technologies such as Virtual Reality (VR). Several <u>startups</u> are working on new training methods in VR, such as training for surgery without practicing on a body. Crews already use forms of VR to learn the operation of robot arms.

It becomes even more interesting if virtual elements can be added to scenarios in reality, also called Augmented Reality (AR) or Mixed Reality (MR). Imagine that the inside of a space station, with the help of special glasses, can be combined <u>with virtual layers</u>, to show vital parameters or offer guidance when performing a <u>medical procedure</u>. Astronauts Scott Kelly and Tim Peake have tested Augmented Reality <u>aboard the International Space Station</u>. The European Space Agency is also investigating how forms of VR, AR, and MR can contribute to <u>training for operational tasks</u>. The <u>future of medical training</u> with Mixed Reality will help doctors on earth, but also astronauts.

What is reality?

In this article I have shared a number of examples of technology and design that offer opportunities for the future of healthcare, both on earth and in space. Aerospace gives us challenges that we have not yet solved - such as the absence of gravity and the presence of radiation - but I believe that the digital health technology we use for health(care) on the planet is also bearing fruit in the space sector.

Digital solutions ensure on-demand availability of care, focused on patients instead of centered around institutions. At the same time, terrestrial health(care) can benefit from solutions that are the result of designs for extreme environments such as space. If we can do it in space, we can do it anywhere! Let us join forces and move towards a healthier world, up there and down below!

Epilogue : Writing this book has been an interesting journey.

The way I produced this book might be different than you'd expect.

I had the ambition to write a new book after the first smaller ones I'd done in 2010 and 2011, so I decided to take on the challenge of using new tools and technologies and new ways of working. I have been writing about a lot of the things I've been doing over the course of the past years on my LinkedIn blog, and many other places as well. So I decided to take those as a resource to start off. Additionally, I wanted to kind of download the journey we as a center (REshape) and me as a person (Lucien) made; from my brain into a book (USB-slot still excluded;-).

So, typically you would start to sit down and start writing, and writing, writing and writing and once you have a bunch of words that are good enough to be named a book, you'll publish it. Apart from my busy schedule that doesn't fit my modus operandi, as I also wanted to combine the traditional way of writing a book with a different approach.

For starters, I turned to fiverr.com, a crowdsourcing platform for finding people to help me with all kinds of tasks, like building a website, doing data-entry work, making graphics, etc. I started to search for someone who would be willing to copy & paste all of my 170+ Blogs into one file. I found Jimmy from

Nigeria to do just exactly that for me in almost no time. This gave me the opportunity to copy and paste from my blogs and make that into a kind of storyboard for the separate chapters I had in mind.

Secondly, I turn to Mirjam Hulsebos, one of the people I've been working with for in the past years. She interviewed me once every couple of months for a magazine. Those interviews typically would take place by phone in my car, driving to or from the university medical center, and would translate into an article. So I scheduled some extra interviews to 'download the things on my mind' on different topics, and get them into articles or chapters. Mirjam turned my words and views into an edited (Dutch) text, following the topics I had chosen.

In parallel I was conducting interviews with some of the people I work(ed) with over the past years, asking them for their perspective on the developments in health(care). You've found these, or brief text contributions of them, as vignettes throughout this book.

Of course, I also needed a cover, and after creating one myself I handed this over to Germancreative from Germany, again on Fiverr.com, asking her to make that into a nice front and back cover, and to offer me two designs. I liked the one you're holding best, as you will imagine by now ;-)

Meanwhile, I was writing and adopting some of my blogs and adding new content to the manuscript. Once the vast majority of the elements of text were present, it came to me that the publication date was very near already, as I wanted to launch the book at the HIMSS Europe 2018 conference in Sitges, Spain. Here many of the targeted group would convene, and I was going to deliver a keynote. One call for help to Jan Jacobs and his two daughters Frederieke and Anna, the three of them running a popular Dutch Healthcare blog Smarthealth, turned their and my schedule upside down. Although it deemed undoable, after setting the stage for the right structure with the three of them, Frederieke and Anna did some realy heavy lifting with me, getting the final structure translated into an edited text that could be translated into English. Again via Fiverr, I found a great Irish guy named Eoin, who translated the Dutch text into English and proofread the ones I had already written in English. Many of these processes were running in parallel.

Aalishaa from India next has been formatting the final file, while I was wrapping up the text you're reading right now, in order to finalize the PDF needed for the printing on demand.

Once ready, the book was available through POD (Print on demand) service IngramSpark, offering every book to be printed in 1 day, so no stock, no huge investments and Amazon for the e-book (and later also the POD version).

So, the book you're holding either in print or digital is the assorted combination of sources, ways to produce, from all kind of places in the world to come together in one product.

My notion here is simple and crisp: health(care) is on the menu, just like the music industry, travel, media and book publishing was not so long ago. The time to play around a bit, to test and experiment without a real change of the model and user interface of health(care) is over. Data will help professionals, patients and industry to create a better outcome, experience, and a more sustainable model.

Time's-up, get on with it!

Lucien

List of (public) REshape projects

3 Disease

Adherence Research Chronisch Myeloid Leukemia (CML) with big data

AED4.EU

Audio recording for patient consultation

Beter Gezond ('Better Health')

Beter uit Bed / Ban Bed Centricity

Biobank serious game on health research

Blockchain technology in healthcare (PGD/Medicatie)

Botuline – me and my cloud self management patients

Cardiology patient-friendly measurements

Center for Remote Monitoring

CloudDx walking the privacy & security street

CMyLife – Platform for patients with Chronic Myeloid Leukemia

Community Child Nephrology

COPD Fast Diagnostics

COPD Net

Chronic Lymphocytic Leukemia (CLL)

Diabetes type 1 with Philips

Dutch Hacking Health

E-health contribution to influencing behavior

E-Health for Spiritual Care

ECG measurements via Smartphone

Empowerment for patients with ADD

EuroGo – Gaucher

Expertise center for pediatrics

Excellence in Clinical Innovation & Technology Evaluation (EXCITE) –
Netherlands affiliate

Facetalk

Fast Track – follow flow HartRitmeVariatie (HRV)

From consent to policy

Game for speech therapy with cleft patients

Global Network of Healthcare Innovation Centers (GNHIC)

Graphic Design in Neurosurgery

Health and Wellness Concept Validation

Healthy Professionals

Health Innovation School – together with the Ministry of Health

Helping patients with Cochlear Implants

How might we alarm T1DM patients before getting hypoglycaemic?

Infection Outbreaks

Innovation Learning Network

LATER Outpatient Clinic

MDL app for research

MedCrowdFund

MijnMedicatie (My Medication)

Mijn Radboud Thuis (My Radboud at Home)

Mirror therapy for cleft patients

Multiple Myeloma

News for the Mews

Obesity – 'prachtwijken'

Patient friendly ECG's

Pilot home-monitoring pregnant woman

Pre-Eclampsia

Questionnaires Geriatric Oncology

Rare diseases: e-Health

REach

REdesign Hecovan

RegioICt – End of Intensive Care

Research for needs – community facial paralysis
Safe-messaging with Kanta
Sensiks Multi Sensor Pod
Smart stickers for physical therapy : Sticky exercises
Spinal cord injury – in the cloud
Startup Track REshapeU
Telehealth / Virtual Clinics
Telehealth with Sensire
Tess – psychological coach (Artificial intelligence)
The New first and Second line
Tooth Extraction Simulation
Tracheostomy Emergency Tools
Virtual personal assistant Diabetes: Susan
Virtual poli: Hidradenitis suppurativa/Acne Ectopica
Virtual poli: Hypertension
Virtual Reality (VR) pain reduction
VisitU

Scientific publications

2018

1. Most response-inducing strategies do not increase participation in observational studies: a systematic review and meta-analysis Authors: Marleen M H J van Gelder, Richelle Vlenterie, Joanna IntHout, Lucien J L P G Engelen, Alina Vrieling, Tom H van de Belt. Journal of Clinical Epidemiology 2018; 10.1016/j.jclinepi.2018.02.019 IF: 2.17

2. REach: a novel platform to use ResearchKit for medical research. Authors: Marleen MHJ van Gelder; Lucien JLPG Engelen; Thijs Sondag; Tom H van de Belt. Journal of Participatory Medicine 2018;IF: new journal

3. A smart all-in-one device to measure vital signs in admitted patients. Mariska Weenk; Harry van Goor; Maartje van Acht; Lucien JLPG Engelen; Tom H van de Belt; Sebastian JH Bredie. PLOS One 2018; 10.1371/journal.pone.0190138 IF: 2.806

4. Using social media as early-warning system for MRSA outbreaks Tom H van de Belt; Pieter T van Stockum; Lucien JLPG Engelen; Jules Lancee; R Schrijver; Rodríguez Baño; E Tacconelli; Marleen MMJ Van Gelder; Andreas Voss.

2017

1. Collaborative writing applications in healthcare: effects on professional practice and healthcare outcomes (Cochrane Review) Archambault PM; van de Belt TH; Kuziemsky C; Plaisance A; Dupuis A; McGinn CA; Francois R; Gagnon MP; Turgeon AF; Horsley T; Witteman W; Poitras J; Lapointe J; Brand K; Lachaine J; Légaré F; The Cochrane Library 2017; 10.1002/14651858.CD011388.pub2 IF: 6.103

2. Continuous monitoring of vital signs using wearable devices on the general ward: Pilot study. Mariska Weenk; Harry van Goor; Bas Frietman; Lucien Engelen; Cornelis JHM van Laarhoven; Jan Smit; Sebastian JH Bredie; Tom H van de Belt. JMIR mHealth and uHealth 2017; 10.2196/mhealth.7208 IF: 5.175

3. Personalized consent flow in contemporary data sharing for medical research. Ester A Rake; Marleen MHJ van Gelder; David C. Grim; Barend Heeren; Lucien JLPG Engelen; Tom H van de Belt. BioMed Research International 2017; 10.1155/2017/7147212 IF: 2.476

4. Stress measurement in surgeons and residents using a smart patch. Mariska Weenk; Sander Alken; Lucien JLPG; Sebastian JH Bredie; Tom H van de Belt; Harry van Goor. The American Journal of Surgery 2017; 10.1016/j.amjsurg.2017.05.015 IF 2.403

2016

1. A new cuffless device measuring blood pressure, a real life study. Tessa S Schoot, MD; Mariska Weenk, MD;

Tom H van de Belt, PhD; Lucien JLPG Engelen; Harry van Goor, MD, PhD, FRCPC; Sebastian JH Bredie, MD PhD. J Med Internet Res 2016;18:e85. URL: http://www.jmir.org/2016/5/e85/

2015

1. What Is eHealth: Time for An Update? EA Boogerd, T Arts, LJ Engelen, TH van de Belt. JMIR Research Protocols 2015;4:e29. URL: http://www.researchprotocols.org/2015/1/e29/.

2. Using Web-Based Questionnaires and Obstetric Records to Assess General Health Characteristics Among Pregnant Women: A Validation Study. van Gelder MM, Schouten NP, Merkus PJ, Verhaak CM, Roeleveld N, Roukema J Using Web-Based Questionnaires and Obstetric Records to Assess General Health Characteristics Among Pregnant Women: A Validation Study. J Med Internet Res 2015;17(6):e149. URL: http://www.jmir.org/2015/6/e149/.

3. Using patient experiences on Dutch social media to supervise health care services: exploratory study. Tom H van de Belt, Lucien JLPG Engelen, Lise M Verhoef, Marian JA van der Weide, Lisette Schoonhoven, Rudolf B Kool. J Med Internet Res 2015;17:1. URL: http://www.jmir.org/2015/1/e7/.

4. Patient Rating Sites for Daily Supervision by Healthcare Inspectorates: Implementation into Practice. Tom H van de Belt, Sophia M Kleefstra, Rudolf B Kool. Iproceedings 2015;1:e14. URL: http://www.iproc.org/2015/1/e14/.

5. Emergency medicine residents' beliefs about contributing to an online collaborative slideshow. Patrick M Archambault, Jasmine Thanh, Danielle Blouin, Susie Gagnon, Julien Poitras, Renée-Marie Fountain, Richard Fleet, Andrea Bilodeau, Tom H van de Belt, France Légaré. CJEM;17:374-386. URL: http://journals.cambridge.org/action/displayAbstract?fromPage=online&aid=9821394.

6. Implementation and evaluation of a Wiki involving multiple stakeholders including patients in the promotion of best practices in trauma care: the WikiTrauma Interrupted Time Series Protocol. Patrick M Archambault, Alexis F Turgeon, Holly O Witteman, François Lauzier, Lynne Moore, François Lamontagne, Tanya Horsley, Marie-Pierre Gagnon, Arnaud Droit, Matthew Weiss, Sébastien Tremblay, Jean Lachaine, Natalie Le Sage, Marcel Émond, Simon Berthelot, Ariane Plaisance, Jean Lapointe, Tarek Razek, Tom H van de Belt, Kevin Brand, Mélanie Bérubé, Julien Clément, Francisco Jose Grajales III, Gunther Eysenbach, Craig Kuziemsky, Debbie Friedman, Eddy Lang, John Muscedere, Sandro Rizoli, Derek J Roberts, Damon C Scales, Tasnim Sinuff, Henry T Stelfox, Isabelle Gagnon, Christian Chabot, Richard Grenier, France Légaré. JMIR Research Protocols 2015;4:e21 URL: http://www.researchprotocols.org/2015/1/e21/.

2014

1. Evaluation of patients' questions to identify gaps in information provision to infertile patients. Tom H van de Belt, Arnolf FW Hendriks, Johanna WM Aarts, Jan

AM Kremer, Marjan J Faber, Willanne LDM Nelen. Human Fertility 2014;17:133-140.

2. Wikis to facilitate patient participation in developing information leaflets: first experiences. Tom H van de Belt, Marjan J Faber, José ML Knijnenburg, Noortje TL van Duijnhoven, Willianne LDM Nelen, Jan AM Kremer. Informatics for Health and Social Care 2014;39:124-139.

3. Social media and rating sites as tools to understanding quality of care: a scoping review. Lise M Verhoef, Tom H van de Belt, Lucien JLPG Engelen, Lisette Schoonhoven, Rudolf B Kool. J Med Internet Res 2014;16:e56. URL: http://www.jmir.org/2014/2/e56/.

4. Collaborative writing applications in healthcare: effects on professional practice and healthcare outcomes. Patrick M Archambault, Tom H van de Belt, Marjan J Faber, Ariane Plaisance, Craig Kuziemsky, Marie-Pierre Gagnon, Alexis Turgeon, Karine Aubin, Julien Poitras, Tanya Horsley, Jean Lapointe, Kevin Brand, William Witteman, Jean Lachaine, France Légaré. The Cochrane Library 2014, issue 11. http://onlinelibrary.wiley.com/doi/10.1002/14651858.CD011388/abstract;jsessionid=A4152DA1E0FA4C7D3B336F08F0FD8A27.f03t04.

2013

1. Wikis and collaborative writing applications in health care: a scoping review. Patrick M Archambault, Tom H van de Belt, Francisco J Grajales III, Marjan J Faber, Craig E Kuziemsky, Susie Gagnon, Andrea Bilodeau,

Simon Rioux, Willianne LDM Nelen, Marie-Pierre Gagnon, Alexis F Turgeon, Karine Aubin, Irving Gold, Julien Poitras, Gunther Eysenbach, Jan AM Kremer, France Légaré. J Med Internet Res 2013;15:e210. URL: http://www.jmir.org/2013/10/e210/.

2. Internet and social media for health-related information and communication in health care: preferences of the Dutch general population. Tom H Van de Belt, Lucien JLPG Engelen, Sivera AA Berben, Steven Teerenstra, Melvin Samsom, Lisette Schoonhoven. J Med Internet Res 2013;15:e220. URL: http://www.jmir.org/2013/10/e220.

2012

1. Wikis and collaborative writing applications in health care: a scoping review protocol. Patrick Michel Archambault, Tom H van de Belt, Francisco J Grajales III, Gunther Eysenbach, Karine Aubin, Irving Gold, Marie-Pierre Gagnon, Craig E Kuziemsky, Alexis F Turgeon, Julien Poitras, Marjan J Faber, Jan AM Kremer, Marcel Heldoorn, Andrea Bilodeau, France Légaré. JMIR Research Protocols 2012;1:e1 URL: http://www.researchprotocols.org/2012/1/e1/.

2. Use of social media by Western European hospitals: longitudinal study. Tom H Van de Belt, Sivera AA Berben, Melvin Samsom, Lucien JLPG Engelen, Lisette Schoonhoven. J Med Internet Res 2012;14:e61. URL: http://www.jmir.org/2012/3/e61/.

2010

1. Definition of Health 2.0 and Medicine 2.0: A Systematic Review. Van De Belt TH, Engelen LJ, Berben SAA, Schoonhoven L, J Med Internet Res 2010;12:e18. URL: jmir.org/2010/2/e18.

Scientific conference abstracts

2016

1. Weenk, A. P. Alken , L. J. Engelen , B. J. Bredie , T. H. Van De Belt , H. Van Goor. Mental Stress of Surgeons and Residents at Daily Activities. Annual Academic Surgical Congress, Jacksonville, Florida. URL: http://academic-surgicalcongress.org/pdfs/ASC2016_Program.pdf

2015

1. Tom H van de Belt, Sophia M Keefstra, Rudolf B Kool. Patient Rating Sites for Risk Identification by Healthcare Inspectorates. Connected Health Symposium 2015, Boston, United States.

2. C. Grim, H.G.B. Nijmeijer, T.H. Van de Belt, M. ter Laan. Effects of using 3D printed models for pre-operative patient education. EANS 2015, Annual Meeting Technological Advances in Neurosurgery, P543.

3. Marleen M.H.J. van Gelder, Richelle Vlenterie, Lucien J.L.P.G. Engelen, Alina Vrieling, Tom H. van de Belt. How to recruit participants into observational studies? A systematic review. Healthy Living 2015, Maastricht, the Netherlands. URL: http://www.healthyliving2015. nl/upload/abstractbook_210615.pdf.

2014

1. Patrick M. Archambault, Jasmine Thanh, Danielle Blouin, Susie Gagnon, Julien Poitras, Renée-Marie Fountain, Richard Fleet, Andrea Bilodeau, Tom H van de Belt, France Légaré. Croyances des résidents en médecine d'urgence concernant leur contribution à une présentation collaborative en ligne. INNOVER en Pédagogie, Manoir Du Lac Delage, Faculté de medicine, Université LAVAL, 2014. URL: http://www.fmed.ulaval.ca/site_fac/faculte/vie-facultaire/nos-activites/journ-ee-annuelle-de-l-enseignement/salon-de-l-innovation/presentations/.

2. Jasmine Thanh, Patrick Michel Archambault, Danielle Blouin, Susie Gagnon, Julien Poitras, Renée-Marie Fountain, Richard Fleet, Andrea Bilodeau, Tom H Van de Belt, France Légaré. Emergency medicine residents' beliefs about contributing to an online collaborative slideshow. Journée annuelle de l'enseignement, Université Laval. March 2014.

3. Archambault, T.Van de Belt,FJ Grajales III, MJ Faber, A Bilodeau, C Nadeau, S Rioux,CE Kuziemsky, M Émond, G Eysenbach, K Aubin,I Gold,MP Gagnon,AF Turgeon, JPoitras, JAM Kremer, M Heldoom,F Légaré, "Wikis and collaborative writing applications in health care: preliminary results of a scoping review" Poster Journée scientifique de la recherche du CHAU de Lévis.

4. Patrick M. Archambault, Jasmine Thanh, Danielle Blouin, Susie Gagnon, Julien Poitras, Renée-Marie Fountain, Richard Fleet, Andrea Bilodeau, Tom H van de Belt, France Légaré, "Emergency medicine residents'

beliefs about contributing to an online collaborative slideshow" Poster Journée annuelle de l'enseignement, Université Laval 2014/02.

2013

1. TH van de Belt, PM Archambault, F Grajales, G Eysenbach, K Aubin, I Gold, MP Gagnon, C Kuziemsky, A Turgeon, J Poitras, MJ Faber, JAM Kremer, M Heldoorn, A Bilodeau, S Gagnon, S Rioux, F Legaré. Wikis and Collaborative Writing Applications in Healthcare: a Scoping Review. Medicine 2.0 Conference London, "Wikis and Collaborative Writing Applications in Health Care: a Scoping Review" Poster Medicine 2.0'13 2013/04

2. Tom H van de Belt, Lucien JLPG Engelen, Sivera AA Berben, Melvin Samsom, Lisette Schoonhoven. Using Social Media in Healthcare: Preferences of the General Population Medicine 2.0 Conference 2013, London, United Kingdom. URL: http://www.medicine20congress.com/ocs/index.php/med/med2013/paper/view/1757.

3. P Archambault, M.Bernier, T.Lalonde, T. Van de Belt, F.Grajales, M.Faber, C.Kuziemsky, S.Gagnon, A.Bilodeau, S.Rioux, C.Fournier, M.Émond, C.Nadeau, K.Aubin, I.Gold, M.Gagnon, A.Turgeon, M.Heldoorn, J.Poitras, J.Kremer, G.Eysenback, F.Légaré."The use of collaborative writing applications in healthcare education- a scoping review" Poster Journée annuelle inter-universitaire de la recherche en médecine d'urgence November 2013 URL: http://www.fmed.ulaval.ca/site_fac/presentations/#c13817.

4. Archambault, T.van de Belt, F.Grajales, M.Faber, C.Kuziemsky, S.Gagnon, A.Bilodeau, S.Rioux, K.Aubin, I.Gold, M.Gagnon, A. Turgeon, M.heldoorn, J.Poitras, J.Kremer, G.Eysenbach, F.Légaré, "Using social media and crowdsourcing to gather important publications for a scoping review about wikis and collaborative writing tools." Poster Journée annuelle de la recherche inter-uniersitaire en médecine d'urgence 2013/11.

5. Bernier,T.Lalonde,T.van de Belt,F.Grajales, M.Faber,C. Kuziemsky,S.Gagnon, A.Bilodeau, S.Rioux, C.Fournier, M.Émond, C.Nadeau, K.Aubin, I.Gold, M.Gagnon, A.Turgeon, M.Heldoorn, J.Poitras, J.Kremer, G.Eysenback, F.Légaré, "The use of collaborative writing applications in healthcare education- a scoping review" Poster 21st Cochrane Colloquium 2013/09.

6. Archambault, T.van de Belt, F.Grajales, M.Faber, C.Kuziemsky, S.Gagnon, A.Bilodeau, S.Rioux, K.Aubin, I.Gold, M.Gagnon, A. Turgeon, M.Heldoorn, J.Poitras, J.Kremer, G.Eysenbach, F.Légaré, "Using social media and crowdsourcing to gather important publications for a scoping review about wikis and collaborative writing tools." Poster 21st Cochrane Colloquium 2013/05.

7. Archambault, T.van de Belt, F.Grajales, M.Faber, C.Kuziemsky, S.Gagnon, A.Bioldeau, S.Rioux, C.Fournier, C.Nadeau, M.Émond, K.Aubin, I.Gold, M-P.Gagnon, A.Turgeon, M.Heldoorn, "Wikis and collaborative writing applications in health care: results of a scoping review" Poster 21st Cochrane Colloquium 2013/05.

8. P Archambault, T van de Belt, F Grajales, M Faber, C Kuziemsky, S Gagnon,A Bilodeau, S Rioux, K Aubin, I

Gold, MP Gagnon, A Turgeon, M Heldoorn, J Poitras, G Eysenbach, J Kremer, F Légaré, "Wikis and collaborative writing applications in health care: results of a scoping review" Poster 8ème Congrès Scientifique du Département de médecine familiale et de médecine d'urgence. Faculté de médecine, Université Laval, Québec. 2013/05.

2012

1. M. Archambault, T.H. van de Belt, F. Grajales, G. Eysenbach, K. Aubin, I. Gold, M.P. Gagnon, C. Kuziemsky, A.F. Turgeon, J. Poitras, M.J. Faber, J.A.M. Kremer, M. Heldoorn, A. Bilodeau et F. Legare, "Wikis and collaborative writing applications in healthcare: preliminary results of a scoping review", Medicine 2.0 Congress: Social Media, Mobile Apps, and Internet/ Web 2.0, Medicine 2.0 Conference, Harvard, United States September 2012.

2011

1. Tom H van de Belt, Marjan J Faber, José ML Knijnenburg, Noortje TL van Duijnhoven, Willianne LDM Nelen, Jan AM Kremer. Wikis as an Opportunity to Improve Patient Participation in Developing Information Leaflets: A demonstration project in infertility patients. Medicine 2.0 Congress 2011, Stanford (California, USA).

2. Van De Belt TH, Engelen LJ, Berben SAA, Schoonhoven L. Social Media in European Hospitals: A Descriptive Study. Medicine 2.0 Conference 2011, Stanford, United States. URL: http://www.medicine20congress.com/ ocs/index.php/med/med2011/paper/view/576

2010

1. Van De Belt TH, Engelen LJ, Berben SAA, Schoonhoven L, Definition of Health 2.0 and Medicine 2.0: A Systematic Reviewm, Medicine 2.0 Congress, Maastricht, 2010, URL: http://www.medicine20congress.com/ocs/index.php/med/med2010/paper/view/455.

During the whole proces of writing I got some great support from the Patreon community that started during my sabbatical. Its members and their support kept me going to write this book so again Thank YOU:

Floris Triest,

Anya Kravets,

Bert Vrijhoef & Isabelle Nefkens,

Irene Pylypenko,

Jaco van Duivenboden,

Stefan Buttigieg,

Dave deBronkart,

Hendrik Ahlen,

Heico ten Cate, ,

Walter van den Broek,

Tim Kroesbergen

Richard Gouw,

Ronald Kleverlaan,

John Sharp,

Jan Jacobs.

What's next?

...